Sino-Soviet Military Relations

Sino-Soviet
Military Relations

EDITED BY
RAYMOND L. GARTHOFF

FREDERICK A. PRAEGER, *Publishers*

New York · Washington · London

FREDERICK A. PRAEGER, PUBLISHERS
111 Fourth Avenue, New York, N.Y. 10003, U.S.A.
77–79 Charlotte Street, London W.1, England

Published in the United States of America in 1966
by Frederick A. Praeger, Inc., Publishers

© 1966 by Frederick A. Praeger, Inc.

Library of Congress Catalog Card Number: 66-18900

Printed in the United States of America

To my father
Arnold Alexander Garthoff

Preface

When the Sino-Soviet rift broke into the open in 1960, it came as a great surprise to most people in the West. Nonetheless, some observers had seen the possibility present in earlier muted signs of friction. Today, several books describe the course of the Sino-Soviet political and ideological controversy. There remains, however, a need to examine in closer detail, and in historical depth, the major causes of the split. Among these are a number of military and politico-military considerations that have contributed to, and been affected by, Sino-Soviet political divergence and conflict. The main purpose of this volume is to illuminate these considerations.

As we stand back from the current world political scene and place recent developments in a broader historical perspective, we see further reason to look closely at Russo-Chinese military relations over the past half century. For Soviet relations with Communist China did not emerge from a vacuum, and are not entirely distinct from Soviet relations with the National Republic of China in earlier decades, or even from relations between Imperial Russia and Imperial China. Throughout Russo-Chinese history, military factors have been significant.

The present work focuses on the salient developments in the politico-military relationships between China and the Soviet Union; it seeks to contribute to a better understanding not only of the specific events reviewed and interpreted, but also of the present and future role of military considerations in Soviet-Chinese Communist relations, and their impact on world politics.

A number of the chapters in this volume have appeared earlier in scholarly journals; * others have been written specifically for

* Chapter 4 has appeared in *Orbis* (Summer, 1966); an earlier version of Chapter 5 appeared in the *Annals of the American Academy of Social and Political Science* (September, 1963), and in the author's *Soviet Mili-*

this book, in order to make its coverage comprehensive and timely. The editor assumes responsibility for the work as a whole; each author is responsible for his particular identified contributions. All contributors affiliated with government agencies and other institutions have written as individual scholars.

The editor wishes to express his deep thanks to the contributors. They form an impressive roster of the few outstanding specialists in Soviet affairs, Chinese affairs, and military affairs who have turned their attention to this specific field. He also wishes to thank the journals that have permitted use of those materials published previously. Special thanks are due to Miss Phyllis E. Pesce, who cheerfully gave of her time to type the manuscript.

RAYMOND L. GARTHOFF

Washington, D.C.
July 1, 1966

tary Policy: A Historical Analysis (1966); Chapter 6 appeared earlier in *The China Quarterly* (April–June, 1964); Chapter 7 in *Orbis* (Summer, 1962); Chapter 8 in *The Journal of Conflict Resolution* (June, 1964); the first part of Chapter 9 in *The Reporter* (May 19, 1966); an earlier version of Chapter 10 in *New Statesman* (October 4, 1963); and Chapter 11 is based on an article in *Wehr und Wirtschaft* (October, 1963).

Contributors

RAYMOND L. GARTHOFF is the author of *Soviet Military Doctrine, Soviet Strategy in the Nuclear Age, Soviet Military Policy,* and other works in the field of Soviet political and military affairs. Dr. Garthoff is presently Special Assistant for Soviet Bloc Politico-Military Affairs, U.S. Department of State, and on the faculty of the School for Advanced International Studies, The Johns Hopkins University, Washington, D.C.

O. EDMUND CLUBB served in the U.S. Foreign Service for twenty-four years, including twenty years in China, Indochina, and the Soviet Far East. He was Consul General at Vladivostok, Mukden, Changchun, and—at the time of the Communist takeover—Peiping. He has taught Asian affairs at various colleges, and is the author of many articles in this field and of the book *Twentieth Century China.*

LIEUTENANT COLONEL JAMES C. BOWDEN, JR., USA, is a graduate of the U.S. Army Command and General Staff College and of the Foreign Area Specialist Training Program of the U.S. Army, where he specialized in Russian studies. He holds a Master's degree in International Relations from The American University, Washington, D.C.

HAROLD P. FORD, a long-time student of Chinese affairs, prepared an extensive study of Sino-Soviet politico-military affairs, from which his present contribution is drawn, while engaged in post-doctoral studies at St. Antony's College, Oxford.

JOHN R. THOMAS is a specialist in Soviet Affairs with the Research Analysis Corporation, McLean, Virginia. A graduate of the Russian Institute of Columbia University, he spent a number of years in the Soviet Union in the 1930's, served as a U.S. Army liaison officer with the Soviet occupation forces in North Korea in the late 1940's, and has been with The RAND Corporation and the Institute for Defense Analyses.

ix

ALICE LANGELY HSIEH, the author of *Communist China's Strategy in the Nuclear Era*, is currently a Senior Staff Member of the Social Science Department of The RAND Corporation specializing in Communist China's foreign policy and military policies. From 1945 to 1955, she served as an officer in the U.S. Foreign Service and Department of State where she dealt with political and politico-military problems in the Far East.

J. MALCOLM MACKINTOSH is the author of *Strategy and Tactics of Soviet Foreign Policy*. A member of the Consultative Committee on Soviet Affairs of the Institute of Strategic Studies, London, he has served in the Foreign Office and as a liaison officer of the British Army with the Soviet Army in Bulgaria during World War II.

LIEUTENANT COLONEL O. FERDINAND MIKSCHE resides in Paris and writes on military problems. He is the author of *The Failure of Atomic Strategy* and other works on military strategy. Colonel Miksche has taught at the Portuguese Army Staff College. During World War II, he served with the Headquarters of the Free French Forces.

Contents

Appendixes

Sino-Soviet Military Relations

by, the renunciation of all rights (and obligations) in other
tries. This act, however, was more a gesture than a policy,
one facilitated by Russian weakness. But China itself was still
political chaos from its own revolution, and the effects of the
sian Civil War were felt in Chinese-Russian relations. As one
lt of the Civil War, several non-Bolshevik, "White" Russian
horities held power for a number of years in Central Asia, Cen-
Siberia, the Maritime Province in the Far East, by "spill-over"
Outer Mongolia and Tannu Tuva, and even, through Russian
ntrol of the Chinese Eastern Railway, in northern Manchuria.
uring this period, moreover, Japan placed tens of thousands of
oops in the Maritime Province. (Partly to offset the Japanese
ove, the United States also sent a few thousand troops to
Vladivostok.)

As the Russian Civil War gradually came to a close, the Bolsheviks established three satellite "people's republics"—a completely artificial "Far Eastern Republic" in eastern Siberia, the
"Mongolian People's Republic," and the "People's Republic of
Tannu Tuva." The first of these was absorbed into Soviet Russia in
1922 (following the withdrawal of American and Japanese
troops); the last named was incorporated into the Russian Soviet
Federated Socialist Republic (R.S.F.S.R.) in 1944; and the Mongolian People's Republic remains, to this day, perhaps the Soviet
Union's most reliable, as well as oldest, protégé.

A Chinese Communist Party was created and held its first congress in July, 1921; in its establishment, two Comintern agents, the
Russian G. N. Voitinsky and a Dutch Communist named H.
Sneevliet (under the psuedonym Maring) played a major role.
Meanwhile, other, more significant Chinese revolutionary groups
had created the Kuomintang Party, and it, too, established ties
with the Soviet leadership and the Comintern. In 1923, the Russian Mikhail Borodin (Gruzenberg) helped to orient and organize
the Kuomintang along Communist lines, and General Chiang Kai-
shek went to Moscow on behalf of the Kuomintang. The Kuomintang, however, maintained its independence. Following tangled
maneuvers by all concerned, Chiang, in 1927, decisively defeated
Communist infiltration in the Kuomintang and nearly destroyed
the Chinese Communist Party. Only after a series of continuing
failures did the Chinese Communist Party eventually, by 1935,
emerge as a force under the leadership of Mao Tse-tung.

After 1931, with the Japanese occupation of Manchuria, Russian interests in the Far East again were in juxtaposition not only

1. Introducti

By RAYMOND L. GARTI

Russia has always been a European power, an
sometimes been questioned by those in Western E
by particular national differences, it has never beer
Chinese. Diplomatic relations between Russia and
established by the Treaty of Nerchinsk in 1689.
tional border between the two countries in the Far E
lished only as recently as the Treaty of Peking in
Central Asia was not set until 1881; recurring fricti
flicts have arisen between the two states over the fro
borderlands, which are sparsely populated by minorit
ties neither ethnically Slavic nor Han Chinese.

During the late nineteenth century, Russia joined the
ropean states in extorting advantages (including a territ
on Port Arthur in 1898) from the weakened Chinese Em
especially after 1895, competed with Japan for econd
political influence in Manchuria and Korea. A shift of Ru
tention from the Balkans to the Far East around the turl
century led to the clash with Japan in the Russo-Japanese
1904–5. In that conflict, Russia, one of the Great Powers
rope, was defeated. After 1905, despite renewed Russian a
in the Siberian and Central Asian borderlands following the
lapse of the Chinese Empire, Russia's attention was primaril
rected elsewhere; her interest turned to internal problems reve
both by the defeat and by the widespread internal political distu
ances of that year—and soon again to her role in Central Euro

Debilitated by the strains of World War I, Imperial Russia c
lapsed in 1917—only six years after the end of Imperial rule
China. One of the first acts of the Bolshevik regime, which ha
swiftly succeeded a short-lived liberal republican Provisional Gov
ernment, was the nullification of all "imperialistic" treaties, and,

there
coun
and
in p
Rus
res
aut
tra
in
co
D
tr
m
V

with China's but also—and more dangerously—with Japan's. This situation existed until 1945. Accordingly, the U.S.S.R. and Japan were constant adversaries, and occasionally engaged in local undeclared warfare. After 1937, the Soviet Union once again gave aid to the National (Kuomintang) Republic of China in its war with Japan. From 1941 until after the defeat of Nazi Germany, both Russia and Japan found themselves engaged in life-and-death war on other fronts. Then, joining the victorious Western Allies, in order to secure private gains, the Soviet Union launched its own short and easy war—defeating Japanese forces in Manchuria, northern Korea, Sakhalin, and the Kuril Islands. To purchase Western acceptance of Russian gains in these territories (and, finally, of Communist rule in Mongolia), the Soviet leadership accepted the National Government as the sole authority in the Republic of China.

In 1945 and 1946, the Russians used their position of temporary occupation of Manchuria to influence events in that specific area, and, more generally, in China. But they did so in an inconsistent way, as their estimates of the capabilities of the National Government and of the Chinese Communists gradually changed, and as American intentions with respect to China became clearer. The Russians aided the Chinese Communists in Manchuria, but not to the exclusion of maintaining an active relationship with, and giving some assistance to, the Nationalists as well. Elsewhere, and subsequently, the Soviet role in the Chinese Civil War of 1946–49 was almost completely passive.

The Chinese Communists emerged victorious in mainland China in 1949, after triumphing over initially stronger odds on the other side. The Soviet regularization of relations with the Kuomintang National Government was replaced, in February, 1950, by a set of agreements with the new Communist People's Republic of China not drastically different from those agreed upon with the Chinese Nationalists just five years earlier.

The shock in the West over the rather sudden shift in China to Communist rule, coupled with the façade of "monolithic" unity among the Communist states established under Stalin's rule and preserved for a time under his successors, led to a decade of American misunderstanding of the nature of Russo-Chinese relations. This misunderstanding extended, in general, to American estimates of emerging relationships in the Communist "bloc" of states and, indeed, in the world Communist movement. Only during the 1960's have the differences, divergencies, and even sharp conflicts among the Communist powers developed for all to see, and been disclosed to be so many and so deep.

Now, it is both possible and necessary to recognize, to analyze, to understand, and to act on the basis of national distinctions and differences among the Communist states—above all, on the differences between the Soviet Union and Communist China.

The studies collected in this volume seek to analyze one of the cardinal strands of Chinese-Russian relations—the role of military and politico-military considerations. The work is addressed primarily to present—and future—relations, but it necessarily examines in some depth and detail past relationships, including those of the Soviet Union with China before the Chinese Communist accession to power.

The chapter immediately following places in historical perspective, and particularly from the Chinese viewpoint, the course of successive conflicts and Russian interventions in the Chinese borderlands. As later chapters also show, such interventions did not cease with the establishment of Communist rule in these areas; they were stopped only through forceful Chinese Communist measures against Soviet politico-military power, although direct military means were rarely used by either opponent.

The third chapter treats the other side of the coin—Soviet support for the Kuomintang in China as a rising independent national force. It was (in Soviet eyes) the only force capable of confronting the Western Powers and Japan in their imperialistic exploitation of China and, later, the only force capable of stopping the Japanese conquest of China and of preventing the emergence of an overwhelmingly strong Asian power center directed from Tokyo. The Soviet leaders were, clearly, more impelled to prevent Japanese power from growing on Russia's flank than they were constrained from aiding the internal foe of the Chinese Communists.

The fourth chapter presents a close-up of Russian intervention in Manchuria during the last days of World War II, and of the opening of the third phase in the Chinese Nationalist–Communist civil war. The Soviet military campaign in August, 1945, was, of course, fought against the Japanese—although the action occurred in China. The Russians' use of their military victory and occupation of Manchuria as leverage on Chinese affairs and, especially, the high priority given to specifically Russian interests as contrasted to those of the Chinese Communists are extremely significant.

A comprehensive review and analysis of Sino-Soviet military relations from 1945 through 1965 appears in Chapter 5. The many aspects of military relations, and of military considerations in political relations, between the two states are brought together in this analysis.

The early phase of rising discord over military and politico-military issues, from 1957 to 1960, while not evident to many at the time, was extremely important. It is, therefore, examined in greater detail in Chapters 6 and 7. (The single most crucial historical event of that period, in all probability, was the revelation in the 1958 Quemoy crisis of limits beyond which the Russians would not go to support their Chinese ally in pursuit of even the highest-priority Chinese interests.)

Since many of the developments in the crucial breakdown of Sino-Soviet military—and political—relations were disclosed rather frankly (although not always accurately) in the course of the public polemics by the Soviet and Chinese leaderships beginning in 1963, it is particularly useful to examine closely and critically the nature of these revelations. Such an analysis is made in Chapter 8, and carried down to 1966 in Chapter 9. (The latter chapter also includes an analysis of a Soviet General Staff journal's discussion of Peking's politico-military "total strategy," the full text of which is given in Appendix D.)

Chapter 10 analyzes, from the Russian viewpoint—particularly from that of the Soviet military leaders—present and future contingencies. There is no comparable treatment of the contemporary Chinese military viewpoint, but earlier chapters do present Chinese views as they have appeared in the past. Perhaps it should be noted that, in the period following Mao's departure from the scene, some Chinese military leaders may again argue—as did Marshal P'eng Teh-huai, unsuccessfully, in 1959—that China must trim its independent policies somewhat so long as it remains dependent on Soviet military support. But, of course, Communist China is devoting great efforts to reducing and, eventually, eliminating such dependence. Basically, after all, the Chinese leaders want to serve Chinese interests, as the Soviet leaders want to serve those of Russia.

The editor of this volume would not predict a Sino-Soviet war. But such a war *is* conceivable, even while both states have Communist rule. Chapter 11 is an imaginative projection of the possibility, sketching a number of the relevant military and geostrategic considerations. While one may differ with particular political and military judgments and assumptions made by the author (as, in fact, does the editor), the discussion is useful as one expert's view of a subject that deserves thoughtful speculation, which so far has been generally lacking.

2. Armed Conflict in the Chinese Borderlands, 1917-50

By O. EDMUND CLUBB

Ever since ancient times, China and Russia have been concerned with their inner Asian frontiers. The two empires met in Northeast Asia in the seventeenth century, and in Central Asia in the nineteenth century. The struggle between China and Russia thereafter focused on the borderlands of China—Manchuria, Outer Mongolia, and Sinkiang. The non-Chinese and non-Russian inhabitants of those borderlands had their own ambitions, which, during periods of imperial stress, they could attempt to serve by siding with one or the other of the chief protagonists; they had, however, little chance of achieving independence, much as they might strive to do so.

In the twilight of the Manchu Dynasty, Tibet was effectively taken out of play by the 1907 convention between Russia and Great Britain, which, recognizing "the principle of the suzerainty of China over Tibet," mutually bound the two signatories "to deal with Tibet only through the Chinese Government." The situation in the borderlands was further changed by the decision of the Manchu throne to open up both Manchuria and Mongolia to Chinese immigration. The Manchu weakness manifested by the concessions to Chinese subjects whetted the appetites of the imperialist powers, who anticipated the breakup of China and the benefits that they might inherit as a result. (Russia's long occupation of Manchuria after the Boxer Rebellion of 1900, for example, was evidence of an imperialistic ambition only lightly veiled.) Russian expansionist ambition was temporarily halted by the Russo-Japanese War of 1904-5, and was only barely stirred again— given the situation in Europe—by the Chinese Revolution of 1911. Then, with the Russian Revolution of 1917, the Russians became

9

concerned first and foremost with internal strife and later with national self-preservation. But the Chinese borderlands were destined to remain arenas of recurring clash of ambition; sometimes the tide of conflict even surged into Russian Central Asia and Siberia.

With the Bolshevik Revolution in October, 1917, Soviet Russia purported to turn over a new leaf in international affairs: it renounced imperialism and the imperialist privileges it might have inherited from Czarist Russia. This policy applied particularly to China. The Karakhan Declaration of 1919 offered the renunciation of the privileged position Russia had enjoyed in China as a result of various earlier "unequal treaties." However, this initial offer found no takers on the Chinese side, since the Peking war lord government considered its interests best served by refraining from the establishment of ties with the Bolshevik Government. By 1919, the Chinese republican house was deeply divided against itself, into North (governed by Peking), South (led in Canton by Sun Yat-sen's intermittent revolutionary Opposition), and still other factions. In Sinkiang and Manchuria, as well as various provinces, largely independent war lords ruled. Outer Mongolia had already, on November 9, 1911, declared its independence of China, and had won legal recognition of its "autonomy."

Russia was torn by civil war. One phase of Russia's civil strife was fought in Siberia, where the situation was further complicated by Allied intervention in 1918–20. Japan had major ambitions in Northeast Asia, and, as early as December, 1917, proposed intervention in Vladivostok with the evident aim of exploiting the situation to its own political benefit. Japan's allies in the European war were naturally interested. The United States, which, more than Britain or France, was becoming a direct competitor of Japan in the rich area of Manchuria, was especially concerned. In December, 1917, the United States opposed intervention. Then, in February, 1918, as a result of Japanese moves and British and French pressure, the U.S. Government shifted its stand; nonetheless, it considered that any intervention should be international in character, rather than be dominated by a single power (particularly Japan) "acting as the mandatory of the others." The Japanese and British had dispatched cruisers to Vladivostok in mid-January; the U.S.S. *Brooklyn* joined them there on March 1. The headquarters of the Japanese Army General Staff had evolved a plan for sending an expeditionary force into Siberia, with two separate forces to occupy the Maritime Province and the Trans-Baikal sector. A contingency plan provided for the possible dispatch of troops to the "central Mongolian area" in conjunction with Chinese troops; this concept envisaged advance into the Trans-Baikal area. The Japanese plan simply ignored outer Mongolia's autonomy as established by the Russo-Chinese-Mongolian Kyakhta treaty of 1915.

The signature by the hard-pressed Bolsheviks of the onerous Treaty of Brest-Litovsk with Germany on March 3, 1918, provided a basis for the belief, then widely held in the Allied camp, that the Bolsheviks were merely veiled instruments of the Germans. On March 25, Peking and Tokyo reached an agreement looking toward joint action against "the steady penetration of hostile [German] influence into Russian territory." On May 16, representatives of the Chinese and Japanese military authorities signed a secret convention by which China and Japan, "realizing the fact that the gradual extension of enemy influence towards the east may jeopardize the peace of the two countries, consider it their mutual duty, as participants in the war, to take concerted action against the common enemy." [1] On the basis of the March and May agreements, Japan moved a total of 60,000 troops into northern Manchuria.

The secret document clearly envisaged Manchuria's becoming a base of operations, and provided (in Article 5) that "Whenever troops have to be dispatched outside Chinese territory, the two countries shall dispatch them jointly whenever necessary," and also contained (in Article 4) a stipulation that "The Japanese troops in Chinese territory shall be withdrawn as soon as operations cease." By July, the Czech prisoners of war, released by the Bolsheviks in March and now strung out along the Trans-Siberian Railway from Kazan to Vladivostok, were in open warfare with the regime that had set them free. In August, the intervention by Japanese, American, and token British and French forces formally began; nominally, it was to protect the eastward movement of the Czechs, and to save the Allied-supplied military stores that had piled up in Vladivostok. The Chinese, concerned primarily with establishing a "presence" in the operation in order to protect their interests in Manchuria and their place at the peace conference to come, also contributed a contingent of troops.

White Russian protagonists of the *ancien régime* were already in the picture in Northeast Asia. By the beginning of May, 1918, the Bolsheviks had gained control of the region from Lake Baikal to Vladivostok, but a counterrevolutionary movement was in course, with Grigory Semënov, a Cossack ataman, early assuming a leading role. With the blessing of the Provisional Government after the February Revolution, Semënov had gone to Siberia to

raise a force of non-Russian troops around a nucleus of Buryat
Mongols. One of the men who joined his banner was a half-
Magyar, half-Russian, Baltic Baron, Roman von Ungern-Stern-
berg. Semënov at the time was just 26, Ungern-Sternberg only 30.
Both became imbued with a romantic idea of a renaissance of the
power the Mongols had wielded in ancient times.

In March, Semënov and another Cossack, Ivan Kalmykov, had
taken the field against Bolshevik positions in the Trans-Baikal
sector, but had been driven into Manchuria by Red forces commanded by Sergei Lazo. However, the situation was soon to
change to the advantage of the extremist elements of the anti-
Bolshevik opposition. In June, 1918, a moderate "All-Siberian"
White government had been established at Omsk. In November,
that regime was overthrown by Admiral Aleksandr Kolchak, who
declared himself "Supreme Ruler of Russia," and soon received
the support of the Americans, British, and French. The Japanese,
for their part, decided to use Semënov as their chief instrument.

This is not the place to recount the whole course of the Siberian
intervention. The year 1919 was to have seen the toppling of Bolshevik power by the combined efforts of the White military leaders
Denikin, Wrangel, Yudenich, and Kolchak, but the ill-coordinated
campaigns failed. In October, Yudenich's drive on Petrograd came
to grief, and in the south Denikin's front collapsed. The 3rd and
5th Red Armies thrust into western Siberia, Omsk fell to the Red
forces on November 15, and Kolchak's power rapidly crumbled.
The general effort to overcome the Bolshevik power had failed. In
April, 1920, the Allied expeditionary force in Siberia withdrew—
with the exception of the Japanese, who remained in the Maritime
Province until 1922. At the same time, the Bolsheviks created a
sham "front" state, the "Far Eastern Republic" (F.E.R.) in the
region east of Lake Baikal, judging that such a satellite would be
less provocative to the Japanese than direct Moscow control.

But the foreign intervention was not without important consequences. The Peking Government, headed by the pro-Japanese
Tuan Ch'i-jui, aspired to recover, as an incidental fruit of the Russian Revolution, the control over Outer Mongolia that had been
exercised by the Manchus in imperial times. Presumably as a development stemming from the Sino-Japanese agreement of May,
1918, Peking, by the end of the year, in violation of the tripartite
treaty of 1915, had increased its consular guard in Urga, the Mongolian capital.

In June, 1919, while the Kolchak-Denikin-Yudenich summer

campaign was in full course, Tuan's ruthless hatchet man, Hsu Shu-cheng, was appointed Commissioner of Northwestern Frontier Development and, concurrently, commander in chief of the Northwestern Border Defense Force. Hsu dispatched a force of some 4,000 troops to Urga, and he himself proceeded there in late October. By a none-too-gentle exercise of the force at his command, he caused the Mongolian Cabinet, on November 16, to submit a petition to Peking requesting cancellation of the 1915 agreement—and of Outer Mongolia's autonomy. The Peking Government on November 22 graciously consented to accept Outer Mongolia back into the Chinese motherland. Hsu became High Commissioner for Outer Mongolian Rehabilitation Affairs, and he swung into action with the evident intention of making Outer Mongolia into something in the nature of a personal empire.

There was, however, competition in Hsu's domain. In February, 1919, a conference had been held at Chita among Semënov, the Japanese Major Suzuki, and a number of Mongols; this meeting had led to the launching of a movement directed toward establishment of a "Great Mongolian State," encompassing all Mongolian lands from the Trans-Baikal sector (Buryat Mongolia in Russian Siberia) to Tibet. A "government" headed by Neisse Gegen, an Inner Mongolian *khutukhtu* or Living Buddha, was set up. This pretender government, however, failed to gain broad Outer Mongol backing. The Japanese officially denied support, and the movement reached a violent end when the Chinese garrison at Maimachen in January, 1920, captured and shot Neisse Gegen and officers of his "Special Manchurian Detachment," and sent 200 captured soldiers to Urga for forced labor.[2] Semënov, however, escaped.

The Chinese action led by Hsu had had additional side effects. Even as Kalmykov's ferocious cruelty had alienated the Siberian population from the "White" cause, and the mutual jealousies of the White generals had inhibited their cooperation against the Bolsheviks, so Hsu's actions had alienated the Mongol princes. Moreover, Hsu's patent ambitions to control all Mongol territory, including that of western Manchuria, aroused the ever-ready suspicions of Chang Tso-lin, the war lord in Mukden. Chang Tso-lin initiated a move that resulted in a démarche in April, 1920, by eight powerful *tuchüns* (war lords) against Peking. In July, 1920, against the background of the collapse of Kolchak's power in Siberia, the Tuan Ch'i-jui government was overthrown—with the political position and policies of Hsu Shu-cheng the issue. Hsu fled to the

Japanese Legation in Peking, and then made his way to the foreign concessions of Shanghai.

Chang Tso-lin, who had succeeded, by 1919, in establishing his control over all Manchuria, had ties with the Japanese of long standing. Japan also commanded the services of Semënov and Ungern-Sternberg. Even if the Japanese had lost out in the Allied intervention, they still saw an opportunity, through use of the military power of Ungern-Sternberg and Semënov, and the "friendly collaboration" of Chang Tso-lin, to implement the concept of pan-Mongolism for their own benefit. A strong base extending over both Manchuria and Outer Mongolia would obviously give Japan a good position against revolutionary Russia, and against China.

In October, 1920, under increasing Bolshevik pressure, Semënov finally abandoned Chita. In the same month, his lieutenant, Ungern-Sternberg, thrust into Outer Mongolia with some 2,000 troops and attacked Urga, then held by a Chinese garrison. The first attack was repelled, but Ungern-Sternberg recruited disaffected Mongol leaders to the anti-Chinese cause and continued his campaign. On February 3, 1921,[3] the combined Cossack-Mongol force of 5,000 men occupied Urga, inflicting heavy casualties on the Chinese garrison (then about 8,000 men). Ungern-Sternberg promptly established an "independent government of Outer Mongolia," and set about consolidating his position by instituting a bloody purge that became a virtual reign of terror.

Outer Mongolia adjoins the strategically important narrow Baikal corridor through which Russia's only line of east-west land communications passes south of Lake Baikal. Ungern-Sternberg's dream of the restoration of a pan-Mongol empire, taken together with his ties to Japan, offered a clear threat both to the Buryat Mongol–populated area in Siberia and to the whole Russian strategic position in Northeast Asia. The Bolsheviks were, naturally, deeply concerned.

An instrumentality was ready at hand for Moscow's use. On August 28 of the previous year, the Mongolian revolutionary Sukhe Bator had addressed a letter to Boris Shumyatsky as head of the Far Eastern Republic government requesting "Russia" to aid in restoring Mongolian autonomy. On March 1, 1921, at Kyakhta— on Russian soil—Sukhe Bator's Mongolian People's Revolutionary Party held its first congress, and on March 13, still at Kyakhta, the Provisional People's Revolutionary Government of Mongolia was established. A "Mongolian People's Revolutionary Army" was formally inaugurated, and quickly proved itself by capturing Maimachen, across the Mongolian border from Kyakhta, on March 18.

Meanwhile, Ungern-Sternberg had gone about crushing potential opposition and building up his power. In May, by which time he commanded about 11,000 troops, Ungern-Sternberg called for a new crusade against the Bolsheviks, and attacked northward from Urga in the direction of Maimachen and Troitskosavsk (in Russia). Peking, on May 30, appointed Chang Tso-lin High Commissioner for the Mongolian Borderlands, with the mission of reasserting Chinese authority in Outer Mongolia; $500,000 (Chinese) was provided to finance his military operations. Chang, however, with his ties both to the Japanese and to the White Russians based in Manchuria, made no move in the direction of Outer Mongolia—although he accepted the money.

The Bolsheviks had a grievance. The Chinese Government not only had taken no action to restrain Semënov and Ungern-Sternberg in the White Russians' forays into Russian territory, but also, in effect, had provided them with bases for military action and, through Chang Tso-lin, had offered aid and encouragement to those enemies of the Bolshevik state. The Far Eastern Republic government at Verkhneudinsk set about formulation of countermeasures.

In the long Russian civil war, one of the Red partisans who had especially distinguished himself was Vasily Blücher (in Russian, "Blyukher"). He had commanded a partisan unit in the Urals, participated in the storming of Perekop in the Crimea, and had subsequently seen action against Kolchak as a division commander. On arrival in the Far Eastern Republic, in 1921, he took over chairmanship of its army's Military Council and assumed the post of Minister of War.[4] In those capacities, he was charged with confronting both hostile forces in the Maritime Province (where a new Japanese-supported puppet government, headed by Spiridon Merkulov, had been set up in May) and with liquidating the flanking threat posed by Ungern-Sternberg, the "mad baron" who, by now, thought himself the reincarnation of Genghis Khan.

Ungern-Sternberg attacked Troitskosavsk on May 20, and was met by units of the Red Army, the F.E.R. "People's Revolutionary Army," and the revolutionary Mongol forces led by Sukhe Bator and Choibalsan. Defeated on June 6, he retreated toward Outer Mongolia. The victorious Red Russian and Mongol forces, numbering approximately 13,000 men, pursued him to Maimachen. On June 15, Commissar for Foreign Affairs Chicherin addressed a note to the Peking Government (which had not recognized the Bolshevik regime) to explain that Ungern-Sternberg's "attacks on the armies of Soviet Russia and of the Far Eastern Republic developed into extensive military operations and forced Russian troops to cross the Mongolia frontier . . ." [5] On June 20, the new Red Mongol regime itself declared that "When the Red Army defeats Ungern, it will return to Russia." [6]

The combined forces of the F.E.R., the Red Army, and the Mongols continued their advance, and took Urga on July 6, 1921. The Mongols promptly moved their provisional government there, and, on July 11, transformed their interim regime into the People's Revolutionary Government. The Mongols had submitted their first request for aid to the Red Army on April 10, while seated at Maimachen. Now, on July 12, the new Mongolian regime formally requested the Moscow Government to retain Red Army units in Outer Mongolia for the purpose of eliminating the White forces. [7] Moscow naturally acceded to the request, and the base for future Russian-Mongolian cooperation was formally laid.

Ungern-Sternberg once more invaded Russian territory, and met defeat at Gusinoe Ozero on August 5. Abandoned by the Mongol troops whom he had dreamed of leading to imperial glory, he was captured on August 21 in the Gobi south of Urga while trying to escape. He was tried by a revolutionary tribunal at Novonikolaevsk (present-day Novosibirsk), and executed on September 15, 1921.

In an important sense the Chinese, by failing to engage Ungern-Sternberg effectively on behalf of their pretended vassal, had let Outer Mongolia half slip from their grasp by default. They had not fulfilled the duties of a suzerain. This legal situation was exploited, to a degree, with the signature, on November 5, 1921, of a secret Russian-Mongol treaty of friendship. Unlike earlier treaties involving Mongolia in the Chinese republican period, this treaty made no reference at all to the suzerainty of China and technically accorded Russian recognition to Outer Mongolia's independence. The Chinese were now out of the picture, and the "soft underbelly" of Siberia was protected. Blücher turned his attention to the Maritime Province in the Far East, and, on October 25, 1922, forces of his F.E.R. army entered Vladivostok. On November 13, the Far Eastern Republic formally opted for union with the rest of Russia. In December, 1922, the Soviet Union was born, with all of Siberia as part of the Russian Soviet Federated Socialist Republic.

When the Russian Revolution began in 1917, refugees from Imperial Russia were already on the soil of Sinkiang. In 1916, the Czar had attempted to conscript Turki tribesmen for service in the European war. This action was in violation of conventions exempting tribal elements in western Turkestan from military service, and the Kazakhs and Kirgizi resisted. As a consequence of the fighting that ensued, approximately 10,000 Kazakhs had retired into Sinkiang. By February, 1917, according to the province's war lord governor Yang Tseng-hsin, some 300,000 Russian subjects had taken refuge in Sinkiang.

Governor Yang had hardly begun to make a dent in the problem of returning refugees when the Russian civil war spread to Russian Turkestan following the October Revolution and an uprising against the Bolshevik power in Semireche in June, 1918. A new wave of refugees flowed into Sinkiang; this time the bulk of the refugees was made up of ethnic Russians. After an initial White success, Red partisans went into action, and a long and bloody struggle ensued in Semireche. With Admiral Kolchak's coup at Omsk in November, 1918, the fortunes of the Semireche White Russian forces became linked to developments in Siberia; Kolchak's fellow naval officer, Admiral Bakich, and the Cossack atamans Dutov and Annenkov played leading roles in the Turkestan imbroglio.

There were also alien complications in the Sinkiang situation. In 1918, a so-called Sino-Japanese Joint Investigation Group arrived in Sinkiang, presumably after signature of the secret agreement of May, 1918, between Peking and Tokyo for military collaboration with respect to Siberia. Yang, in December of that year, noted in one of his communications that nationals of "a certain country" (Japan?) had several times proposed the stationing of (Japanese?) troops in Ili and Chuguchak to assist with respect to the matter of border defense, and had, moreover, urged him to dispatch troops to attack the Bolshevik forces. But Peking had given a behind-the-scenes assist to Yang by instructing him that China itself bore responsibility for the defense of Sinkiang.

The Bolsheviks had alienated many of the peasants and nomads of Russian Central Asia by their policies, but, about March, 1919, Moscow adopted a more favorable line, which began to be imple-

mented with the taking over of Bolshevik command on the
Turkestan front by Mikhail Frunze in August, 1919. The Bolsheviks, as they made headway against the White forces in Semireche,
began to exert more political pressure on Yang Tseng-hsin in
Sinkiang. Yang's harboring of "counterrevolutionary elements"
was naturally an issue with the Red authorities, but he cagily
watched the course of developments in the Russian civil war, and
acted accordingly. In September, Ataman Dutov was defeated, and,
with the collapse of the Kolchak regime at the end of 1919, the
White Russians in Semireche were on their own. Yang Tseng-hsin
would offer no support to a lost cause.[8]

Frunze began mopping up the Kolchak remnants in Semireche,
and on March 10, 1920, an advance was ordered on Kapal, then
held by the Cossacks. The White leader Boiko surrendered on
March 18. Admiral Bakich crossed the Chinese border with several thousand troops, together with families and a number of merchants, to reach Chuguchak. In early June, a new movement of
peasant opposition to the Soviet power developed as a result of
Bolshevik grain requisitions; there was a full-scale revolt in the
vicinity of Alma-Ata. Cossack forces moved quickly to join in the
struggle, but the Bolsheviks moved even more rapidly and with
greater strength, getting three infantry and two cavalry regiments
to the threatened area by June 18. In a telegram of June 20,
Frunze was able to report that the revolt had, in the main, been
put down. Soviet power was brought even more heavily to bear
upon the remnants of White power in Semireche; defeated Cossacks
and large numbers of peasants opposed to or fearful of the Bolsheviks began now to stream across the Chinese frontier into Sinkiang. Semipalatinsk fell to the Red forces that summer, and the
last Cossack leader, Annenkov, who had stubbornly been holding
a position near the Ili border, finally crossed the border into
Sinkiang with his hungry, typhus-ridden troops.

In theory, as dictated by international law, the retreating Cossack forces were disarmed by the Chinese authorities; in fact, the
arms turned over to the Chinese comprised only a few relatively
worthless pieces of equipment. The Cossacks buried or otherwise
hid the bulk of their matériel in Russia for possible future use, and,
apparently, retained some arms out of sight of the Chinese. They
also maintained their military organization. The seeming indulgence of Yang Tseng-hsin was easy enough to understand, for
Sinkiang's own military forces were neither numerous nor especially effective. But now there was in Sinkiang a White force that

might offer a threat to the Red power established in Semireche. There were some 11,000 White Russian troops concentrated in the Chuguchak region, with Admiral Bakich in command, and in the Borotala region, near the Sinkiang-Russian border, Annenkov could still count some 2,000 to 3,000 men (though hardly in good fighting shape) of his original force of 20,000. Ataman Dutov had also fallen back into Sinkiang. In all, there were now some 15,000 to 20,000 White Russian military refugees in the Chinese province.

The final act of the drama was soon played. Admiral Bakich's lieutenant, Sidorov, had been killed by Kazakhs near Kuldja. Bakich himself went into winter quarters on the Emil River, near Chuguchak, and remained there until March, 1921. However, early in 1921, the Bolsheviks had requested permission from Yang Tseng-hsin to enter Sinkiang and take action against the Chuguchak force, and Yang had granted the desired permission, with various qualifications that did not in the slightest impair the essential freedom of action of the Red Army. The Red forces, accordingly, crossed the Sinkiang border, and arrived at Chuguchak on Easter Day. One Red detachment surrounded the Cossacks they found there, and herded the captives back to Russia. Several other engagements followed. Bakich and his hard-core force retreated to Sharesume, where the final battle was joined in September, 1921. After a bitter fight, the Bolsheviks won the field, taking many prisoners. In the final operation in Sinkiang, Yang's troops collaborated with the Red Army to prevent White forces from escaping elsewhere in Sinkiang. However, Bakich escaped to Mongolia and joined the forces of Ataman Semënov, and Annenkov and other White officers and men made their way down country to China proper. The battle at Sharesume, on Chinese soil, was the last big battle between the Red and White forces in Central Asia. The long, bitter struggle had been won by the Bolsheviks. With their Russian opponents subdued, the Bolsheviks could now turn their attention to Enver Pasha and the Turki Basmachi, to complete the consolidation of their rule in western Turkestan. The White Russian officers and men remaining in Sinkiang settled down to the task of building a new foundation for their existence. Their military life was ended—at least for the time being.

The year 1921 thus marked a turning point in Sino-Russian relations. The bases from which White Russian forces might threaten the Bolshevik power had been effectively eliminated from Sinkiang, Manchuria, and Outer Mongolia, and the international support upon which China had depended in part for its campaign to rescind Czarist Russian privileges in China had largely withered away as the several powers went their respective ways in the service of their own interests. The Bolsheviks turned to the revolutionary offensive, and in July, 1921, with the Comintern acting as midwife, the Chinese Communist Party was born.

In 1924, while aiding the revolutionary Kuomintang Nationalists at Canton,* Moscow at last also succeeded in signing treaties with both the Peking Government and—because he claimed independence of Peking—with Chang Tso-lin in Manchuria. In the treaty with Peking, Moscow recognized Outer Mongolia as "an integral part of the Republic of China," and, moreover, committed itself to withdraw its troops from Outer Mongolia—but at such time as might be agreed upon at a special conference. In Outer Mongolia, a few months later, upon the death of the Jeptsun Damba Khutukhtu, there came into being the Mongolian People's Republic (M.P.R.). In 1925, the U.S.S.R. withdrew its forces from the soil that had in fact become Mongolian, not Chinese.

In 1927, breaks occurred in Soviet relations both with Chang Tso-lin, now set up in power in North China, and with the Nationalist power that had established itself in the Yangtze Valley. Upon the overthrow of Chang's war lord government in 1928, there were no regular diplomatic relations remaining between the Soviet Union and China proper—only with Manchuria, Sinkiang, and, of course, Communist Outer Mongolia.

The victorious Kuomintang Nationalists, looking for new fields to conquer, in 1929 turned to the Soviet position in Manchuria. An earlier attempt by Chang Tso-lin to seize by force the Sungari River flotilla of the Chinese Eastern Railway in August, 1926, had proved unfruitful. Now, after Chang Hsueh-liang (son of Chang Tso-lin) had in December, 1928, shifted his allegiance to the Nationalist camp in defiance of Japanese "advice," Nanking and Mukden conspired to attack the Soviet position as being, seemingly, the weakest of the privileged "imperialist" positions in China.

The first move was a Chinese police raid May 27, 1929, on the Soviet Consulate General at Harbin, resulting in the arrest of 39 visitors, chiefly representatives of Soviet organizations (including the Chinese Eastern Railway) found on the premises. The Harbin

* See Chapter 3.

police announced the following day that "a session of the III International" had been in progress at the consulate. Acting Soviet Commissar for Foreign Affairs L. M. Karakhan protested on May 31. On July 10 and 11, the Chinese proceeded to seize the Chinese Eastern Railway and carry out widespread arrests of Soviet citizens throughout Manchuria. Operation of Soviet trade organs was suspended, and the offices of *Sovtorgflot* (the Soviet Mercantile Fleet) were closed. The Chinese claimed that evidence discovered at the time of the raid on the Soviet Consulate General showed that the trade organs and their personnel had been engaged in carrying on propaganda dangerous to the Chinese Government. In a communication of July 13 to the Chinese Chargé in Moscow, Karakhan proposed a conference to settle outstanding questions, but also demanded an immediate restoration of the *status quo ante* on the Chinese Eastern Railway and immediate release of the arrested Soviet citizens. He ended with a clear warning: "The Government of the Soviet Union hopes that the Mukden Government and the Government of the Republic of China will carefully consider the serious consequences of opposing these proposals made by the Soviet Government." [9] He said that his government expected a response within three days.

On July 16, the Chinese Government replied, in effect contending that it was the Russians, not the Chinese, who were guilty of violation of the 1924 agreement. On July 17, the U.S.S.R. announced that it was recalling all Soviet diplomatic, consular, and commercial personnel from Manchuria, withdrawing Chinese Eastern Railway personnel from China, suspending rail communications between China and the U.S.S.R., and ordering Chinese diplomatic and consular representatives to depart the Soviet Union at once. Even earlier, the Russians had arrested and detained a large number of Chinese resident in Soviet territory.

China was already following its chosen course. American Minister MacMurray at Peking reported on July 17 that several divisions of troops from Kirin and Heilungkiang provinces, in northern Manchuria, had been sent on July 8 and 10 (before the move against the Chinese Eastern Railway) toward the Manchurian-Soviet border. According to a Moscow charge, denied by the Chinese, White Russian émigré and Chinese forces between July 18 and August 18 made eight attacks on Soviet installations and territory.[10]

The Russians began early to move their own troops, and by a decision on August 6 of the Revolutionary Military Council, a Spe-

cial Far Eastern Army (ODVA), with headquarters at Khabarovsk, was created.[11] The new command consisted of two army
corps, each comprising three rifle divisions, one cavalry brigade,
and from 30 to 35 planes, with a total strength of 113,000 men.
Soviet troop strength in that area before the Chinese action against
the Chinese Eastern Railway had been only about 34,000. The
buildup in strength had been accomplished by expansion of various units to war strength through recruitment, and by the transfer
of two rifle divisions from western Siberia. General Vasily Blücher,
lately military adviser to Chiang Kai-shek, was placed in command.

The Russians moved the 21st Territorial and 12th Rifle Divisions up to Chita. The Chinese side continued to procrastinate—
all the while holding on to the Chinese Eastern Railway. Reput-
edly, there was harassment of Soviet shipping on the Amur River.
On October 12, at 5:30 A.M., units of the ODVA in conjunction
with the Soviet Amur Flotilla struck at the Chinese fleet and land
positions at Lahasusu, at the junction of the Sungari and Amur.[12]
Five Soviet gunboats engaged four Chinese gunboats, sinking three
within the first hour or so. The Chinese crew abandoned the big ex-
German gunboat *Li Chi,* which the Russians then took in tow. The
chief of the Amur River flotilla and 16 men were killed aboard the
Soviet gunboat *Kalmyk,* but the Russians lost no vessels or planes.
Under the Soviet battering, on the morning of October 13, the Chinese garrison at Lahasusu retreated "in complete disorder" to
Fuchin, up the Sungari about 30 miles, and looted the town. Soviet
forces, for a time, pursued the fleeing Chinese troops, inflicting
heavy losses on them. Meanwhile, the Russians loaded barges with
captured Chinese military equipment and stores, and evacuated
Lahasusu on the 17th, leaving two gunboats on guard at the
mouth of the Sungari nearby. Soviet casualties were given as 275
killed and wounded, Chinese casualties as 964, including 373 sai-
lors and marines lost with the gunboats.

This defeat gave the Chinese pause. China had already made various public references to the 1928 Kellogg-Briand Pact of Paris,
and on October 30, Minister C. C. Wu invoked the intervention of
the Pact signatories. On October 31, the Soviet Amur Flotilla, with
a landing party from the Soviet 2d Division, attacked the Chinese
positions at Fuchin, destroyed them in short order, and, on November 2, returned to Khabarovsk in Russia.[13] Meanwhile, elements of the 1st Pacific Ocean Division and the 9th Independent
Cavalry Brigade struck at Mishan, 40 kilometers inside eastern

Manchuria, and smashed the 1st Fengtien Cavalry Division and a White Russian regiment.

The ODVA also struck in the west. There, the Russians had organized a special task force comprising 6,000 infantry and 1,600 cavalry, with modest support in the form of artillery, tanks, and aircraft.[14] On November 17, the Soviet forces surrounded the frontier post of Manchouli and its garrison, while other troops farther east assaulted the Chinese position at Chalainor, taking that town November 18. Manchouli fell to the Soviet attack on November 20. Some Chinese troops had broken out of the encirclement, but the Soviet task force destroyed the 15th and 17th Composite Brigades, and took over 8,000 troops prisoner.[15] The Russians gave their own losses as 123 dead and 405 wounded.

The Soviet air forces bombed Chinese concentrations of reserves at Tsokang but, so far as the retreating Chinese troops were concerned, the Russians contented themselves with harassment by single planes—evidently just to keep the Chinese moving. The Soviet ground forces occupied Tsokang on the 23rd. The Chinese troops were generally deserted by their officers when they reached Hailar; demoralized, they fired the town, and then fled in disorder eastward toward the Hsingan mountain range, looting various points along the railway en route.[16] The Soviet forces occupied Hailar on the 27th. In Washington, the Chinese Minister on November 21 informed the U.S. Government that the U.S.S.R. had invaded Chinese soil in the Manchouli-Chalainor sector with nearly 30,000 troops and a large number of tanks, and that China proposed to lay the matter before the League of Nations.[17] However, the U.S. Consul at Harbin stated in a report of November 27 that, although there had been some severe fighting at Chalainor with heavy damage to the local coal mines, there was "no indication of any large Soviet troop movements then or now." The chief fear of the Chinese populace, he said, centered on the undisciplined Chinese soldier mob.

China won no substantial help from the signatories of the Pact of Paris, some of whom naturally viewed the Chinese attempt to seize the Chinese Eastern Railway against the background of their own vested interests in China. Nor was China encouraged to lay the matter before the League of Nations, of which the Soviet Union was not a member. On November 26, instead, Chang Hsuehliang wired full acceptance of preliminary conditions that had been communicated to him through China's diplomatic commissioner at Harbin, Ts'ai Yun-sheng, who was in touch with the Soviet People's Commissariat for Foreign Affairs by telegraph. Maxim Litvinov, successor to Chicherin as Foreign Affairs Commissar, in his reply gave Moscow's conditions for settlement; basically, the conditions were those set forth four months earlier by Karakhan. According to the U.S. Consul's report of December 2 from Harbin, of the original 40,000 Chinese troops between Pokotu and Hailar, nothing now remained but the disarmed force at Manchouli and a few thousand cavalry troops near Hailar.[18] Nothing stood in the way of a complete Soviet victory. On December 22, 1929, at Khabarovsk, on Russian soil, the issue of the Chinese Eastern Railway was settled when the Chinese signed a protocol with the Russians providing effectively for restoration of the *status quo ante*.

The dénouement impressed, among others, the Japanese. Those ambitious empire-builders had evidently been taking into account, on the one hand, Chinese designs, and, on the other, the effectiveness of countering Soviet military action, and had formulated plans vis-à-vis China accordingly. Increasingly, the Japanese high command focused its attention on the U.S.S.R. as the prime enemy. In 1930, according to the later testimony of a staff officer on the Japanese Army General Staff, a revised plan of war operations against the Soviet Union, with emphasis on the strategic offensive and a sudden attack, was prepared.[19] In September, 1931, the Japanese Kwantung Army began its campaign of mainland conquest with the occupation of Manchuria, and in 1932, the new puppet state of Manchukuo was established.

The organization of the ODVA under Blücher in 1929 had marked a beginning of substantial strengthening of the Soviet military establishment east of Lake Baikal. From 1931 onward, the ODVA underwent continuing expansion. In 1932, the Nanking Government, seeing now a need for Soviet support against Japan, re-established diplomatic relations with Moscow. But the U.S.S.R., far from taking up Nanking's struggle with Japan, went on to buttress its own position. On November 27, 1934, while the Mongolian Premier was visiting Moscow, a secret agreement was reached for Soviet aid in defense of the Mongolian People's Republic. In 1935, the U.S.S.R. liquidated its vulnerable position in Manchuria by selling the Chinese Eastern Railway to Manchukuo. On March 12, 1936, the Russians and Mongols signed, at Ulan Bator, a public "Protocol of Mutual Assistance," by which both agreed, *inter alia,* "in the event of a military attack on one of the contracting parties to render each other every assistance, including military assistance." Soviet military forces shortly afterward again took up station in the Mongolian People's Republic. The Soviet Union was strengthening its defenses in Northeast Asia against anticipated trials to come.

Upon the violent death of war lord Yang Tseng-hsin in July, 1928, Chin Shu-jen, a local military man, had seized power in Sinkiang. But his misrule of the Turki peoples soon had Sinkiang seething with unrest. In February, 1931, the Sarts of southern Sinkiang rose in revolt, under the leadership of Yollbars Khan and Khoja Niaz. They called for help from the hardfighting Dungan general Ma Chung-ying, and Ma entered the Sinkiang lists.

Chin Shu-jen enlisted the service of White Russian refugee troops and officers, chief of whom was Colonel Papingut, an old Dutov officer, against the tough Muslim fighters. Chin's chief of staff was a Manchurian, Sheng Shih-ts'ai. The tangled power struggle continued sporadically, manifested by military and political measures, with Nanking's representatives involved in the conflict, until April, 1933. Then, Chin was in turn ousted from power at Urumchi by the disaffected Cossacks he had himself enlisted in his service. The man who benefited from the coup was Sheng Shih-ts'ai, whom the White Russians put into power.

Political negotiations between Sheng and Ma Chung-ying for a *modus vivendi* broke down, and by January, 1934, Ma stood with his forces at the gates of Urumchi. He was supported on the west by the Ili garrison commander, Chang P'ei-yuan, now advancing on Urumchi. In the north, near Chuguchak, was one of Ma's lieutenants, Ma Ho-ying. A few thousand Chinese troops, retreating in late 1932 into the U.S.S.R. from Manchuria in the face of the Japanese thrust, had been promptly disarmed by their Soviet hosts, but, in 1933, had been "repatriated"—to Sinkiang. Sheng commanded the support of those troops. He was, nevertheless, too weak to withstand the onslaught of the attacking Muslims, and stood in grave danger of being overthrown. In October, 1933, Sheng, who had come to power by his own efforts and owed nothing to and could expect nothing from the National Government, had sent a mission to Moscow with a request for economic aid and military supplies. The mission had returned from Moscow in December accompanied by the able Soviet political agent Garegin Apresov, acting as consul general. Now, in January, 1934, with defeat literally knocking at his gates, Sheng contacted Apresov and called for direct Soviet military assistance.

Two GPU (Soviet state security police) brigades [20] and Red

Army units entered the fray, in uniform but without any insignia, as "men from the Altai." Soviet artillery, cavalry, armored cars, and aircraft on January 24 surprised Ma Ho-ying en route south from Chuguchak and virtually destroyed his force. They launched a heavy attack on Ma Chung-ying's forces in the environs of Urumchi, and the Dungan general, unable to face up to the superior Soviet arms, began to withdraw in the direction of Toksun. The Soviet forces continued their pursuit until Ma crossed the T'ien Shan range and entered southern Sinkiang. Behind him, Chang P'ei-yuan's forces were ambushed in the vicinity of Manas, west of Urumchi, and almost totally destroyed. Chang himself, with his defeat manifest, and capture and disgrace staring him in the face, committed suicide.

The motives behind the unusual Soviet intervention in support of a Chinese war lord against a revolutionary Asian nationalist may not appear on the surface, but they are not hard to uncover. As early as 1918, it will be remembered, a Sino-Japanese mission had visited Sinkiang with the aim of exploiting the anti-Bolshevik forces then present in Central Asia. The Bolsheviks had experienced considerable trouble with the pan-Turanian movement of Enver Pasha in adjoining Russian Turkestan, and had experienced the threat of a Japanese-sponsored pan-Mongolism led by Seménov and Ungern-Sternberg. Ma Chung-ying was reported by the Swedish explorer Sven Hedin, who had the misfortune of meeting up with him in Sinkiang, to be another man dreaming of empire. Ma had in his entourage both a Japanese agent, one Onishi Tadashi, and a Turk named Kemal Kaya Effendi.[21] The implications were clear: Ma, if successful, would not have limited his violent activities to Sinkiang, but would have endeavored to embroil all Central Asia; moreover, the farther Ma went, the more dependent he would have become on the Japanese for financial and military assistance, and the more probably he would have been made into an instrument of Japanese imperial policy. Moscow chose national security over support of a fiery brand of Asian nationalism.

The story of Ma Chung-ying had a strange ending. He and his Dungans had already parted company with their fellow Muslims, the Sinkiang Sarts led by Khoja Niaz and Yollbars Khan. In November, 1933, an "Eastern Turkestan Republic" had been established at Kashgar, headed by Khoja Niaz. Ma Chung-ying, driving into southern Sinkiang in defeat, possessed sufficient residual strength to overthrow the rebel Muslim republic, already riven by internal dissension. Then, in July, 1934, he handed the command of his remaining forces over to his brother-in-law, Ma Hu-shan, and, lured by none-knows-what Soviet promise, proceeded to disappear into the Soviet Union in the company of the Soviet consular officer Konstantinov and several members of *Sovsintorg,* the Soviet trade agency in Sinkiang.

A natural political development derived from the 1934 intervention: Sheng Shih-ts'ai oriented Sinkiang toward the U.S.S.R. Sheng still was not sufficiently concerned with the welfare of the Turki peoples to give them full satisfaction, however, and in late 1936 a brief flash revolt against his rule occurred. This time the rebellion was led by Ma Hu-shan, who had succeeded to the control of the remnants of Ma Chung-ying's battered force, with the support of Yollbars Khan, Khoja Niaz, and Ma Shao-wu. The rebellious movement made some headway, gaining an especially important increment in strength when the formidable Kazakhs of the Altai threw their support to the campaign in hope of ousting Sheng Shih-ts'ai. Again the anti-Chinese movement demonstrated a potential for achieving its objectives. And again in May, 1937, the Russians intervened with military force to save their protégé. This time, it sufficed for Soviet planes to go into action against the mounted riflemen, and the rebel movement collapsed. The explanation for the Soviet action on this occasion is easily divined. In December, 1936, as the price for his release, Chiang Kai-shek had promised his dissident Nationalist captors at Sian that he would abandon prosecution of the civil war and undertake resistance against the Japanese; and in April, 1937, Soviet Ambassador Bogomolov had opened conversations looking toward Sino-Soviet cooperation in that effort. For Moscow, resisting the major enemy, Japan, was of much greater importance at that stage of developments than promoting the disappearance of the Chinese "presence" from Central Asia.

By its 1935 sale of the Chinese Eastern Railway, the U.S.S.R. had withdrawn from its politically exposed salient in Manchuria, in order to avoid a confrontation with Japan. It had further solidified its position in the Mongolian People's Republic through the mutual defense protocol of March 12, 1936. And it had built a base in Sinkiang that not only enabled it to exclude Japanese influence from the area, but also to build up its own influence. Finally, it had proceeded to strengthen its military establishment in the Soviet Far East. In a world of increasing tensions, the U.S.S.R. had buttressed its position in Asia.

Developments had not proceeded entirely smoothly. On June 9, 1935, under continuing heavy Japanese pressure, the Chinese had entered upon the Ho-Umetsu agreement, by virtue of which the Chinese ceded still more of their authority in North China. Relieved of that much more of the threat on their flank, the Japanese proceeded to implement their plans for development of an "autonomous" Japanese-leaning Inner Mongolia, where they would, patently, be in a good position to threaten the Mongolian People's Republic from the south; the M.P.R. was already under threat from the Japanese position in Manchukuo on the east. Manchukuo put forward a demand, rejected by the M.P.R., for a revision of the boundary line in the region of Buir Nor in the vicinity of Khalkhin Miao, with the aim of fixing that line to the south of Buir Nor— in territory claimed by the M.P.R. Then the Japanese demanded that the frontiers of the M.P.R. be opened to Japanese subjects and that Japan have the right of maintaining representatives in the M.P.R. From the beginning of 1935, a number of Manchukuo border incidents were provoked by the Japanese. A clash at Grodekovo, in the Siberian Maritime Province, on January 30, 1935, had been especially serious. Finally, on July 4, a Mongolian delegation, in Manchukuo for negotiations regarding border questions, was given an ultimatum: The Japanese Government demanded permission to send "military observers" into the M.P.R. with the right to establish their own military telegraph system on Mongolian territory for "better connections with Japan and Manchukuo." [22] The Ulan Bator Government naturally rejected that demand, and threats from the Japanese-Manchukuo side followed. Troops of the M.P.R. in the fall of 1935 repelled an assault by a combined Japanese-Manchukuan force. At the beginning of 1936, the Japanese mounted new efforts to exert military pressure against the M.P.R., and on February 12 there occurred an engagement in which the Mongol forces thrust the Japanese-Manchukuan attackers back. Exactly a month afterward, to the day, the U.S.S.R. and the M.P.R. signed their mutual aid protocol.

Stalin's vast purge of the Red Army, begun in 1937, did not at first seriously affect the officer corps on the Far Eastern front. Blücher, who in 1935 had been one of the five military leaders named Marshal of the Soviet Union when that new rank was created, was a member of the military court that tried Marshal Tukhachevsky in June, 1937. The Special Far Eastern Army had, in 1935, been separated from the Trans-Baikal Military District. In February, 1937, it was reorganized as the Far Eastern Red Banner Front. Blücher now commanded a total strength of twenty rifle divisions and three cavalry divisions, supported by large formations of armored cars, tanks, and aircraft—at least 240,000 men.[23]

But the military purge spread to Blücher's command in June (when Blücher was in Moscow), and the Japanese were perhaps not to be blamed for thinking (as did the Germans) that the Soviet military establishment must necessarily have been gravely weakened. Japan was, however, too astute to proceed on that assumption without testing it; a fresh "border incident" soon provided an opportunity. Soviet troops on June 21, 1937, occupied two small islands in the Amur River about 70 miles down river from Blagoveshchensk. On June 30, the Soviet forces were engaged by Japanese and Manchukuan forces, with both sides supported by gunboats. One Soviet gunboat was sunk, at Senukha Island. The Russians ordered withdrawal of their troops and gunboats on July 2, in accordance with an agreement providing for mutual withdrawal reached at Moscow. On July 6, however, the Japanese occupied Bolshoi Island, and remained, despite a Soviet protest. The U.S.S.R. made no effort to evict the presumed trespassers, and the Japanese military were evidently convinced that Soviet military capabilities in the Far East had been seriously damaged.[24] U.S. Ambassador Joseph E. Davies, at Moscow, recorded that a high Japanese official had told him the incident had been staged to test Soviet resolution and preparedness.[25]

The time for final decisions on the implementation of Japanese strategy had come. The kidnapping of Chiang Kai-shek by nationalistic officers at Sian in December, 1936, and the shift in Chinese political strategy that followed, had crystallized the situation. On July 7, 1937, the second Sino-Japanese War began. Then the Soviet relationship with Sheng Shih-ts'ai paid off; Moscow was able to dispatch, with Sheng's acquiescence, a heavily armed mixed brigade to take up station at Hami, the vital eastern gateway to Sinkiang, to block any possible Japanese move in that direction. That brigade, misleadingly designated the "8th Regiment," was made up entirely of Soviet troops, and officered by Russians—but they conscientiously wore Chinese uniforms and insignia. The National Government at Nanking, on August 21, had reached a non-aggression pact with Moscow that was, in effect, the forerunner of credits for the purchase of Soviet military supplies, which had to be transported to China over the highway passing through Hami. There is little doubt that Nanking was not only privy to the arrangement, but had approved it in the first instance.

Soviet planes and fliers were soon in the air over China fighting the Japanese.* Japan's protests were rejected by Moscow. Hostility between Japan and the U.S.S.R. increased, and the "border incidents" multiplied. (Japan, in 1938 alone, gave an accounting of 2,400 such incidents.) According to the Soviet Consul General at Harbin, there occurred, on January 30 and 31, 1938, four clashes near Hunchun and Aigun in which Soviet troops had been forced to fire on trespassing Japanese troops.[26]

In the summer of 1938, while their Yangtze Valley drive was in course, the Japanese military confronted a new situation on the U.S.S.R. border. Near the junction of the frontiers of Manchuria, Korea, and the Soviet Union at the Tumen River, on the east side of the river, there are two modest heights bearing the Russian names Zaozërnaya and Bezymyannaya. The hills, although of small dimensions (Zaozërnaya, the higher, has an elevation of approximately 500 feet above sea level), possessed strategic value because of their relationship to the international frontiers and to Lake Khasan to the east, [27] and because of a reconnoitering range extending to Posyet Bay (U.S.S.R.) and to the port of Rashin (in Korea). Oddly, neither height appears to have been held previously by border guards. But Zaozërnaya (which would soon be better known to the non-Russian world by its Chinese name, Changkufeng) now became the subject of dispute. The issue was whether the boundary followed the ridgeline in that sector, as contended by Moscow, or whether it fell between the ridgeline and Lake Khasan, thus leaving the hills in the possession of Manchukuo (and, in effect, of Japan).†

Trouble began on July 6, 1938. On that date, a party of three Soviet horsemen reconnoitered the peak. A few days later, a working party of approximately 40 Soviet troops arrived and set about constructing a military position on the western slope of the hill. The U.S. Consulate General at Mukden reported on July 15 that,

* See Chapter 3 for a fuller account of Soviet military assistance to Nationalist China at this time.

† It has sometimes been considered that the issue was whether the hills were Soviet or *Korean*. That the interpretation employed here is correct seems clear in the light of (1) Japan's protests to Moscow in behalf of Manchukuo, (2) Moscow's citation of a convention between Russia and *China* in support of its claim, and (3) a map published in *Izvestiya* (Moscow) on August 6, 1939, showing that the Soviet Union there bordered on *Manchuria*. A sketch map given in Erickson, *op. cit.*, p. 496, follows generally the *Izvestiya* portrayal of the border issue in point. Korea does lie west of the Tumen River, but the narrow slip of land between the river and the reference ridgeline was Manchurian soil.

according to urgent Japanese dispatches, Hsinking (Changchun, the capital of Manchukuo) was greatly aroused at the occupation and fortification of the hill in point, described as being 4 kilometers (about 2½ miles) within Manchurian territory and 40 kilometers (about 25 miles) east and south of Hunchun, and the Manchukuan Government was reported to have protested to the Soviet Consul General and to have requested withdrawal. The Japanese Embassy at Moscow had evidently also protested the alleged incursion into the territory of Manchukuo almost simultaneously, because the U.S. Chargé at Moscow reported that the Soviet Foreign Office had informed the Japanese Embassy on July 15 that the territory in point was Soviet.[28]

It would appear that there was soon another exchange, for it is recorded that a protest of the Japanese Ambassador was rejected on July 18, with the citation of the Hunchun Protocol of 1886 between China and Russia and the delivery to him of a copy of that convention, accompanied by an attached map showing Changkufeng in Russian territory.* [29] At this juncture, the military attaché of the U.S. Embassy at Tokyo reported an interesting bit of information. An Embassy communication of July 25 reported his view that one school of Japanese thought was advocating suspension of hostilities beyond Hankow and strong action respecting the border situation, combined with an attempt to bring about the political downfall of Chiang Kai-shek; another group, according to his report, contended that border operations should be avoided to the end that there might be complete destruction of the Chiang regime, "and with it the likelihood of future Russian operations in support of that government." [30] It would appear, from subsequent developments, that Japanese thinking actually fell between two stools.

Tokyo, on July 16, had instructed the Japanese Army Commander, General Nakamura, to move troops into the vicinity of Changkufeng, and elements of the 19th Division under General Suetaka, who had already put a patrol force on the west bank of the Tumen opposite Changkufeng, were moved forward. By July 19, an infantry regiment of four battalions, and artillery and engineers, were in position.[31] Upon receipt of the Soviet rejection of the Japanese demand, the Japanese forces were at first withdrawn, but, on July 26, the Japanese reached a decision "to gamble, but

---

* The 1886 protocol was a supplement to the Sino-Russian Hunchun Convention of 1869, delimiting the border agreed to in the Treaty of Peking in 1860.

cautiously." [32] The 19th Division, with a strength of about 20,000 men, moved up. On July 24, the Russian 1st Army, stationed in the Posyet area, was ordered to concentrate the reinforced battalions of the 118th and 119th Rifle Regiments and of the 121st Cavalry Regiment in the vicinity of Zareche in full battle readiness. [33] On July 29, an eleven-man squad of Soviet frontier guards moved onto Bezymyannaya, lying roughly a thousand yards due north of Changkufeng, and began work on the western slope. The Japanese attacked with a company of frontier guards and overcame the Soviet group, all of whom were rendered casualties. Later the same day, a Soviet force moved up and recaptured its neighbor height. Suetaka deployed two infantry battalions, an engineering regiment, and half a battery of artillery of the 19th Division, together with two companies of border guards, across the Tumen. The Russians, also, evidently were reinforced, but apparently still with border guards. They were reported to have held Changkufeng on July 31 with only 300 men, who were, however, well equipped and well entrenched. The Japanese laid down a heavy artillery barrage and then, on July 31, the 19th Division forces took both hills and penetrated to a depth of 4 kilometers (about 2½ miles) inside Soviet territory. [34] That penetration would have corresponded to Hsinking's original claim that Changkufeng was 4 kilometers deep in Manchukuan territory.

At that time, Blücher was still in command of the Soviet Far Eastern forces. On August 1, he moved up regulars of the 1st Army, and infantry of that unit, supported by tanks and planes, joined the battle the same day. Japanese estimates put the number of Soviet forces in the area at 3,000, with artillery and armor. Soviet planes, by Japanese report (denied by Moscow), began to fly deep sorties into Manchurian and Korean territory, without Japanese resort to counteraction.

On August 4, according to a TASS report of the following day, Shigemitsu called on Litvinov and stated that the Japanese Government proposed to settle the incident in the vicinity of Lake Khasan as a local incident, by peaceful measures. Litvinov, in response, demanded withdrawal of such Japanese forces as might remain on Soviet territory, whereupon the Soviet Government would be prepared to entertain for diplomatic consideration such proposals as the Japanese Government might wish to submit. However, according to the report of the U.S. Embassy at Moscow, Litvinov further stipulated that "the inviolability of the Soviet frontier established by the Hunchun Agreement and the map annexed thereto must be preliminarily guaranteed." [35] In submitting this report, U.S. Chargé Kirk quoted Japanese Ambassador Shigemitsu as saying that Japan had now for the first time seen the map appended to the Hunchun Agreement.

By August 6, the entire 40th Rifle Division of the 1st Army, supported by tanks and planes, had been concentrated in the battle area. About that date, Marshal Blücher was removed from command of the Special Far Eastern Army and Corps Commander (General) Grigory Stern, in command of the 1st Independent Red Banner Far Eastern Army, took charge of operations.[36]

The Japanese were beginning to get worried. Shigemitsu saw Litvinov again on August 7, and found the Soviet position unchanged. The Japanese Ambassador at Washington called on Secretary of State Cordell Hull on August 9 and, while holding that the treaty of 1886 left the hill Changkufeng "on the Japanese side" (that is, the Manchurian side) and characterizing Litvinov as "incorrigible," reported with some evident foreboding that the U.S.S.R. already had 250,000 troops in the Pacific region and "have since" (the attack on Changkufeng?) increased the number to 300,000 and were moving up even more troops from the interior of the U.S.S.R. Hull recorded that the Ambassador emphasized "Japan's extreme desire to restrict this clash to a local incident." [37]

Another development was unfavorable to the long-range Japanese position. Moscow had, a few days earlier, demanded the closure of the Japanese consular office at Khabarovsk, and on August 6, under protest, the Japanese Consul General departed for Vladivostok.* Later, it was learned that German Foreign Minister Joachim von Ribbentrop, in the early days of the hostilities, had first avoided receiving the Japanese Ambassador and then, after the Ambassador had at last succeeded in getting a meeting and subsequently conveyed to the press the impression that von Ribbentrop had given assurances of more than moral support for Japan, called the envoy back and informed him that the press reports differed from the actual conversation; in the words of U.S. Embassy Moscow's report, "Germany would not only not render material assistance but counseled Japan's moderation in relation to the incident." [38] By further report, the German and Italian Am-

---

* In 1938, Moscow completed a sweep of its strategically sensitive Far East by forcing all Japanese, Chinese, and Korean civilians residing in the Maritime Province to choose between returning to their homelands or removing to Soviet Central Asia.

bassadors on August 6 informed the Japanese Government at Tokyo that their governments viewed the time as unpropitious for a clash between the Anti-Comintern Powers and the U.S.S.R.[39]

After the Soviet 40th Rifle Division had completed its concentration, an infantry assault, supported by 216 attack aircraft, was undertaken on August 6. It failed, owing to a combination of bad weather, inadequate artillery preparation, and impediments to tank operations in the marshy environ of Lake Khasan.[40] Heavy fighting continued August 7–9. A communique of the 1st Army published at Moscow on August 10 reported that the Japanese forces had launched attacks on Changkufeng on the 9th, but had been thrown back with heavy losses. According to that communique, the Japanese held a wedge about 650 feet deep inside Soviet territory at the height Bezymyannaya, while Soviet forces had driven a wedge about 1,000 feet into Manchurian territory.[41]

The Japanese diverted the 104th (Kwantung Army) Division, under orders to proceed to the South China front, to the battle area. The Russians built up their own force to about 27 infantry battalions, plus several regiments of artillery and numerous tanks —altogether, about 20,000 troops.[42] Both Tokyo and Moscow were obviously exercising restraint, with the aim of keeping the affair localized. The Imperial Headquarters in Tokyo had instructed the Japanese Army in Korea to avoid an enlargement of the conflict; and Headquarters had informed Minister of War Itagaki, in response to a request for clarification of policy, that it was proposed "to make every effort to effect a local settlement of the issue even though the Japanese may have to withdraw from the line which the U.S.S.R. claims to be the frontier in the vicinity of Changkufeng." [43]

The Russians, although they had apparently suffered the greater losses to date, occupied a superior political and military position. For one thing, they had in hand the protocol of 1886, and Japan at best was acting as surrogate for their clients of Manchukuo; for another, they had heavier battalions in Northeast Asia, while Japan was deeply involved in its campaign against China. Soviet attacks had recovered at least part of the lost ground, and a Japanese counterattack of August 9 had failed. On August 10, Suetaka's Chief of Staff bypassed normal communications channels to wire the Chief of Staff of the Japanese Army at Tokyo: "Appropriate diplomatic measures are immediately imperative." [44]

The Russians bent somewhat from their previous adamant position, and, on August 10, Shigemitsu, meeting once again with

Litvinov, reached an agreement for a cease-fire effective 12:00 noon local time, August 11, with troops of the two sides to remain in the positions occupied by them as of midnight, August 10. It was provided with every show of fairness that redemarcation of the frontier in dispute was to be effected by a mixed commission of two representatives from each side, with an umpire selected by the two parties from citizens of a third state. But the vital provision was found in article 4 of the agreement: "The Commission for the redemarcation shall work on the basis of agreements and maps bearing the signatures of plenipotentiary representatives of Russia and China." [45]

The affair had seemingly ended in a draw as of August 11, with the Japanese still on the crest of Zaozërnaya and the Russians only on the eastern slope.[46] But it soon became evident that, if the agreement at Moscow had incorporated a face-saving device for Japan, it provided victory for the Soviet Union. Suetaka on August 11 sent a colonel to meet with General Stern in the *Soviet* fortifications. Subsequent meetings were held on August 12 and 13, but they were only a formality. The Imperial Headquarters at Tokyo on the afternoon of August 11 had already instructed the Japanese Army in Korea to pull the 19th Division back across the Tumen River;[47] the Japanese had accepted the boundary claimed by Moscow, and the Russians were left on both Zaozërnaya (Changkufeng) and Bezymyannaya.

The Japanese set forth an accounting of 158 killed and 740 wounded on their side in the fighting, and put Soviet casualities at 4,500; Moscow, for its part, admitted 236 Soviet dead and 611 wounded, while estimating Japanese casualties at 3,100. Each side evidently offered a low estimate of its own losses, and a high estimate for the enemy. (Japanese medical statistics, for instance, showed 517 Japanese dead and 922 wounded—the real figures were probably greater still.)[48] It would, in the final analysis, appear that the Soviet Far Eastern army had won "a convincing victory." [49]

U.S. Chargé Kirk, reporting August 14 on opinions circulating in foreign circles in Moscow, said that "it is suggested that as the incident developed the Japanese were not averse to making a reconnaissance of the present fighting ability and morale of the Red Army at the present time and that furthermore the Kwantung Army for its part was ready to engage in a reconnaissance of this nature on the Far Eastern front." [50]

The Russians presented their case respecting the Changkufeng affairs to the International Military Tribunal for the Far East that judged Japanese war crimes in 1948, supporting their argument with a photostatic copy of Annex I of the Hunchun Protocol. Majority opinion held that the Japanese had been guilty of initiating the hostilities at Changkufeng.[51]

After the Changkufeng affair, the Soviet forces east of Lake Baikal were reorganized. There were two Red Banner armies in the Soviet Far East, and the Trans-Baikal Military District forces. In addition, with headquarters at Ulan Bator in the M.P.R., was the 57th Russian Rifle Corps. The Japanese General Staff estimated the total strength of the Soviet force to be 24 divisions, 1,900 tanks, and 2,000 planes.[52] Marshal Blücher was no longer in the picture. On November 9, 1938,[53] even as Tukhachevsky before him, he was executed on fabricated charges.

A new major incident occurred on the western border of Manchukuo, in the vicinity of Buir Nor, the following summer. As earlier related, already in 1935 there had been portents of impending events in that sector. A Soviet work contends that it was the Japanese design to cut the Trans-Siberian Railway by a thrust through the Mongolian People's Republic, and thus to deprive Moscow of the possibility of transferring armed forces from European Russia to the Soviet Far East for defense purposes.[54] General Stern, of Lake Khasan fame, in a speech in mid-March, 1939, charged that the Japanese were preparing an attack on the Mongolian People's Republic.[55] In any case, the Japanese did again test the Russians.

East of Khalkhin Gol (river) there are some hillocks, the highest of which is called Nomonhan. How the trouble involving that height began is not entirely clear. The U.S. Chargé at Tokyo, in due course, reported that the clash had come about following a dispute arising out of a Japanese denial to Mongolian nomads of the right to attend a trade fair in territory to which they traditionally traveled, but which was now claimed by Manchukuo; the nomads finally undertook to go to the fair with a herd of several thousand sheep, under escort of Soviet troops, and on May 8, after crossing the Halha (presumably, Khalkhin) River, this mixed company was intercepted by Japanese troops, and the two sides exchanged fire.[56] Another version has the affair beginning on May 4.[57] The Soviet version states that, on May 11, M.P.R. border guards stationed southeast of Buir Nor, twenty kilometers east of Khalkhin Gol (which site would have been about the location of Nomonhan), were subjected to a sudden attack by Japanese troops.[58]

Having taken the Mongols by surprise, the Japanese succeeded in penetrating Mongol territory and nearing the Khalkhin Gol. Here, a battle took place between the attacking Japanese and the Mongol border guards. It can readily be inferred that the Mongols were driven to the west bank of the Khalkhin Gol.

The Japanese at this time had concentrated some elements of the Kwantung Army in eastern Manchuria with the aim, according to testimony at the 1948 War Crimes trial in Tokyo, of occupying strategic points in the lower Maritime Province by a lightning strike, and then going on to the capture of Khabarovsk and Blagoveshchensk.[59] Both sides reinforced their positions, and on May 31, Soviet Foreign Minister V. M. Molotov in his report to the Supreme Soviet proclaimed, to the Japanese, that the U.S.S.R. would defend the territory of the M.P.R. as resolutely as it would defend its own.

The Russians came promptly to the aid of their Mongol allies, and Soviet-Mongol forces numbering about 950 men (cavalry, artillery, engineers, and armored cars but no tanks) [60] were soon facing over 2,500 Japanese along the Khalkhin Gol. In heavy fighting on May 28–29, the Soviet-Mongol forces, strengthened by the 149th Regiment, which had been moved up from Tamsag-Bulak, something over 60 miles away, held the attacking Japanese. Reinforced with the 8th (Mongolian) Cavalry Division and the 11th Tank Brigade, the 36th Motorized Rifle Division (minus one regiment), the 7th, 8th, and 9th Mechanized Brigades, a heavy artillery battalion, and 100 fighter planes, the Soviet-Mongol force then had a strength of 11,100 men, with 186 tanks.

By the end of June, the Japanese had moved up the 7th and 23rd Divisions and additional Manchukuan cavalry. Heavy fighting began on July 2, when the Japanese put a force of 24,700 troops, 250 planes, 140 tanks, and 300 artillery pieces (including 100 antitank guns) into action against the combined M.P.R.–U.S.S.R. forces in the vicinity of the height Bain Tsagan on the west bank of the Khalkhin.

Both sides made extensive use of air power, and cavalry played an important role. The first Japanese assault took Bain Tsagan, but the height was retaken on July 5 after a three-day battle and the Japanese retired to the east bank of the Khalkhin Gol. They resumed the offensive on July 8, but were again pushed back,[61] and, apparently, the Soviet-Mongol forces, at this time or soon afterward, established a bridgehead on the east bank of the Khalkhin. The Japanese, between July 23 and July 25, conducted an intense artillery bombardment in an effort to reduce that bridgehead. The importance of the air arm in particular was indicated by the Japanese claim that 715 Soviet and Mongol planes had been destroyed up to July 28, and in the Russians' counterclaim that they had downed 199 Japanese planes between May 8 and June 12. The Russians further asserted that they had inflicted 5,500 casualties (2,000 dead, 3,500 wounded) on the enemy, and captured 254 prisoners, in the fighting between July 6 and July 12 alone.*

At that juncture, General Georgy Zhukov was given command of the 1st Army Group, and he set about concentrating forces adequate to the task of defeating the Japanese. The U.S. Ambassador at Moscow on August 10 forwarded to Washington the military attaché's report of the movement over the preceding six weeks or two months of "considerable" quantities of military supplies and "some" troops, presumably to the Trans-Baikal area, in connection with the border troubles.[62]

The movement had been bigger than remarked at the time. By August 20, having used every possible effort at concealment, Zhukov had deployed 35 Soviet rifle battalions and 20 cavalry squadrons against 25 Japanese infantry battalions and 17 cavalry squadrons. Notably, Zhukhov had 498 tanks, 346 armored cars, and 500 aircraft. His aim was to encircle the enemy in a battle of annihilation.

The Japanese launched their biggest offensive to date on August 17, when the specially formed 6th Japanese Army heavily attacked the Soviet-Mongol positions near the Khalkhin Gol. The main Japanese offensive was fixed for August 24. On August 20, however, Zhukov launched his own carefully prepared offensive, attacking along the entire enemy front east of the Khalkhin Gol. Attacking incessantly and making heavy use of tanks and aviation, the Soviet-Mongol forces achieved an initial encirclement, and, on the night of August 28, hammered the Japanese force to pieces.

Simultaneously, a political situation of major importance for the world balance of power—and for the German-Japanese relationship—had been developing. On August 23, to the undisguised

---

* This report gets some substantiation from the previously cited July 26 report of the U.S. Chargé at Tokyo, which stated that the Japanese had by then engaged the greater part of the two divisions and admitted the loss of 35 per cent of their effectives and 30 planes since the fighting began three weeks earlier.

surprise of Tokyo, Molotov and von Ribbentrop, on behalf of the Soviet Union and Nazi Germany, signed a nonaggression pact. The U.S. Chargé at Tokyo reported, on August 25, that he had been "most reliably" informed the day before that the Soviet Government had submitted to the Japanese Ambassador at Moscow a proposal for a Soviet-Japanese nonaggression pact.[63] On September 1, 1939, the German invasion of Poland started, and the European War had begun. Japan's grand strategy had suffered a severe wrench.

The end of the "Nomonhan Incident" came in essentially the same pattern as the end of the Changkufeng affair. On September 16, TASS announced at Moscow that, as a result of conversations between Foreign Affairs Commissar Molotov and Japanese Ambassador Togo Shigenori, it had been agreed that hostilities between the Japanese-Manchukuan and Soviet-Mongol sides would cease at 2:00 P.M. Moscow time that date, with troops to remain in the positions they occupied at 1:00 P.M., Moscow time, September 15. Military representatives of the two forces engaged should implement those provisions, and should immediately arrange for an exchange of dead and prisoners. A joint border commission would be set up, with two representatives from each side, to demarcate the border in the region of the recent conflict as soon as possible.[64] On June 9, 1940, it was announced simultaneously at Moscow and Tokyo that agreement had been reached for demarcation of the disputed border between Manchukuo and the Mongolian People's Republic. The Japanese Foreign Office said that this agreement had been achieved by "mutual concessions and compromises." Japanese casualties had probably numbered 55,000. Japan itself officially characterized the affair as "a disastrous, bitter battle," and admitted 18,000 casualties.[65] It seems probable that the Russians' claim that they had destroyed the Japanese 6th Army was correct.

The Japanese had suffered a major reverse, and the Soviet-Mongol forces consolidated their positions on the borderline claimed by the M.P.R. The troop strength engaged on the two sides in that practically uninhabited plains region had been substantially greater than that in the fighting at Lake Khasan: the Japanese defeat was the greater. At Moscow, Zhukov was given the award of "Hero of the Soviet Union" for his victory. His employment of artillery and tank forces had been a presage of victories to be achieved with those arms in World War II.

The Nomonhan affair was followed by a stabilization of Soviet-

Japanese relations. The September 15, 1939, agreement led logically to the signature, on April 13, 1941, of a nonaggression pact between the two countries, which permitted each to pursue its own national ends unhindered by the other. An agreement of June, 1940, between Ambassador Togo and Molotov had defined the Manchukuan–M.P.R. boundary in general terms. In May, 1942, the common frontier was formally demarcated. At that time, the U.S.S.R. was heavily engaged with the Germans, and Japan was deep in war in the Pacific with the United States, Britain, and the Netherlands. But the common frontiers between the Soviet Union and the Japanese-controlled regions of China were quiet—temporarily.*

With the entry of the United States into the war as an ally in 1941, the Chinese National Government turned promptly to exert pressure on the Soviet Union to withdraw its forces, and its influence, from Sinkiang. Sheng Shih-ts'ai, who thought he foresaw Russian defeat in Europe, turned to Chungking. The involved political maneuvers of 1942 were attended by ultimate success for the Chinese, and, in 1943, Moscow pulled out of Sinkiang, lock, stock, and barrel. The "8th Regiment" finally left Hami.

There was an incidental denouement of some interest. Sheng Shih-ts'ai, in line with his pro-Soviet policy, had, in 1937, requested that the Communists at Yenan lend him the services of some cadres, and a number of important Chinese Communists had been sent to help Sheng construct the "New Sinkiang." The first leader of the group, Teng Fa, special services chief, was replaced in 1939 by Ch'en T'an-ch'iu, one of the founding members of the Chinese Communist Party (under the alias Hsu Chieh). Among the cadres was Mao Tse-min, the younger brother of Mao Tse-tung, under the name Chou Pin. According to Sheng Shih-ts'ai, Mao Tse-min actually served as Sheng's "personal adviser and assistant," but he occupied the official post of provincial Commissioner of Finance. In early 1942, apparently sensing the way things were going in Sinkiang, Ch'en asked Sheng's permission for the group to return to Yenan, but Sheng refused the request. Ch'en thereupon asked that the group be permitted to proceed to Moscow, only to meet a new refusal—and the group was put under surveillance. In April, 1942, Ch'en, Mao, and about 100 other Communists were arrested. There followed a widespread purge of Communists in the

* For further review of Soviet-Japanese relations with respect to Manchuria during World War II, see Chapter 4.

province on the basis of the general charge, issued publicly only in December of that year, that there had been a Communist conspiracy to overthrow Sheng's government. Such was the secrecy of Sheng's regime that dates and detailed circumstances are not known; but it is known that among those executed were Ch'en T'an-ch'iu and Mao Tse-min.

By its refusal to share political power, the new Kuomintang-dominated regime in Sinkiang succeeded in quickly alienating the sympathies of the Kazakhs, the Mongols, and the Turki peoples of the province. In early 1944, a Kazakh rebellion began in the Altai region; in November of the same year, a parallel Uighur revolt broke out in the Ili district. The two rebellions joined forces, and in January, 1945, an "Eastern Turkestan Republic" was organized in Ili. Athough there was no clear evidence of direct Soviet intervention in the affair, the Soviet interest was unmistakable.

As the revolt developed, the new Kuomintang governor of Sinkiang, Chang Chih-chung, enlisted the mediation of the Soviet representative in Urumchi, and, thanks to Soviet efforts, it proved possible to obtain a truce based upon the concept of a coalition provincial government in which the Turki, Kazakh, and Mongol peoples should be duly represented. But the able Chang Chih-chung was replaced by a "tame" Uighur, Masud Sabri, a Kuomintang hack of many years' standing. The program based upon a sharing of political power with the non-Chinese people was aborted, with the coalition government at Urumchi breaking apart in July, 1947. The revolt resumed, to the accompaniment of worsening Sino-Soviet relations.

Immediately before, in June, 1947, the "Peitashan" affair had occurred on the borders of Sinkiang and the M.P.R. The boundary line in that area had been considerably adjusted in Sinkiang's favor since the advent of the Republic of 1912, but there was open dispute about its exact location. In April, 1946, one of the early Kazakh rebels against the Kuomintang power, Osman Bator, had broken relations with Ili and moved to the Peitashan area. In February, 1947, he took the field *against* Ili, but after some initial success was pressed back in mid-April into the Peitashan area, with only a hundred men remaining under his command. There, he was approached by an Urumchi emissary with a proposal to serve the Chinese cause, and he evidently accepted. At the beginning of June, Osman, with his small body of horsemen, joined Chinese troops in an attack on a Mongol command post, overrunning it and killing the Mongol commanding officer. However, Mongol planes and cavalry on June 5 promptly launched a counterattack, and the forces of Osman and the Chinese were thrust back. The Chinese Government claimed that Soviet planes had participated, but this claim could have been in error, given the similarity of the red star markings used on the planes of the two countries. M.P.R. authorities charged that the battle in point had occurred about 9 miles inside their frontiers, whereas the Chinese claimed that it had taken place some 120 miles inside Sinkiang.[66] In the end, the Chinese were found outside the line claimed by the M.P.R. as the frontier.

The Sinkiang rebellion was finally resolved only in 1949, as the civil war between the National Government and the Chinese Communists drew to a close in China proper. There was, at the end, an interesting reversal of roles. In August, 1944, as central government pressure upon his political position became unbearable, Sheng Shih-ts'ai had sent his chief of staff to the Soviet Consulate General in Urumchi requesting military intervention in his behalf yet again, for a consideration.[67] At that late date, with no illusions, now, regarding Sheng's "friendship for the Soviet Union," the Russians made no reply. Five years later, the Chinese Communists forces advanced into neighboring Kansu, and, according to an unnamed "reliable source," the Soviet Consul General at Urumchi approached the commander of the Chinese Nationalist forces, General T'ao Shih-yueh, and urged him to declare Sinkiang independent. Thereupon, according to the report, the Russians would direct the Chinese Communists to halt their advance into the province, and, following a Red victory, autonomous Sinkiang could be incorporated into a federal (Chinese) republic.[68]

The new governor of Sinkiang, Burhan Shahidi, actually reached an agreement that resulted in the turnover of T'ao Shih-yueh, and Sinkiang, to the Communist side on September 29, 1949. The rebels at Ili were thus left without an enemy—but also effectively without a friend, for Moscow was looking toward the establishment of friendly relations with the Central People's Government destined to come into being at Peking on October 1, 1949. The Kazakh-Turki rebellion that had begun in 1944 came to a miserable end. The leading advocates of Turki nationalism died in a mysterious "air accident" while en route to Peking to attend the September conference, at which they had been supposed to construct a political platform for the new regime. Osman Bator, found on the Nationalist side when the turnover came, rose up in revolt again, and took to the field against the Communist forces. He shielded the retreat of many of his people out of Sinkiang, and Kazakh refugees flowed into Kashmir, and eventually to Turkey; Osman Bator himself was captured in the Tsinghai-Tibetan borderland in February, 1951, taken to Urumchi, and there executed.

Thus, the third effort in a century to establish an "Eastern Turkestan Republic" resulted in failure, and Sinkiang began to undergo a radical transformation to fit into the new Chinese mold, as an integral part of the Chinese People's Republic. In 1955, it became the Sinkiang-Uighur Autonomous Region—but, in fact, it possessed no real autonomy.

The Soviet declaration of war against Japan on August 8, 1945, and the launching of a joint Soviet-Mongol drive into Manchukuo and Inner Mongolia, brought about a new Soviet occupation of Manchuria, but this time the occupation was made, initially, with the full agreement of Nationalist China.* The National Government's formal recognition, on January 5, 1946, of the independence of the Mongolian People's Republic was also effected. (Neighboring Urianghai, which had become Tannu Tuva when Soviet Russia recognized its independence in 1921, had, meanwhile, quietly been incorporated into the Soviet Union on October 13, 1944.) The "Mongolian Question" entered a new phase.

The Peking regime has undertaken to direct a flood of Chinese peoples into Tibet and Sinkiang, as into Manchuria and Inner Mongolia in earlier days, with the aim of achieving a true ethnic amalgamation. Sinkiang will soon be more Chinese than Turki. Now it is the Chinese who look across their frontiers with the idea of reincorporating the Mongolian People's Republic into the Chinese empire, and of making good various claims on the Russian borderlands. For the visible future, they plainly lack the strength to fulfill their ambitions. Nevertheless, the Chinese borderlands have clearly taken on a new aspect, and will never be the same again.

* See Chapter 4.

3. *Soviet Military Aid to Nationalist China, 1923-41*

By JAMES C. BOWDEN

The Soviet Union extended a considerable amount of aid to Nationalist China during the period 1923–41, while at the same time giving severely limited support to the Chinese Communists. An interesting aspect of this little-known development, which helps to explain its obscurity, is that not much has been written about this selective Soviet aid either by the Chinese Nationalists or by the Chinese Communists. A Soviet writer has been prompted to note that "the work of our advisers in China during the period 1924–27 has not been sufficiently publicized by the Chinese press." The Soviet critic added that "only one short article, which included only fragmentary material, is known to us." [1]

What was once thought by many to be a world-wide Communist monolith is disintegrating, and the most important element of this disintegration is the bitter schism that has grown between the Soviet Union and the Chinese Peoples' Republic. The roots of current Sino-Soviet discord are deeply embedded in several layers of the fertile soil of the past. Before the advent of Communism—which briefly cemented the two countries together—the Russian and Chinese peoples had been engaged in a centuries-old struggle for political and economic control of central and northern Asia. The seeming indifference of the Kremlin toward the struggling Chinese Communist Party during its long years of struggle to power renewed Chinese suspicion and even hatred for the Russians. There is ample evidence that, during this period, as well as since, the Soviet Union always has had its national interest foremost in mind, and has always been ready to sacrifice the interests of the Chinese Communists when it would be of advantage to the U.S.S.R.

Soon after the Bolsheviks came to power in 1917, they began to turn their attention to the spread of Communism throughout the countries of Europe and Asia. The precarious situation in China appeared to the leaders in Moscow to offer great possibilities. It is a well-known Soviet tactic to infiltrate an indigenous movement in a country with which it is maintaining diplomatic relations. Thus, it appeared to the Russians that the nationalist movement headed by Dr. Sun Yat-sen offered a good opportunity for Communist infiltration. Soviet publications comment favorably on Sun Yat-sen, and build up his role in inviting Soviet support for the Kuomintang. According to the Soviet *Political Dictionary,* Sun Yat-sen "welcomed the October Revolution and under its influence and the influence of the growing worker's movement in China decided to establish closer relations with the Russian Communist Party." [2] A Soviet military historian has quoted a letter of August 28, 1921, which Sun Yat-sen sent to the Soviet Ministry of Foreign Affairs, saying, "I am extraordinarily interested in your affairs, especially in the organization of your soviets, your army, and educational systems." [3]

In answer to Sun Yat-sen's inquiries, the Soviet Union in 1923 sent to China a delegation that included Mikhail M. Borodin. Sun Yat-sen was faced with the problem of organizing China, and became convinced that "the Russian Communist Party with its history and achievements would be a good example." [4] The advice of Borodin, who was sent to help organize the government and the military, was very welcome.

Chiang Kai-shek, a rising military aide to Sun Yat-sen, visited the Soviet Union in 1923 on his leader's behalf, and, during this visit, called on military schools, and was briefed on Soviet military organization and procedures. Upon his return to China, he indicated that he favored the adoption of Soviet methods in the organization of the infant Kuomintang army. [5] In 1924, the reorganization of the Chinese army was initiated under Soviet guidance, and an influx of Soviet military aid and advisers began. [6]

Among the recommendations that Chiang Kai-shek submitted to Sun Yat-sen, after returning from the Soviet Union in 1923, was a proposal for the establishment of a military academy to train officers for the revolutionary army. Such an academy was opened at Whampoa in 1924. The initial class consisted of approximately 500 cadets recruited from all over China. [7] In his speech at the opening ceremonies, Sun Yat-sen declared:

Six years ago Russia started a revolution and at the same time organized a revolutionary army. This army developed by stages and was able to destroy the old forces and external dangers and achieved great successes. Opening this academy, we follow the example of Russia. In the academy the principles of the building of the Red Army of the Soviet Union will be studied and an Institute for Party Commissars will be established. In the future this system will be incorporated into the remainder of the units of the revolutionary army.[8]

This warm welcome set the stage for the Soviet advisers who soon came into China. Sun Yat-sen had made an agreement with the war lords in Canton to have 300 Mauser rifles sent to the Academy, but only 30 had been sent—scarcely sufficient even for the guards. So Sun Yat-sen turned to the Soviet Union for aid. Soviet military ships arrived in Canton on October 8, 1924, with a shipment that included 8,000 rifles, with 500 rounds of ammunition for each. Within a year, the Chinese received an additional 15,000 rifles, machine guns, and artillery pieces.[9] It is estimated that the Russians advanced a total of 3 million rubles for the initial expenses of the Academy.[10]

The influence of the Soviet advisers, headed by General Galen (Blücher), was very strong in the Whampoa Military Academy. A Soviet general, A. I. Cherepanov, who served as an adviser in China during this period, clearly outlined the tasks of the Soviet advisers in a memoir published in 1964:

> Our group of advisers consisted of commanders who combined practical experience with solid theoretical preparation. We had participated in two wars and all of this was strengthened by theoretical preparation in the Academy [Frunze Military Academy in Moscow]; therefore, we were able not only to organize the studies of the cadets in class, but also to demonstrate the practical aspects of training. Much was done so that the first steps of the training of the cadets would master the maximum of practical skills. We desired that the future commanders would understand the importance of field training, coordinated actions, good appearance, careful preparation, and would master all aspects of military service.
>
> The duties at the school were divided among the Soviet advisers, with the senior adviser supervising the academic portion and two other advisers working with drill, weapons firing, and tactical preparation. . . . In the process of military training, we turned our greatest attention to the individual training of each cadet. However, if a Chinese cadet acquired some habit which was a little

different than our regulations required, we would ignore it so as not to complicate training. As far as tactics (combat, intelligence, observation, etc.) and rifle instruction were concerned, we went entirely by our manuals, taking into consideration their modest armament: rifles, two to four machine guns, and one cannon per regiment. In order to improve rifle marksmanship we ourselves made simple instruments for checking, sighting, and aiming. . . . On tactical exercises we taught the cadets to attack swiftly in coordination with fire, and as there were never enough troops this was especially important when flanking the enemy. In the defense we also demanded maximum movement, attempting to prevent enemy attack through the use of counterattack.

Cherepanov also described the many difficulties which confronted the Soviet advisers at the Whampoa Academy:

Our work was especially complicated by the apprehension of the teachers, as the officers and cadets did not know that all the academic courses were in fact developed by the advisers. The teachers were afraid of "losing face." Not wishing to worsen relationships, we made sure that all of the basic work was conducted according to our plans, but we avoided the limelight. Slowly, however, we won over the confidence of the instructors and were able to give orders directly to the officer or cadet as necessary to complete the exercise or to organize a course of instruction.

The biggest difficulty which we met in the beginning was the lack of interpreters. We spoke English and Chinese very poorly and could not, naturally, check the theoretical training or listen to the lectures and make the necessary corrections. In addition, we could not personally conduct any classes. Much time was lost convincing stubborn teachers that the Russian methods were the best.[11]

The support given to the Chinese by the Russians in establishing the Whampoa Academy was of inestimable value to the Kuomintang. The graduates of this Academy became the core of the National Revolutionary Army. However, it must be noted that, in due time, many of them became leaders in the Chinese Communist army.

One facet of Soviet organization that was transferred *in toto* to the newborn Chinese army was the control mechanism of "political commissars." In October, 1923, Borodin pointed out the importance of political work in the army to Sun Yat-sen. After a detailed explanation by Borodin of the structure and military life of the Soviet army, Sun Yat-sen declared: "We do not have an army like that. It is necessary to form one." [12] The school at Whampoa played an instrumental part in the inculcation of political reliability into the Chinese army. One Soviet author has noted that "in the military academy at Whampoa the political department gave the young commanders excellent political preparation. The seed, planted in the school, soon began to yield a harvest." [13] The Soviet advisers at Whampoa succeeded in having Chou En-lai, an avowed Communist, appointed to an important role in—some sources say for a time as head of—the political department.[14] A mandatory political curriculum was established at Whampoa. It included the following socioeconomic disciplines: political economics, the theory of imperialism, the three principles of Sun Yat-sen, the history of China, and the history of the revolutionary movement in the West. There was a lack of qualified instructors for these courses, and, occasionally, a theoretician from the Kuomintang came and presented lectures.[15]

Emphasis on political control was extended to the rest of the army in 1924, with "political administrations formed to strengthen educational work, and political departments established in corps to oversee the political commissars and cells of the Communist Party." [16] These commissars were designated all the way down to regiments, battalions, and companies. Although ostensibly the political officers were supposed to concern themselves only with propaganda and agitation, they actually had the power to countermand the orders of the military commanders.[17] According to an agreement with Sun Yat-sen, these political officers were to indoctrinate the troops with the principles of the Kuomintang, but, in reality, they covertly cultivated Communist doctrine.[18]

Under the guidance of the Russians, the Chinese began to think about conducting propaganda campaigns among the civilian populace. Prior to the outset of the first major campaign to reunify China, the First Eastern Expedition in 1925, the workers in the propaganda department in Whampoa prepared 500,000 pamphlets to be given to the soldiers, and 100,000 leaflets to be spread among the peasants, plus 50,000 texts containing revolutionary songs. This material was distributed during the campaign. In the large population centers, meetings were organized under such slogans as "Organize Peasant Unions" or "Lower the Rent." The peasant unions developed through this propaganda were able to provide communications and intelligence, and they were also able to cause disorganization in the enemy's rear areas. The peasants used every opportunity to accumulate weapons for use in future operations when the landlords would be weak enough so that the peasants could attack.[19] The Northern Expedition, during the period 1926–27, also showed the results of the influence of the Soviet advisers. A vast political apparatus was formed to accompany this march to spread propaganda among the troops and populace. The propagandists even had a huge printing press that they took with them for printing proclamations, posters, and newspapers.[20] The propaganda conducted during both these campaigns considerably facilitated the forward movement of the Kuomintang armies.

As has been shown, the Soviet advisers soon assumed influential roles in the reorganization of the army. These experienced officers passed on their knowledge in tactics, logistics, and organization in an attempt to prepare the Kuomintang army for the forthcoming battles. The First Eastern Expedition was scheduled to begin in January, 1925. The chief Soviet adviser, General Blücher, had drawn up the plans for the campaign, and had had them approved only after a great deal of opposition from several Chinese generals. These Chinese generals conducted their part of the campaign with a noted lack of enthusiasm, and were accused by Blücher of exhibiting a criminal lack of responsibility. However, the campaign was not prevented from progressing satisfactorily.[21]

The Soviet advisers were not always successful in instituting Russian methods in the Chinese army. Cherepanov mentions that the Chinese were accustomed to marching for two or three hours and then taking a long break of from 15 to 20 minutes, whereas the Soviet army usually took a 10-minute break after each 50 minutes of marching. Nor did the Chinese stop for lunch, as they had no accompanying kitchen trains, but, rather, they ate in the morning before the march, and in the evening. A Russian attempt to shorten the period between the soldiers' meals was not crowned with success. The Chinese were advised to cook two portions in the morning—the food consisting basically of rice and some kind of greens—and issue them to the soldiers for breakfast and lunch. However, the soldiers always ate the portion prepared for lunch long before the designated time, and the Chinese soon went back to the old method.[22]

Particularly vulnerable on the march was security for the advancing march column, as there was no means for reconnaissance except by patrols of foot soldiers. The Chinese had no aviation or horses available at this time, and the Chinese officers met the Soviet advisers' suggestions with indifference, which resulted in many misfortunes. These misfortunes finally forced the Chinese officers to ask the Russians for their recommendations on route security.[23]

The influence of the Soviet advisers reached its zenith in the spring and summer of 1925. There were then over 1,000 Russian advisers in China. By that time, operational leadership of the Kuomintang forces was almost completely in the hands of General Blücher; Blücher himself wrote many of the directives, which were then translated into Chinese and sent to the field commanders. If there was not sufficient time to have the orders translated, they were forwarded to the Soviet advisers in Russian and then, in turn, given to the Chinese commanders.[24]

In the fall of 1925, Blücher was, for a time, recalled to Moscow. His absence considerably weakened the influence of the Soviet advisers in the strategic and operational preparation for the Second Eastern Expedition, and the main role at that time passed to Chiang Kai-shek. Despite the temporary diminution of Soviet influence, by the end of 1925 there were Soviet officers officially heading the Chinese Navy and Aviation bureaus, as well as the very important post of Communications Department of the General Staff.[25] In January, 1926, critical references pertaining to the Soviet advisers appeared in Chiang Kai-shek's diary.[26] Chiang knew that he would have to take measures to bring the revolutionary movement back under the control of the Kuomintang. His first step to reduce Soviet influence was made on February 17, 1926, when he insisted on the reorganization of the General Staff, and on the removal of the Russians from top administrative posts in the Navy and Aviation bureaus.[27] However, his action had little effect, as was clearly pointed out by a Soviet adviser in his report to Moscow:

> The changes put into effect by Chiang Kai-shek early in 1926 did not materially reduce Soviet influence. Russian advisers were in fact at the head of all departments of the General Staff, although officially they were called advisers. The reason the Russians reverted to the positions of advisers was that it is politically inconvenient for our advisers to hold official posts and our influence does not suffer in the least by their becoming advisers again.[28]

Aware that Soviet influence continued unabated, on March 20, 1926, Chiang Kai-shek took stronger measures. Chinese Communists in the army were arrested, and the quarters of the Soviet advisers were surrounded by loyal Kuomintang troops.[29] General

Stepanov, Soviet adviser with the Chinese First Army, reported the reversal to Moscow, and then candidly described the mistakes that the Soviet advisers had made in their relations with the Chinese:

> The Russian advisers pursued erroneous tactics by pushing the centralization of military organs too rapidly and by grabbing too much direct control over various organizations. This, combined with their excessive supervision of the Chinese generals and neglect of Chinese etiquette, aroused resentment among the Chinese military officers. Furthermore, the Russians failed to disseminate suitable propaganda in the army.[30]

Chiang Kai-shek still needed Soviet support for the forthcoming Northern Expedition, and therefore did not push matters far enough to rupture completely Chinese-Soviet relations. The Soviet advisers had been surprised by Chiang's moves, and Mikhail Borodin, the leading Soviet official in China, requested instructions from Moscow. At that time, Stalin was busy consolidating his power in the Kremlin against Trotsky's group, and he insisted that the Russians in China continue to support Chiang Kai-shek. In an attempt to ameliorate the situation, Borodin announced that Chiang Kai-shek had taken correct action against those who were "too far to the left." [31] However, after the setback in March, the Soviet Government adopted a more cautious approach to China, and curtailed Soviet aid. The aid that China did receive was meager, and of low quality, with the U.S.S.R. selling outdated Japanese and German arms to the Chinese for high prices.[32]

There is considerable variance between Communist and non-Communist writers as to the role of Soviet advisers in the subsequent Northern Expedition. F. F. Liu reports that Soviet aid was minimal, and that Blücher's contribution consisted mainly of criticism of the Chinese operation plan. Although Blücher's help in the field of logistics was welcomed by the Chinese, Liu contends that "Blücher seldom formulated or made any attempt to direct the expedition's course himself." [33] Soviet writers, however, insist that Blücher played a very important role in developing the plans for the Northern Expedition. His detailed planning, they claim, included the supply of provisions, ammunition, warm clothing, preparation for radio and telephone communication, and arrangements for medical care. On the tactical side, Blücher emphasized coordinated action of the attacking units. At his direction, Soviet pilots flew air support missions dropping "219 bombs . . . and several hundred pounds of leaflets" on the enemy positions. Blücher wrote the attack orders, with specific instructions to the corps, and these orders were then translated into Chinese and signed by Chiang Kai-shek as Commander in Chief. In addition, Blücher paid much attention to political work in the armed forces. He insisted that the troops be informed about the mission of the Northern Expedition and its significance for the national revolution.[34]

The Northern Expedition got under way in July, 1926, with fifteen Russian officers, under the direction of Blücher, advising. The Chinese army consisted of 100,000 troops organized in ten corps, with Soviet officers in strategic advisory positions in each of these corps.[35] The Russians claim that if these advisers had not accompanied the Chinese units many of the Chinese generals would have turned their units into partisan groups, the formation of which would have led to the disintegration of the Kuomintang forces.[36]

The Northern Expedition was successfully completed in less than one year. However, during this period, the subversive activity of the Communists continued unabated, with attempts to spread Communism among the soldiers, peasants, and workers.

The Chinese Communist Party had been founded in July, 1921, and soon came under the control of the Comintern, which had its headquarters in Moscow. This fledgling Party was instructed by the Comintern to form a coalition with the Kuomintang.[37] The Soviet advisers in China helped the Chinese Communists acquire positions of influence within the Kuomintang, for example, as has been noted, by having Chou En-lai appointed to the political department of the Whampoa Military Academy. However, the increase in the number of Chinese Communists in the Kuomintang army was slow. By the middle of 1926, there were only 1,000 Communists in the National Revolutionary Army, with up to 60 or 70 per cent of them in the school at Whampoa.[38] The number of Communists in the army did, however, increase rapidly during the Northern Expedition in 1926 and 1927.

Chiang Kai-shek realized that, in order to rid himself of Communist influence, he would have to sever all relations with the Soviet Union. On April 12, 1927, Chiang Kai-shek purged the Kuomintang of all Communists, and, soon thereafter, established a government at Nanking.[39] In July, the rival Left Kuomintang government at Wuhan also purged itself of Communists. All Russian political and military advisers then departed from China. By December, 1927, all Soviet consulates in Kuomintang-controlled

territory were closed, and relations were severed between the Soviet Union and the Kuomintang National Government.[40]

The Soviet Union made no effort to come to the aid of the Chinese Communists, and George Kennan maintains that the ruthless
destruction of the Communists by Chiang Kai-shek marked a crucial turning point in Sino-Soviet relations. From that time on, Mao
Tse-tung was "an ally, but not a satellite." [41]

A Soviet historian, M. F. Yurev, dates the birth of the Red
Army of China as "in the beginning period of the Second Civil
War [1927–37]. This army was formed from defectors from the
National Revolutionary Army, which had successfully completed
the Northern Expedition." [42] During much of the next decade, the
Chinese Communists were fleeing from the Nationalist army, and
it was difficult for the Russians even to maintain communication
with them. Also, during this period, the U.S.S.R. was in the throes
of collectivization and, later, the purges of the Party and the Red
Army, and was more concerned with internal affairs than with the
Chinese Communists.

After breaking with the Soviet Union, Chiang Kai-shek was in
dire need of military assistance. He turned to the Germans, who
quickly appointed an aide to Chiang. The German Government
was pleased to fill the void left by the sudden departure of the Soviets, and began the task of reorganizing the Chinese army along
German lines.[43] German influence continued until 1937.

The assistance given by the Soviet advisers during the period
from 1923 to 1927 was a major contributing factor in the victory
of the Chinese Nationalists. General Cherepanov summed up the
work of the Soviet advisers in the following manner:

> An uncompromising attitude in the basic questions of operational
> and military-political preparation was encouraged by Blücher. How-
> ever, if the adviser attempted to interfere in all the little details
> and thus worsen his relationship with the Chinese commander,
> Blücher would correct this in short order, sometimes transferring
> the officer to other duties.

> The bulk of the activity of the advisers consisted of daily work in
> the troop units, larger units, and headquarters. The advisers made
> all possible efforts to deepen their knowledge of troop conditions,
> to become acquainted with commanders and the mass of soldiers.
> They actively participated in the military training of the lower
> military units (platoon through regiment), and in the preparation

of periods of instruction. Often, the adviser would lecture the officers and organize the practical work accompanying the lectures. The advice of our comrades was most of the time unquestionably put into practice. All advisers strove to put into effect measures of centralizing the army under the basic principle of unity of command and organization.[44]

In 1932, the Soviet Union and China re-established diplomatic relations, in mutual recognition of a common interest in countering Japanese moves in the Far East. The fact that they were now trying to normalize relations with the same government that had slaughtered the Chinese Communists only five years previously evidently did not deter the Russians. Again, they put national interest ahead of ideological considerations.

On August 21, 1937, the Soviet Union and the Nationalist Government concluded a nonaggression pact and a barter agreement with the Chinese, trading foodstuffs, wool, tungsten, silk, and other Chinese products for Russian arms and ammunition. Chiang complained about the difficult terms demanded by the Russians, and stated that, in many instances, the weapons that the Soviet Union sold the Chinese were not accompanied by sufficient spare parts.[45] Probably about the same time (but announced only in September, after two years of negotiation), the Chinese Communists and the Kuomintang Government joined in an uneasy alliance against the Japanese invaders.

A. A. Martynov, a Soviet author, has described Soviet aid to China during the period 1937–41 as follows:

> The friendship of the Soviet Army with the Chinese people and their army was further increased and strengthened during the period of the Chinese people's war for freedom against imperialist Japan. . . . In the fall of 1937, the Soviet Union signed a treaty of nonaggression with the Government of the Chinese Republic, and in 1938–39 loaned China the equivalent of 250 million American dollars. Following signature of the treaty of 1938, Soviet voluntary pilots and other Soviet military specialists were sent to China to aid the Chinese in conducting military operations. . . . Thanks to the aid of the Soviet pilots, by 1940—in 40 months of battle against the Japanese invaders—986 Japanese planes were destroyed. More than 100 Soviet hero-pilots . . . were killed in these battles.[46]

By the end of 1939, more than 1,000 Soviet planes had been furnished China, and more than 2,000 Soviet pilots had rotated

through the air units. The Russians also started to train Chinese
pilots during this period. In addition to Russian airplanes and
pilots, the Chinese received tanks, artillery, trucks, and fuel.[47] By
1941, most of China's combat planes were Soviet-made, and Russian pilots were still much in evidence, as the Chinese did not yet
have enough trained pilots to wage war against Japan.[48] Soviet air
units defended Nanking, Hankow, Chungking, and Lanchow. In
addition to Russian pilots, there were other Soviet advisers attached to the Chinese army. They counseled the Chinese on military and technical matters, as well as instructing in the various
officer-training camps. However, Chiang Kai-shek was still wary of
Soviet intentions, and the influence of the Soviet advisers was
never as great as it had been during the period 1924–27. Chiang
informed the Russians that he wanted only military advice, and he
handled matters of strategy and political affairs within his own
staff, making sure that political instruction was controlled by his
own political department.[49] The U.S.S.R. had sent many top-
notch officers to China, including Generals Zhukov, Chuikov,
Cherepanov, and Vlasov. As soon as the Russians ascertained that
their political manipulations were to be closely restricted by the
Nationalists, many of the top personnel were recalled to Russia.[50]
From all indications, Soviet aid ceased in 1941, partially as a result of a treaty of nonaggression between the Soviet Union and
Japan, but primarily because of the Russians' desperate battle for
survival against Germany.

Soviet sources consistently emphasize the importance of Soviet
aid. Virtually all of this aid to China between 1937 and 1941, as
in 1923–27, was for the Nationalist forces. There is no evidence
of direct Soviet aid to the Communist forces under Mao Tse-tung.
The Chinese Nationalists did send some money and ammunition to
the Chinese Communists during at least the early period of collaboration against the Japanese. Mao Tse-tung repeatedly requested arms, but his requests were denied.[51] The only aid the
Chinese Communists received from the Soviet Union was in the
form of the training of selected Chinese specialists by the Russians.

The Soviet Union appears to have considered the Chinese Communists as pawns to be played in accordance with the best interests
of the Russians. Mao Tse-tung had become aware of this as early
as 1927. Ever since that time, he has played an increasingly independent role in the Communist world. Plainly, he feels that he
owes little to the Soviet Union. And indeed, it is clear that the So-

viet Union has not ever given the Chinese Communists the degree of "fraternal aid" that it has been capable of giving. One is led to conclude that the U.S.S.R. has never desired a strong China—Communist or not—on her borders.

4. *The Soviet Intervention in Manchuria, 1945-46*

By RAYMOND L. GARTHOFF

The most direct and large-scale Soviet military involvement in the Far East—the Soviet campaign for Manchuria, in August, 1945—occurred in China, although the Russians fought the Japanese. That campaign is of considerable interest as the main Russian military move in the region since the coming to power of the Bolsheviks, and because of its impact on Soviet relations with both the Chinese National Government and its Communist successor on the mainland.

The German attack on the Soviet Union on June 22, 1941, either coincided with, or led to, Japanese consideration of the possibility of making war on Russia. However, at an Imperial Conference on July 2, 1941, it was decided to proceed with occupation of French Indochina, putting aside for the time the question of possibly undertaking operations against the Soviet Union.[1] The Russians claim that, in October, 1941, Japan developed a secret "Plan for Administering the Territories of Greater Eastern Asia," which included Soviet territory. The Maritime Province, reportedly, was to be made part of Manchukuo, and Russian deportees were to be replaced by Japanese colonists.[2] Whether or not that particular Soviet allegation is true, we do know that, beginning in August, 1941, the Japanese in two months doubled their forces in Manchuria (from nearly 400,000 to nearly 700,000 men) under cover of so-called special maneuvers, and, by January 1, 1942, had placed fully one-third of the Japanese Army—1,100,000 men—in Manchuria and Korea.[3] And this military build-up occurred at the time of full Japanese commitment in China, and after initiation of war with the United States.

The Japanese contingency build-up in Manchuria would have

permitted Japan to move rapidly if the Germans had been victorious in the West. Since the Japanese Navy was, at that stage, bearing the burden of the Pacific and South Seas offensives, the possibility of making such a move may have seemed a feasible option for Tokyo to keep open. But the Germans were turned back short of Moscow, and the United States showed no disposition to settle for a *fait accompli* of Japanese mastery of the western Pacific. Accordingly, despite the fact that the Soviets had been compelled to withdraw large forces from Siberia for the German front, the Japanese decided not to attack the U.S.S.R.

There was a tacit, general Soviet-Japanese moratorium on hostile actions toward one another from April, 1941, until late 1944. The Russians, however, claim that the Japanese illegally detained 178 Soviet vessels, and sank three, in the years 1941 through 1944.[4] The first small armed border incident since 1939 occurred at Wuchiatzu (near Lake Khasan) in July, 1944; judging from Japanese records and the general situation, it apparently reflected the start of Soviet probing. Other similar incidents occurred at Mongoshili on the Mongolian border in August, again on the eastern border of Manchuria at Kuangfengtao in October, and at Hutou in December, 1944.[5]

Soviet cordiality toward Japanese diplomats in Moscow noticeably declined during 1944. It did not pass without notice in Tokyo that, while Foreign Minister Vyacheslav Molotov himself had greeted the Japanese Ambassador at the reception on November 7, 1943, his deputy Andrei Vyshinsky substituted on May Day, 1944, and by November 7, 1944, only the chief of the Far Eastern Bureau of the Foreign Office, Dmitri Zhukov, deigned to be seen with the Japanese plenipotentiary. In the summer and fall, articles on such themes as Japanese barbarity in the intervention at the time of the Russian civil war appeared in Soviet publications. Finally, in his speech of November 7, 1944, Stalin castigated Japan as an "aggressor."

In talks with his Western Allies, Stalin had taken the initiative in stating, at the Moscow Conference in October, 1943, that the U.S.S.R. would join the war against Japan after Germany was defeated. At Tehran, in November, 1943, Stalin added that, while Soviet forces then in the Far East were adequate for defense, a threefold increase would be required before they would be ready to initiate offensive operations. Also at Tehran, President Roosevelt presented Stalin with several questions prepared by the Joint Chiefs of Staff, including both a request for Soviet military intelligence on Japan, and a request for the Russians to indicate what "direct or indirect assistance" they could provide in case the United States launched an attack on the northern Kurils. Subsequently, the Russians provided intelligence information, but deferred discussion of the "other questions," including the Kurils.[6]

In October, 1944, Stalin accepted, for the Soviet military forces in the Far East, missions that had been suggested by the United States—mainly, occupation of Manchuria and southern Sakhalin. Stalin stated that Soviet forces would be ready to move about three months following the end of the war in Europe, after doubling the number of their divisions in the Far East. In October, Stalin accepted the idea of American operations in the Kurils before the Soviet Union entered the war. He again agreed to the American requests for bomber bases and for uses of the Petropavlovsk naval base. In general, throughout most of 1944, the Russians agreed, in principle, in repeated discussions, to later American use of bomber bases in Siberia for B–29 raids on Japan, but on December 16, General Alexei Antonov gave a completely negative answer on the question of bases, reflecting either a new, or (more likely) newly revealed, firm Soviet decision against that long-standing American request.[7]

On December 14, 1944, Stalin for the first time spelled out, to Ambassador W. Averell Harriman, the Soviet war aims: annexation of southern Sakhalin and the Kuril Islands, "restoration" of former Russian holdings in Manchuria, and recognition of the *status quo* (Communist rule) in Mongolia. On February 8, 1945, at the Yalta Conference, the Western Powers accepted these Soviet claims, and agreed to urge their acceptance by Chiang Kai-shek, as well.[8]

There has been much postwar controversy in the United States about the Yalta agreements. It is, therefore, perhaps worth noting that, in November, 1944, and again on January 24, 1945, immediately prior to the Yalta Conference, the Joint Chiefs of Staff stated that, while they no longer considered Russian participation in the war as essential, "We desire Russian entry into the war against Japan at the earliest date commensurate with her ability to engage in offensive operations and are prepared to offer the maximum support possible without prejudice to our main effort against Japan." The Joint Chiefs' assessments also contained the observation that, in any case, the Soviet Union would no doubt enter the war in its own self-interest, regardless of the U.S. position.[9]

By February 27, 1945, the Japanese had received their first intelligence on Soviet troop movements to the Far East. On March 5, 1945, they had learned about the Soviet promise at Yalta to attack three months after the defeat of Germany. (Japan had its intelligence on this point confirmed by von Ribbentrop in Berlin, from German intelligence.) On April 5, 1945, the Soviet Union publicly denounced the Soviet-Japanese Neutrality Pact, which was due to expire on April 26, 1946, but could be denounced at any time, to be effective one year after the denunciation (in other words, the Russians were still legally bound not to attack Japan until April 5, 1946). From May through June, in addition to intelligence on Soviet movements of troops and supplies across Siberia, the Japanese took note of the recall of an unusual number of Soviet diplomats and dependents from Japan.[10]

Despite these growing indications of Soviet intent to attack, in April, 1945, the Japanese began extending peace feelers through Moscow.[11] These overtures were not, however, transmitted by Stalin to the United States.

In April, the United States gave up the effort to get Soviet agreement to American use of Siberian air and naval bases, and the projected Pacific supply route. On May 28, Stalin assured Harry Hopkins that the Soviets would attack during August. He also declared Soviet desire to receive the Japanese surrender in northern Hokkaido, and to participate in the occupation of Japan. Finally, he noted Soviet intentions to occupy the Kurils, since their annexation by the Soviet Union had already been agreed upon.[12]

On May 21, 1945, in reply to a query from the Secretary of State, the Secretary of War stressed that the Russians would enter the war against Japan for their own purposes, and that the most the U.S. could hope for was to get some political concessions toward China. A War Department assessment concluded that the United States could not, in any case, preemptively intercede in the areas of intended Soviet military operations, except in the Kurils —and there, only at the expense of other planned operations against Japan.[13] The United States, therefore accepted the Soviet decision to occupy the Kurils, but declined the Russian request to take the surrender in northern Hokkaido, and insisted that all questions with respect to the occupation be left to the Supreme Allied Commander, General Douglas MacArthur—in effect, rejecting the Soviet demand to share in the occupation of Japan.

On June 18, the Secretary of War and the Joint Chiefs of Staff met with the President to decide on the proposed invasion of Kyushu. The invasion ("Olympic"), by three-quarters of a million men, was agreed upon, and set for November 1, 1945. The Chiefs informed the President that Soviet entry into the war would have a major impact on the Japanese, and "may well be the decisive action levering them into capitulation at that time or shortly thereafter if we land in Japan." [14]

At the Potsdam Conference in July, 1945, the Soviet Chief of Staff stated that the Russians planned to attack late in August, depending on the timing and success of their negotiations with the Chinese.[15] (The Russians thus revealed their great desire to tie down the Yalta agreements by getting Chiang Kai-shek's concurrence; as long as China did not agree, there would always be a loophole for the United States to disavow its commitment at Yalta, which was explicitly—if ambiguously, and only formally— conditioned on Chinese concurrence. In fact, the Soviet-Chinese Treaty of Friendship and Alliance was signed only on August 14.) On July 26, the Potsdam Proclamation, with its call for unconditional surrender of Japan, was publicly issued. On July 18 and 28, Stalin informed the United States of two official Japanese bids to send a delegation led by Prince Konoye to discuss ending the war; he tended to dismiss the first bid as too imprecise, and stated that he would, of course, reply negatively to the second since it did not include acceptance of the Potsdam Proclamation. Stalin was clearly very anxious not to see the war end before Soviet entry. The Japanese could not have selected a worse medium to open surrender talks, as their Ambassador in Moscow repeatedly advised Tokyo.[16]

In early 1945, after Yalta, the Japanese had expected Russia to enter the war at the same time the United States invaded. They believed that the U.S. invasion was planned for April, 1946, and assumed that the one-year grace period after Soviet denunciation of the Pact in April, 1945, confirmed this expectation. On May 17, 1945, the Imperial General Headquarters concluded that the Soviet attack might come in August or September. In May, the Kwantung Army Intelligence Division still estimated that war with Russia in 1945 was *not* likely, but, after Potsdam, reversed this judgment and concluded, in late July, that war was very likely "in the early fall." The last official Japanese estimate, on July 31, was that the Russians would probably attack in late August or early September, 1945.[17]

The Japanese noticed a distinct improvement in diplomatic relations with the Russians in the early summer of 1945. There were no more major border incidents after December, 1944, until one

on August 6, which was not, however, regarded as significant.[18]
When Japanese Ambassador Hoatake Sato was called in by Foreign Minister Molotov on the night of August 8, he was expecting to receive the Soviet reply to the July 25 Japanese proposals that the U.S.S.R. undertake to mediate peace between Japan and the Western Powers.

On August 6, 1945, the first atomic bomb was dropped on Hiroshima.

At about midnight, on August 8–9, Ambassador Sato in Moscow was given the Soviet declaration of war with Japan. At ten minutes after midnight, the Soviet military offensive in Manchuria began. On the same day, the second American atomic bomb was dropped on Nagasaki.

After the German attack on Russia in June, 1941, the Soviet Army in the Far East had been depleted (especially of trained divisions) to meet the need in Europe. By the time major Soviet transfers westward ceased, at the end of 1942, the estimated order of battle stood at 19 infantry divisions, 10 infantry brigades, 750,000 men, 1,000 tanks, and 1,000 aircraft.[19] Approximately these force levels were maintained until the end of 1944. A Soviet build-up began in February, 1945. During the four months from April to August, 1945, the Russians moved 39 divisions and brigades and other units from Europe to bolster their forces already in the Far East.[20]

Soviet forces available when the campaign began on August 9 comprised three Fronts (Army Groups), having eleven combined arms armies, one tank army, and three air armies—in all 80 divisions (including 2 tank and 6 cavalry), 4 tank and mechanized corps (of U.S. armored-division size), and 40 tank and mechanized, and 6 infantry, brigades. The total in military manpower (excluding the Navy) was 1,577,725 men, of whom 1,058,982 were in combat units; 26,137 artillery pieces and mortars; 3,704 tanks and 1,852 self-propelled guns; and 5,368 aircraft, of which 4,807 were combat planes.[21]

By August 9, 1945, the Japanese had 24 divisions and 11 brigades in Manchuria, 7 divisions in Korea, and 3 divisions and 1 brigade on Sakhalin and in the Kurils.[22] Over-all Japanese strength in these areas, including Manchukuan and Inner Mongolian satellite troops, totaled a little over 1 million men, of which 787,600 were in the Kwantung Army in Manchuria. The Japanese had, in all, about 1,215 tanks, 1,800 aircraft, and 6,700 artillery pieces and mortars in the theater.[23] But these figures do not tell the whole story. The Kwantung Army had been bled white of trained units and of first-line equipment. Virtually all its matériel was obsolete. For example, the most "seasoned" division (the 107th Infantry) had only been established in the spring of 1944. As late as July 1, 1945, the Kwantung Army in Manchuria had only 11 divisions. Eight of the 24 divisions, and 7 of the 9 infantry brigades—comprising over one-quarter of the total Japanese military manpower in Manchuria—had been mobilized only ten days before the Soviet attack! One of the only two weak tank brigades in the whole area (both were in south central Manchuria) had not been formed until July, 1945. Reinforcements were in the process of being transferred from China, but some of the divisions had only one out of the nine prescribed artillery companies. The 149th Infantry Division had not a single artillery piece. There was practically no artillery heavier than 75-mm. caliber, no modern anti-tank guns, and no rocket artillery. Most of the Japanese tanks were very light (14-ton), and obsolete. The tactical aircraft were all obsolescent, and much inferior to the Soviet airplanes. In all, the Japanese rated the real effectiveness of their 24 divisions in Manchuria at only 7 or 8 effective divisions (and the 7 in Korea at 2). Thus, the Japanese were woefully unprepared, even though, after June 14, they had been rapidly attempting to rebuild their strength in Manchuria, with a "deadline" goal of late September.[24]

By late July, the Soviet build-up of men and units was virtually completed, but the Russians were still bringing in aircraft, anti-aircraft artillery, rocket guns, vehicles, and fuel. The Soviet higher staffs completed their disposition only on August 8. In fact, it seems clear that the Russians had not completed their preparations for the offensive by August 9.[25] There are considerable grounds to conclude that the Soviet decision to launch their campaign was suddenly precipitated somewhat earlier than they had planned. This writer would assume that the decision was prompted by the first American atomic attack on Japan on August 6. Moscow simply could not afford to let Japan surrender before launching her offensive. Thus, the offensive was launched almost immediately after the first atomic bomb.

A special High Command of Soviet Forces in the Far East had been set up under Marshal Alexander M. Vasilevsky, former Chief of the General Staff. Three Army Groups were established: the

Trans-Baikal Front under Marshal Rodion Ya. Malinovsky, the
1st Far Eastern Front under Marshal Kyril A. Meretskov, and the
2d Far Eastern Front under General of the Army Maxim A.
Purkayev (the Far Eastern commander during most of the Soviet-
German war). Admiral Ivan S. Yumashev was Commander in
Chief of the Pacific Fleet.[26]

The strategic plan was simple, though some elements of its execution were complicated and bold. The two main thrusts would be
made by the Trans-Baikal Front from the east, cutting through
most of Manchuria to Mukden and Changchun, and by the 1st Far
Eastern Front from the west, breaking through the Japanese forti-
fied area facing the Maritime Province, and moving to Kirin and
on to Changchun. The 2d Far Eastern Front in the north would
make a lesser thrust down the Sungari toward Harbin.[27]

The main striking force of the Soviet offensive was Marshal
Malinovsky's Trans-Baikal Front, deployed mainly in Mongolia.
This Front had six field armies, including the 6th Guards Tank
Army. In all, nearly half of Soviet military power in the Far East
was assigned to this Front, which faced only weak Japanese concentrations, but had unusually challenging terrain and a difficult
supply problem. The Russians calculated (and authoritative Japanese sources have subsequently confirmed) that the enemy would
not expect a major offensive over hundreds of miles of the Gobi
Desert in Inner Mongolia, and across the Great Hsingan mountain
range.

By the time of the Japanese surrender on August 15, Marshal
Malinovsky's Front had crossed the desert, surmounted the Great
Hsingan range, and reached its initial phase objectives. Apart from
a major shortage of fuel, this Front was prepared to move on to
the south-central Manchurian industrial centers of Changchun,
Ssuping, Mukden, and Anshan. The opposing Japanese 3d Area
Army had, however, withdrawn the bulk of its forces in good
order, and concentrated them in those areas. (Only two Japanese
divisions and one brigade were actively engaged, and overcome, by
the massive thrust of the Trans-Baikal Front.) [28]

In the east, Marshal Meretskov's 1st Far Eastern Front faced
the strongest Japanese concentrations and fortifications. It had,
however, a great superiority (all the opposing Japanese forces
totaled fewer divisions than just one of the four field armies of
Meretskov's Front). By the time of the Japanese capitulation, the
Soviet forces had taken the forward Japanese defense line, and
threatened the main defense concentration at Mutanchiang. But

the Japanese 1st Area Army on this front retained about two-thirds of its effectiveness, and was withdrawing to a planned and prepared defense redoubt in southeastern Manchuria.[29]

Complementing the main thrust of Marshal Meretskov's forces into Manchuria, one army of his Front moved down the coast of northeastern Korea. "Naval infantry" were landed in several small Korean ports: Yuki, Rashin, and Chongjin (and, after the surrender of Japan, Odaejin and Wonsan). These were small-scale operations, and against little opposition, except for the landing at Chongjin, where the initial Soviet landing force was pinned down, and only the hasty commitment of the entire available marine force, an infantry brigade, secured the landing.[30]

In the north, General Purkayev's 2d Far Eastern Front had the missions of making auxiliary offensive thrusts down the Sungari River and across the Amur at Aigun, with defense along the remainder of the long northern frontiers with Manchuria. Although this was the weakest of the three Soviet Fronts, it faced the weakest Japanese forces, and had a tremendous superiority. The very modest Japanese forces opposing were pushed back, but had not been overcome by the end of hostilities.[31]

At the beginning of the campaign, Soviet forces on northern Sakhalin and Kamchatka were ordered to assume defensive positions. In view of the initial success in the campaign in Manchuria, Marshal Vasilevsky decided, on August 10, to proceed with an invasion of southern Sakhalin, and, on August 15, to mount operations to occupy the northern Kuril Islands.

On Sakhalin, the Japanese held their narrow defense line near the border for nine days before being defeated by much stronger Soviet forces. Two small landings were made on the west coast of the island from the mainland, and a third landing to the south after the Japanese surrender (to prevent withdrawal to Hokkaido).

The only combat operation in the Kuril was a bitterly contested landing, and subsequent battle, on the northernmost island, Shimushu, from August 18 to 23. In this case, uniquely, Soviet and Japanese forces on land were about equal, 8,824 men against 8,480 (the Russians had matériel superiority, except in tanks, but the Japanese had prepared defensive positions). The other islands of the Kuril chain were occupied from August 23 to September 6, without combat.[32]

Air and naval operations played only a secondary—even minor—role. In all, the Soviet air forces flew a total of 14,030 combat sorties, and 7,427 noncombat sorties, and dropped 2,773 tons of bombs. (The entire Manchurian theater was plagued, from August 11 through 20 with rain, which greatly hampered air activity.) Perhaps most important of the air operations was reconnaissance, which accounted for more than one-quarter of all sorties. Air transport, particularly of fuel for armored units, was also extremely important. In all, the air forces transported 16,497 men, 2,777 tons of gasoline and oil (2,456 tons of it to units of the Trans-Baikal Front), 549 tons of munitions (over half to the 2d Far Eastern Front), and 1,496 tons of other supplies to all three Fronts. There was no "strategic" bombing.[33]

Japanese air activity was even less significant. The Japanese had a total of about 1,200 aircraft of all types in Manchuria, including a small Manchukuan element, plus about 600 in Korea. Almost all, however, were obsolete. The 2nd Air Army, controlling all tactical military air forces in Manchuria, had only 360 aircraft available for combat: 225 fighters, 40 bombers, 45 reconnaissance planes, and 20 attack aircraft. Furthermore, most of the effective air defenses—fighter aircraft—as well as anti-aircraft artillery— had been deployed in southern Manchuria in the year preceding the Soviet attack, to meet the U.S. B–29 raids, which had begun with a raid on Anshan in July, 1944.[34]

Upon notification of the outbreak of war on August 9, the 2d Air Army was ordered to implement its standing war plans, and, on that basis, began reconnaissance, bombing of advancing Soviet forces in the west, and fighter defense—but all on a very modest scale. Plans to attack Soviet forces in Mongolia, and the Trans-Siberian Railway near Chita, were—for reasons unknown—never actually attempted. There is little information available on Japanese air activity in the campaign, but, judging from both Soviet and Japanese accounts, it was not great. Japanese air units were concentrated in the Changchun—Ssuping—Mukden—Anshan area of south central Manchuria. Reconnaissance was conducted on both fronts, with priority given to the western front, where Marshal Malinovsky's attack was under way. On August 12, in what was probably the maximum effort, 184 fighter sorties were mounted on the west against Linhsi and Lichuan. The Japanese claims for that day's operations (on which Soviet reports are not available) were destruction of 42 trucks and 27 guns, and an estimated "500 men and horses" (sic) casualties. On August 13, bad weather hampered operations, and only seven attacks were mounted; on the 14th, only 29. On the morning of August 15, 39 fighters attacked Taonan, claiming destruction of 23 aircraft on the ground at the air field, and 135 trucks, and estimating 300 casualties inflicted. Some suicide missions were flown on that front.[35]

At noon on August 15, the Imperial order on the cease-fire was received by the 2d Air Army headquarters, and all planned air combat operations were canceled. While ground operations continued in some sectors, there was no further air action except for reconnaissance. In all, unofficial, and probably incomplete, Japanese estimates of their own air losses in August were only ten aircraft lost owing to enemy action, and about fifty lost owing to other causes. Following a revolt of Manchukuan units along the Sungari River on August 19, after cessation of hostilities against Soviet forces, Japanese air attacks were made that day against the rebelling Manchukuan units. (The Japanese Air Academy, located in Manchuria, succeeded in evacuating to Japan with most of its aircraft, but the other air units remained to surrender.) [36]

Naval operations were even less notable. The Pacific Fleet was given the following initial missions: (1) to disrupt Japanese maritime communications in the Sea of Japan, (2) to prevent Japanese naval use of the northern Korean ports, and (3) to assist the Army in preventing any Japanese landings in the U.S.S.R. Later, it was given the additional—and, in the event, its primary—mission: to take by assault Japanese ports in northern Korea, southern Sakhalin, and the northern Kuril Islands.[37]

The Pacific Fleet at that time consisted of 2 Kirov-class cruisers, 11 destroyers, 19 destroyer escorts, 78 submarines, 49 subchasers, and 204 motor torpedo boats. Pacific Fleet Aviation had 1,549 land-based fighter, attack, reconnaissance, and light bomber aircraft. Most of the fleet was based at Vladivostok, but a "Northern Pacific Flotilla" was based, in part, at Sovetskaya Gavan on the west coast of the Tartar Straits, and, in part, at Petropavlovsk on Kamchatka. The opposing Japanese naval and air forces were insignificant: 1 old light cruiser, 1 destroyer, 45 small patrol and mine-warfare craft, and 170 aircraft. Most of these were in the northern districts of the Japanese home islands, and were kept there. (For example, the Japanese had only 7 military aircraft in the Kurils, and none on Sakhalin.) As already noted, the Soviet landing operations were all unopposed at sea. There were no naval battles at sea. The Soviet fleet sank one Japanese destroyer.[38]

The surrender came in stages. On August 14, a junior staff officer in 3d Area Army Headquarters misunderstood a message from

Kwantung Army alternate headquarters at Tunghua, noting unofficial radio reports of Japanese surrender, and issued a cease-fire order; the order was subsequently rescinded by General Otozo Yamada, the Commander in Chief. On August 16, the Imperial Rescript on capitulation was formally received by Kwantung Army Headquarters, where it became the subject of debate. A majority wanted to resist to the last,* but General Yamada and General Hikosaburo Hata, his Chief of Staff, decided that they must obey any order from the Emperor. Japanese Imperial Army Order No. 2544, dated August 16 (received August 17), formally directed General Yamada to negotiate a surrender, and, on the 18th, this order was read to the hastily assembled Chiefs of Staff of all Area Armies and Armies. General Hata then flew to the field headquarters of Marshal Vasilevsky to arrange the surrender. Arrangements to surrender were formalized on August 19, with a technical effective date of August 25, but, in fact, were put immediately into effect in most areas. On August 19, by Soviet order, the Headquarters of the Kwantung Army ceased to function. On August 23, Stalin announced the successful conclusion of the Manchurian operation. On September 2, the Japanese surrendered formally on the U.S.S. *Missouri.* On September 5, General Yamada and almost all Japanese general officers in Manchuria were flown to the U.S.S.R. On September 13, the Imperial General Headquarters in Tokyo formally dissolved the Kwantung Army, effective September 17.[39]

So ended the Manchurian campaign. Soviet victory would doubtless have come soon, even if the surrender of Japan had not precipitated it. But the Japanese forces might have held up the Soviet forces for some weeks in their planned redoubt area in south-

---

* It is interesting to note that Japanese Military Intelligence, even as late as August 15–16, grossly underestimated the weight of the Soviet attack. On the Trans-Baikal Front, where there had been extensive aerial reconnaissance, but very little direct combat contact, the Soviet force—actually numbering 6 field armies—was estimated by the Japanese at 4 infantry divisions, 2 tank divisions, 3 tank brigades, and 1 cavalry division! The 2d Far Eastern Front in the north was estimated at 4 infantry divisions and 1 tank brigade. The 1st Far Eastern Front, which had been most heavily engaged, was estimated at 10 infantry divisions, 1 tank corps, 1 tank division, and 2 tank brigades. Thus, the total Soviet force was believed to be about 24 divisions and 6 brigades, while, in fact, it numbered 80 divisions and 46 brigades. (Hayashi, *Kogun,* p. 217, for the Japanese estimate.)

eastern Manchuria and northern Korea. The bulk of the Kwantung Army was never committed to battle, and was concentrated in a position to impede the Soviet advance and defend the redoubt area.

The Far Eastern Campaign was far less demanding than the Soviet High Command could prudently have anticipated. Perhaps the chief indicator of the intensity of the combat (since real casualties are not known) is the amount of munitions used. Figures are not available on the full Soviet ammunition stock established for the theater, but it is known that, in addition to munitions already in the Far East and those brought in during the last few months of intensive preparations, from December 1, 1944, to April 1, 1945, more than 3.2 million shells and 410 million small-arms cartridges were transferred from European Russia to the Far East. The total ammunition expended during the campaign, on all fronts, was only 361,079 shells and 1,023,697 bullets.[40]

The Russians estimate Japanese casualties at 83,737 killed and 594,000 prisoners. (Unofficial, and perhaps incomplete, Japanese estimates are about 21,000 Japanese killed.) Acknowledged Soviet losses, probably understated, were 8,219 killed and 22,264 wounded. Data on captured Japanese weapons and matériel are not entirely consistent. Official Soviet claims in September, 1945, were that 925 aircraft, 369 tanks, 2,566 artillery guns and mortars, 4,836 machine guns, and 300,000 rifles were captured. The recent major Soviet multivolume history of World War II does not give comparable over-all figures, but lumps together booty of the Trans-Baikal and 1st Far Eastern Fronts as 861 aircraft, 600 tanks, 3,704 artillery guns and mortars, and 11,988 machine guns —larger numbers of tanks and guns for these two Fronts than the earlier official grand total.[41]

Virtually all of the nearly 600,000 Japanese prisoners of war were taken to the Soviet Union (and several thousand to Mongolia) for several years of forced labor. During the period from 1948 until 1950, 513,139 were repatriated.[42]

The capitulation of Japan came before the final battles between the opposing sides could be joined. But if there are qualifications to the Soviet record, it also was impressive in many respects. Mounting it only three months after being bled for four years in Europe represented a major achievement. In addition, it may be worth noting the current Soviet view of the campaign; in the words of the official Soviet war history, "The defeat of the Kwantung

Army was a model of a real lightning strike, accomplished by the
Soviet armed forces." [43]

The Manchurian military campaign was successful. Were Soviet
political objectives in undertaking the Manchurian campaign realized?

The underlying ambition was to establish the U.S.S.R. as the
major Far Eastern power in the vacuum left by the defeat of
Japan. More specifically, Soviet objectives were as follows: (1) to
incorporate southern Sakhalin and the Kuril Islands into the Soviet
Union, (2) to gain international acceptance of the Mongolian satellite, (3) to get a foothold in Manchuria and Korea, (4) to keep
the United States off the continent in northeastern Asia, and to
counterbalance American presence in China, and (5) to get a
foothold in Japan. The first two objectives were attained; the third
at least for a time; the fourth only in part. The fifth was not. Today, Japan is united and non-Communist, and allied with the
United States. Even the status of the Kurils is disputed by Japan,
and there is no Soviet-Japanese peace treaty. Korea is divided; the
more important southern half is strongly anti-Communist, allied
with the United States, and host to American military presence.
Mongolia is widely recognized, a member of the U.N., and a faith-
ful ally to the U.S.S.R. All Soviet presence in Manchuria, including
the base at Port Arthur, is of course now removed—the Soviet
Union does not even have a consulate there.

In the immediate aftermath of the war, the key question, with
respect to Manchuria, was the nature of the Chinese succession to
the temporary Soviet occupation. As the most industrialized and
economically advanced region of China, Manchuria was of particular economic, as well as political, importance to the Chinese National Government—and to the Chinese Communists. In addition,
the Russians had made clear by their demands for "restoration" of
former Russian rights in Port Arthur and Dairen, and in the management of the railways, that the U.S.S.R., too, intended to exercise some continuing direct role there. And, though involved less
directly, the United States was committed to assisting the Chinese
National Government. Consequently, a complex multisided period
of maneuver ensued.

The Treaty of Friendship and Alliance Between the (National)
Republic of China and the U.S.S.R., signed on August 14, 1945,
affirmed "the principles of noninterference in the internal affairs of
the other contracting party." In an exchange of notes on the same

day, it was specified that: "the Government of the U.S.S.R. regarded the Three Eastern Provinces [Manchuria] as part of China and reaffirmed its respect for China's full sovereignty over the Three Eastern Provinces and recognized their territorial and administrative integrity." An additional Agreement, signed on the same day, governed relations during the period of Soviet military presence in Manchuria, noting that a Chinese National Government representative and staff would "establish and direct the administration for the territory cleared of the enemy," and that "as soon as any part of the liberated territory ceases to be a zone of immediate military operations, the Chinese National Government will assume full authority in the direction of public affairs." [44] The duration of the Soviet military presence was not agreed upon, but Stalin assured the Chinese that it would be not more than two or three months. In the treaty negotiations, the Russians had attempted to extract more for themselves than had been agreed upon at Yalta but, bolstered by the United States' advice, the Chinese Nationalist representatives held out successfully against these additional demands. [45]

On August 31, the National Government announced the framework for the new administration of Manchuria, named General Hsiung Shih-hui as the chief of this administration, and charged him with liaison with Marshal Malinovsky, who had been placed in command of all Soviet forces in Manchuria. [46] Chiang Ching-kuo, son of Chiang Kai-shek and for over ten years resident in the Soviet Union, was, soon after, named Special Foreign Affairs Commissioner for the Northeast. After October, he had the chief role in negotiating with the Russians. Chiang Kai-shek was wary of moving into Manchuria too precipitately, despite his eagerness to reestablish Chinese National Government rule. Accordingly, while he had sent some 500 officials under General Hsiung to Changchun by early October, he held back from any premature attempt to send troops there until he could move up in force his élite, American-trained armies from Yunnan. General Tu Yü-ming was named commander in chief of Nationalist military forces for the Northeast (Manchuria) only in mid-October, and arrived in Changchun with a small staff only on October 29. [47]

Meanwhile, the Russians had been violating at least the spirit of the recent treaty by permitting a substantial influx of Chinese Communist soldiers from Lin Piao's 8th Route Army in northern China and from Ch'en Yi's New 4th Army in Shantung Province (as well as some others resident in the Soviet Union, including the

long-exiled leader Li Li-san). By November, at least 100,000 men
had been infiltrated, and, by November, the Chinese Communist
military forces in Manchuria numbered 200,000 men, plus local
auxiliaries. The Russians did not officially "recognize" these
forces, and most of them entered in small units, many without
arms. The Communists were, however, permitted to recruit personnel from the disbanded ex-Manchukuo Army, which had numbered 187,000 men. Moreover, they were permitted to obtain large
stocks of captured Japanese small arms, and some artillery; the
Russians even went through an elaborate charade of conniving to
permit "unauthorized" Chinese Communist "seizures" of "inade-
quately guarded" stockpiles of Japanese weapons.[48]

The first in a series of crises between the Chinese National Government and the Soviet authorities came on October 6, when the
Russians objected to Chinese Nationalist plans to disembark
troops at Dairen, on the clearly trumped-up grounds that such an
action would be contrary to the Sino-Soviet Treaty, since it guaranteed Dairen would be a "commercial port." Marshal Malinovsky
himself, however, suggested that use of the other Manchurian
ports, Yingkow or Hulutao, would be acceptable. However, upon
arrival at these ports, the U.S. Seventh Fleet found them already
occupied by Chinese Communist forces, the Soviets having departed. The Fleet was compelled to disembark the Chinese Nationalist armies it was transporting at American-held Chinwangtao in
north China.[49]

Thus, in September and October, 1945, the Russians indirectly
harassed the entry of Chinese Nationalist troops, and facilitated a
thinly veiled build-up of Chinese Communist military power in
Manchuria. Also, at about that time, as the U.S. Observer Group
at Chinese Communist headquarters in Yenan reported, the Russians established direct communication and liaison with the Chinese Communists.[50] But, in some respects, the most gross interference of the Soviet occupation forces was the assistance to the
Chinese Communists in gaining control over the local administration in Manchuria. This assistance is a subject on which there is
little concrete information, although the general procedure was
evident at the time. The Soviet naval newspaper, on September 6,
1945, contained the first Soviet press admission of Russian aid to
"progressive" local political forces in Manchuria.[51] Far more revealing have been several recent Soviet admissions, prompted by
Russian desire, in their polemic with the Chinese Communists, to
show that they did their duty in assisting their Chinese comrades at

that time—and that the Chinese Communist successes owed much to the Soviet aid. For example, one such account cited several specific cases to illustrate its general statement that: "In creating the new Chinese police [in Manchuria] the Red Army command relied on fighters of the [Chinese Communist] 8th Army." [52] The same account notes that, as early as August 17, a new Provincial Committee of the Chinese Communist Party for Northern Manchuria was established in Harbin by fifty-four underground Party Members, and that, subsequently, city Party organizations were established in Mukden, Dairen, Port Arthur, and elsewhere.

The second crisis in Soviet-Nationalist relations arose in early November, when Chinese Communist armed units surrounded and disarmed the local police and administration, which had been established by the Nationalists in Changchun—in the face of Soviet occupation forces. Chiang Kai-shek on December 9 withdrew his mission from Changchun altogether, and placed full responsibility upon the Soviet Union.[53]

The National Government of China, and the Soviet Government, had to face up to the situation. The Nationalist troops in north China began to push north from Chinwangtao on November 11, took Shanhaikuan (where the Great Wall meets the sea) on the 15th, and went on to take Hulutao on the 22d, and Chinchow on the 26th. There Chiang Kai-shek held them.[54] General Albert C. Wedemeyer had recommended to the Generalissimo that he concentrate first on consolidating control in North China between the Yangtze and the Great Wall, but Chiang was determined to move into Manchuria as soon as he could.[55]

The Russians, too, changed tactics at this juncture. On November 13, they agreed to allow the airlift of 1,500 Chinese Nationalist troops per day into Changchun, and, on the 17th, they disclaimed any assistance to the Chinese Communists at Changchun. They agreed to a request of Chiang's that they postpone their departure from Manchuria again (as they had in November) from December 3 to January 3, 1946, in order to allow more time for the National Government to establish its authority. Chiang Ching-kuo was sent to Changchun to talk with Marshal Malinovsky, and, on December 5, Malinovsky agreed to the airlift of one Nationalist division to Changchun and two others to Mukden, *and promised to guarantee their security.* On December 9, the Russians further agreed to postpone Soviet departure until February 1, 1946.[56]

The Russians had, in the meantime, introduced an entirely new element into the picture—one which helps explain their new policy of limited assistance to the Nationalists. On November 24, M. I. Sladkovsky, the economic adviser to Malinovsky, formally presented to Chang Chia-ngau, the Chairman of the Economic Commission of the Northeast (Manchuria) Headquarters for Manchuria, a proposal for joint Sino-Soviet operation of 80 per cent of the heavy industry in Manchuria. The Chinese replied, a few days later, that they could discuss economic cooperation only after Soviet withdrawal was completed. Sladkovsky then, on December 7, raised the new argument that all industry that had "assisted" the Japanese war effort was booty, subject to unilateral Soviet removal. On January 16, Malinovsky said that he could not predict the date of Soviet withdrawal until the economic cooperation question had been settled. By now, the situation, with respect to continued Soviet occupation, had reversed itself. The Nationalists now wanted the Russians to withdraw, but the Russians, unilaterally, postponed the agreed February 1 deadline to March 1—raising obvious excuses about bad weather, insufficient fuel, and the like. On January 21, the Soviet Ambassador brought up the issues of joint Manchurian industrial control and war booty in Chungking, too. On February 9, the United States addressed identical notes to the Soviet and Chinese Governments protesting the Soviet arguments on reparations and booty. On March 27, the Russians asked fifty-fifty Sino-Soviet administration of the major mines, industry, and airfields of Manchuria for thirty years. The Chinese rejected this further demand outright. Subsequently, the issue tended to die out; meanwhile, the Russians had been stripping much of Manchurian industry. The Pauley Commission, which investigated in May and June, 1946, found that Soviet confiscation (and attendant damage) totaled $858 million, or $2 billion replacement value.[57]

The extensive Soviet stripping of Manchurian industrial facilities, and attempts to gain Chinese Nationalist long-term concessions, strongly indicate that the Russians did not expect the Chinese Communists to be able to consolidate their control in Manchuria. In any case, the Chinese Communists could scarcely have appreciated this Soviet action. Nonetheless, the pro-Soviet Chinese Communist Li Li-san approved the Soviet actions by saying that the machinery removed by the Soviet Union was "not a large amount compared with its war losses [in Europe!]."[58] One recent Soviet account has been so bold as to note that the Soviet Command "uncovered" many cases of alleged Japanese industrial enterprises nominally held by Chinese, which were "thus preserved for the Chinese people." [59] No doubt there may have been some such cases of masked Japanese control, but any Chinese administration would scarcely have given them to the Japanese, and, considering what the Russians did to "Japanese" assets in Manchuria, it is brazen to recall such actions with the claim that the Soviet authorities were doing a favor for the Chinese.

Another issue that had become intertwined with the matter of Soviet withdrawal was the question of withdrawal of U.S. military forces from China. By October, 1945, there were 113,000 U.S. marines and soldiers in China, including 53,000 marines in Peiping, Tsingtao, Tientsin, Chinwangtao, and a few other coastal centers in North China. At the Moscow Conference of Foreign Ministers, Secretary of State James F. Byrnes rejected a direct link of American and Soviet withdrawals sought by the Russians, but he did agree to a vague formulation that, at least, tied together reference to Soviet and U.S. military withdrawals. The Russians continued, through February, to link Soviet with U.S. withdrawal. When Chiang Ching-kuo visited Moscow in December, 1945, Stalin told him bluntly that it would be difficult to settle the Manchurian question if a single American soldier remained in China. In fact, the Russians did not maintain this stand, although, when they did complete their withdrawal, the United States had already begun to reduce its military forces in China. [60]

Thus, the Russians attempted to use their occupation as leverage to remove U.S. presence in China, and to gain economic concessions from China, as well as to bolster the Chinese Communists as a counterweight to the nationalists.

In January, 1946, the Chinese Nationalist armies moved farther into southwestern Manchuria. A truce between the Nationalist and Communist forces in China itself was signed on January 10, and it provided explicitly that the cease-fire did "not prejudice the movements of the National Army into or within Manchuria which are for the purpose of restoring Chinese sovereignty." It is just possible that the Chinese Communists, confident in their ultimate victory over the Nationalists, were themselves somewhat alarmed over the long Soviet occupation, and the Soviet demands for long-term concessions giving the Russians the benefits of the Chinese economy. In any case, the Russians and the Chinese Communists did not interfere with Chinese Nationalist troop movements from January to April, 1946. On January 5, troops were airlifted to Changchun. Chinese Nationalist officials, with Soviet approval, were sent to the ten main cities in Manchuria, including even

Harbin. On March 12, the Soviets withdrew from Mukden, and, on the 15th, the city was formally occupied by the Chinese National 52d Army, without incident. By that time, there were 137,000 Chinese National troops in Manchuria and adjoining Jehol.[61]

In March, the Russians stepped up their withdrawal in ways that again aided the Chinese Communists. Although, on March 22, the Russians announced they they would complete their withdrawal by the end of April, they refused to provide a schedule of evacuation to the National Government Representatives. On March 17, they evacuated Ssuping, permitting the Chinese Communists to take over. On March 26, the Russians announced that they could not delay their withdrawal from northern Manchuria any longer, and would, therefore, turn over authority to whatever authorities were present—thereby turning over the whole of Manchuria north of Changchun to the Communists. The situation was increasingly explosive, and, on April 14, it ignited. The Russians withdrew on that date from Changchun, leaving it in the hands of from 12,000 to 14,000 Chinese Nationalist troops. A Chinese Communist force of from 20,000 to 30,000 men attacked the following day, and, after bitter fighting, on April 18 took Changchun.[62]

This flagrant Communist violation of the truce gave Chiang Kai-shek an opening to press ahead while he had an advantage. The Chinese Communists had from 250,000 to 300,000 men in Manchuria by April, 1946. But, during March and April, the United States transported seven Nationalist armies—228,000 men—to Manchuria, and, with the troops already there, Chiang had an edge.[63] The Communist seizure of Ssuping and Changchun, even though these cities could not be held for long, did serve to tie down the Nationalist forces completely. Consequently, while the Russians completed their withdrawal from the north and east in April, the Communists were able to take over Tsitsihar, Harbin, Kirin, and the major part of Manchuria.

On May 3, the Russians announced the completion of their withdrawal from Manchuria. At that time, the future Chinese control of the region was moot. While assisting the Chinese Communists (especially those under Li Li-san engaged in political consolidation, and the local guerrilla leader Chou Pao-chung, in the north and northeastern portions of Manchuria), the Russians had, in the last analysis, handed over south central Manchuria, the population and industrial center, to the Nationalists. They had failed to get the long term economic concessions (beyond the railway, Port

Arthur, and rights at Dairen) that they had sought, but they had taken the most valuable industrial machinery. It was, by that time, clear that the United States would not place any troops in Manchuria, and, in fact, was reducing those already in China (from a high of 113,000 in October, 1945, to 12,000 by the end of 1946).[64] The Russians had, however, clearly been inhibited in their actions during the occupation by concern over possible American counteraction, and extension of direct American influence on the continent. In addition, the Russians had initially overestimated the strength of the National Government, and underestimated that of the Communists. It would appear that they had seen the optimum opportunity for their own maneuver in a situation giving the Li Li-san and local Communists control in a buffer northeastern half of Manchuria, with the Nationalists in southern Manchuria, and with Mao Tse-tung's Communists in north China between Manchuria and National China.

The Chinese National armies had assumed the offensive on April 16, and took Ssuping on May 19, and Changchun on May 23. This operation was the first in which the Chinese Nationalist forces used airpower (B–25's and P–51's based at Mukden). The United States was seeking to restore the truce, but Chiang pleaded inability to maintain contact with his forces, which continued to advance toward Kirin and Harbin. The Nationalists took Kirin on May 28, and a bridgehead over the Sungari river below Harbin. Then, on June 6, they agreed on a truce, which lasted uneasily until October.[65]

General George C. Marshall's mission continued, through 1946, to seek a coalition of the National and Communist sides.[66] During the year, the Chinese Nationalists built up their forces, but they remained concentrated in the main cities of south central Manchuria. The Communists consolidated their control in the northern and northeastern two-thirds of Manchuria. In April, 1946, a "North Eastern Democratic Liberation Army" had been formed in northern and northeastern Manchuria. The Communist army in China was, in July, 1946, named "The People's Liberation Army." [67]

The truce in China proper collapsed in July, 1946. In October, the National armies launched an offensive that took most of Chahar and Jehol provinces adjoining Manchuria, and Antung in southeastern Manchuria. In the wake of the latter operation, a Chinese Communist force that was compelled to withdraw into Soviet-occupied northern Korea was "interned," but, soon after, released (with its weapons) some 150 miles to the northeast to reenter Manchuria.[68] This flagrant un-neutral act was the only known Soviet intervention in the Chinese civil war in Manchuria after the end of the Soviet occupation.

By the end of 1946, the Chinese National Government reached the high point of its postwar fortunes in Manchuria. All the major cities, except Harbin and Tsitsihar in the north, Hailar in the west, and Mutanchiang in the east, were in Nationalist hands. There were some Communist guerrilla forces, and even civil administration in some rural areas, in south central Manchuria. But an offensive to clear Harbin and the north was planned for the spring. It was necessary, first, to clean out a pocket of Chinese Communist forces on the eastern flank in the Chang Pai Mountains, and by January, 1947, Nationalist forces were concentrated for that clearing operation. Suddenly and unexpectedly, the Chinese Communists launched an offensive from the north, across the frozen Sungari. In late February, a second Communist offensive was launched in the north, and, in March and April, yet two more. These offensives were important and successful only in that they kept the Nationalist forces off balance.[69]

Then, on May 11, 1947, the Communists launched major coordinated offensives on several fronts. Changchun, Kirin, and Ssuping were cut off from one another, and isolated completely. The Communists took Chihfeng in the west, and Antung in the east, in May and June. The Communists claim that in fifty days the Nationalists lost 89,000 casualties in these battles. New Communist offensives followed in July and September, and in the final offensive of the year, launched on December 15, and carrying on to March 15, 1948, the Communists took Ssuping, Kirin, and Anshan, and claimed to have inflicted another 150,000 casualties. Some of these gains, notably the seizure of Kirin, followed partial Nationalist withdrawals to reinforce their main centers at Changchun and Mukden. By the end of 1947, the National armies in these, and a few other, centers were isolated, and could only be supplied by airlift.[70]

The year 1948 spelled the complete defeat of Nationalist China in Manchuria. In March, at the close of the major winter Communist offensive, U.S. Major General David Barr advised Chiang Kaishek to withdraw gradually from Manchuria—but the Generalissimo was aghast at the very idea. Alternatively, Barr recommended offensive action to open up the route for sea and land supply to central Manchuria, but, even though Chiang accepted this concept and gave orders accordingly, the Nationalist generals in the field failed even to attempt to do so. All during 1947 and 1948, a "Maginot malaise" afflicted most of the Nationalist commanders in Manchuria (and frequently elsewhere in China, too).[71]

As early as July, 1947, General Wedemeyer had been sent back to China, and again recommended, in September, 1947 (as he had in November, 1945) the completely unacceptable idea of a five-power (U.S., U.S.S.R., U.K., France, and China) "trusteeship" over Manchuria. The United States did not make this proposal known to anyone at the time.[72]

In January, 1948, the Soviet Union privately offered the Chinese National Government mediation in the Civil War.[73] At the time, such mediation must have seemed entirely out of the question; in retrospect, one wonders whether, in fact, Stalin saw it as the last chance to keep a weak and divided China as a neighbor, subject to various Russian influences.

On September 12, 1948, General Lin Piao opened the final offensive of the Chinese Communist Manchurian campaign. A parallel operation in nearby Shantung Province led to a major Nationalist defeat at Tsinan on September 24, with 80,000 men lost—a major portion of them by defection. At Hulutao, in Manchuria, part of the 93d Army defected, and the Nationalist Command feared to commit the remainder. On October 15, Chinchow fell, with eight divisions and some 120,000 men. On October 17–18, the 60th Army—some 26,000 men—defected near Changchun. On the 19th, the 39,000 men of the New 7th Army surrendered in Changchun. The Mukden garrison, once 200,000 strong, had dallied and stayed inactive while the other National garrisons were picked off one by one. Too late, an attempt was made to break out from Mukden to Chinchow, but the 100,000 men who made the attempt were surrounded and defeated by October 30. On November 2, Mukden itself surrendered. The port of Yingkow, the last Nationalist-held city in Manchuria, fell on November 5. By the 27th, the Nationalists had lost Shanhaikuan and Chinwangtao below the Great Wall. These losses were followed by the critical battle of Hwai-Hai, the fall of Tientsin, and, on January 31, 1949, the fall of Peiping.[74]

The fall of Manchuria was the turning point of the civil war, in more ways than one. Nationalist losses from September 12 to November 5, 1948, totaled 472,000 casualties and prisoners. And for the first time, in November, 1948, over-all Chinese Communist troop strength outnumbered Nationalist forces (3 million to 2.9

million, compared with 2.8 to 3.6 million in September, 1948).[75]
Moreover, Lin Piao's Army in Manchuria could now pour into
China proper. Perhaps most important of all was the heavy blow
to Nationalist morale, and the concurrent rise in Communist élan.

Manchuria under Communist Chinese rule (with Li Li-san participating in the leadership until he was removed in 1949, followed
by Kao Kang until he was purged in 1954) necessarily had a
different relationship with the Soviet Union. The U.S.S.R. negoti-
ated a new "Treaty of Friendship, Alliance and Mutual Assistance" with the Chinese People's Republic, signed on February 14,
1950. In auxiliary agreements, the U.S.S.R. undertook to give up
its role in the Chinese Changchun Railway, and its naval base at
Port Arthur, upon the conclusion of a peace treaty with Japan or,
in any event, by 1952. (The agreement on Port Arthur was
amended in September, 1952, during the Korean War, to extend
the Soviet base rights indefinitely until a peace treaty with Japan;
in October, 1954, the Soviet Union agreed to give up the base
completely, and did so on May 1, 1955.) [76]

Thus, by 1955, a decade after the Soviet military campaign,
nothing remained of the Soviet special rights and presence in Manchuria. In 1962, even the last Soviet consulates in Manchuria
(and all of China) were closed by the Chinese Communists. By the
early 1960's, border incidents again marred the Soviet-Manchurian
frontier as they had in the 1930's.

In Order of the Day No. 247, September 3, 1965, Marshal
Rodion Malinovsky, now for many years Minister of Defense of
the U.S.S.R., admitted the assistance of the Allies and the Chinese
Communist armies (and the Mongolian People's Revolutionary
Army), while crediting mainly the Soviet armed forces, in the defeat of Japan in 1945.[77] The Chinese Communists are less generous; the *Liberation Army Daily,* on the same twentieth anniversary, claimed that the Chinese Communist armies "played the
main role in defeating Japanese imperialism and winning the war,"
and did not even mention the Western Allies or the Soviet Union.
Another commemorative article, carried in all major Chinese
Communist newspapers, did note that the Soviet Union had declared war on Japan, but it, too, did not even mention that the
Russians had waged a military campaign, much less credit the Soviet Union with any major contribution to Japanese defeat or
Chinese Communist victory. This marks quite a come-down for
the Russians from Mao Tse-tung's statement, in August, 1945,

that the Soviet entry into the war was "the decisive factor in Japan's surrender." [78] But such are the fortunes of Communist politics and "history."

The Soviet Manchurian campaign had, without question, considerable impact on the subsequent course of political relations in the Chinese upheavals of the late 1940's. Apart from its longer-run effects for the Soviet position—some of which, as noted, have been short-lived—it remains of considerable interest for its indication of military, politico-military, and foreign political aims, and means, of Soviet policy.

5. Sino-Soviet Military Relations, 1945-66

By RAYMOND L. GARTHOFF

The Soviet Union and Communist China are both drawn together and divided by ideology, national interest, military alliance, and political collaboration. The military is only one strand in a complex pattern of relationships. Military frictions have aggravated the serious rift between the two powers; even more significantly, the military has been the victim of political and ideological conflicts.

Chinese Communist–Soviet military relations have passed through four more or less equal periods. First is the background period from the Soviet occupation of Manchuria in August, 1945, through the Chinese Civil War, to the establishment of Communist rule in Mainland China and the signing of the Sino-Soviet treaty of alliance in February, 1950. The second period can be traced from that date through the Korean War until late 1954, following the visit of Khrushchev and Bulganin to Peking. Their subsequent succession to power in Moscow in February, 1955, marks the beginning of a period of growing but strained cooperation. The current period began in mid-1960 with the sudden cut-off of Soviet military and other assistance. This phase has been distinguished by the virtual absence of military relations in any form. Each of these periods is sufficiently distinctive, and sufficiently significant, to merit close attention.

The full story of Soviet relations with the Chinese Communists during the postwar phase of the Chinese Civil War is not yet clear, but the features relevant to the present inquiry are known. Stalin cautiously reinsured Soviet influence by his "correct" diplomatic dealings with the Nationalist Government, while he gave some assistance to the Communists. The Soviet policy of double-dealing may be explained by Stalin's uncertainty as to the outcome of the

Civil War, but it is also entirely possible that he wanted China to remain divided for a long period, and therefore chose to aid both sides in different ways.

During the critical years from 1945 through 1948, Soviet assistance to China was limited. Military assistance consisted in allowing the Chinese Communists to gain strategic footholds and to acquire captured Japanese ordnance in Manchuria; political assistance was initially given to the Nationalist Government by the 1945 Treaty of Friendship, which clearly recognized it as the government of all China; * and economic "assistance" was limited to stripping Manchuria of its industrial assets at the expense of both Chinese rivals. The Soviet looting of Manchurian "reparations" is inconsistent with the contention that the Russians handed Manchuria over to the Chinese Communists so that they could have a base to defeat the Nationalists. If that were the case, why destroy the major part of the great Mukden arsenals which could have given the Chinese Communists the wherewithal to fight? † Finally, there is evidence that, in 1945 and 1946, Stalin urged the Chinese Communists to form a coalition with the Nationalists.[1] Mao did not do so, not only because he may have been more aware of the opportunities than Stalin, but because his one objective was to seize complete power and build a strong Communist China. The Soviet objective was to win concessions and influence for the U.S.S.R. from a weak China, and to keep China weak through a nominal Nationalist role in which the Russians had powerful leverage through the Communists (and through other elements such as dissidents in Sinkiang, and various war lords).

The Russians, therefore, permitted the Chinese Communist Eighth Route Army to enter Manchuria, harassed (but did not prevent) the arrival of Chinese Nationalist troops, and allowed the Communists to "seize" captured Japanese military equipment and supplies in raids on lightly "guarded" stocks. In all, the Russians captured from the Japanese about 300,000 rifles, nearly 5,000 machine guns, 1,226 artillery pieces, 369 tanks, and 925 aircraft. Much of the artillery and small arms, and some of the tanks and aircraft, were then acquired by the Chinese Communist forces in the spring of 1946. This equipment included their first tanks and combat aircraft in the whole Civil War. The Russians also released the ex-Manchukuo Army personnel, a number of whom were re-

* See Appendix A for the full text of the Treaty and other pertinent corollary agreements.
† See Chapter 4.

cruited by the Communists. The Russians withdrew from Manchuria in May, 1946, leaving the Chinese Nationalists in nominal
control—but the Communists in effective control of the northeastern two-thirds of the region.* [2]

There is no evidence of further Soviet military assistance to the
Chinese Communists during the four years of Civil War. The Chinese Communist forces were equipped with a conglomeration of
U.S. and Japanese-produced weapons, most of them captured
from the Nationalist forces. Chinese Communist claims for *gross*
capture during the whole period from mid-1946 to 1950 were
3,160,000 rifles, 320,000 machine guns, 55,000 artillery pieces,
622 tanks and 389 armored cars, 189 military aircraft, and 200
small warships.[3] Assuming these figures are correct, it is evident
that the Russians permitted the Chinese Communists to seize only
small amounts of tanks and aircraft in Manchuria. The Chinese
Nationalists took much larger quantities of captured Japanese
ordnance in 1945–46 than the Russians did—twice as many rifles,
six times as many machine guns, and ten times as many artillery
pieces.[4] The items the Communists seized from the Nationalists,
including the U.S. matériel originally supplied to the Nationalist
armies, and not Soviet-supplied weapons, provided the Chinese
Communist forces with the implements for winning the Civil War.

By the end of the Civil War in 1950, the People's Liberation
Army (as it had been renamed in 1946) was a poorly equipped
and ill-balanced infantry force of about 5 million men (many from
the Nationalist or war-lord armies) formed loosely into four "field
armies" with a total of 215 "divisions." [5] Air, naval, armored, and
technical units were few and miscellaneous. When, in 1949, the retreating Nationalists stood their ground at Quemoy, the Chinese
Communists were not even able to take that modestly defended
offshore island.

A Treaty of Friendship, Alliance, and Mutual Assistance between the U.S.S.R. and the C.P.R. was signed in Moscow on February 14, 1950.† An economic development loan of $300 million
from the Soviet Union was included in the agreements.[6] Protocols
for military assistance were not known or published, but it is clear
that arrangements were made for the Soviet Union to supply
matériel and training. Under these arrangements, a Soviet military

* See Chapter 4 for details.
† See Appendix B for the full text of the Treaty and other pertinent corollary agreements.

mission was established in Peking and an estimated 3,000 Soviet military advisers were sent to China.[7] Some Chinese military men may also have been sent to the U.S.S.R. for specialized training.[8] Hundreds of obsolescent Soviet La-9 and La-11 piston fighters and Tu-2 twin piston-engine light bombers appeared in China. Thus, a program of military aid was begun.

In his exhaustive analysis of Chinese policy on the eve of the Korean War, Dr. Allen Whiting finds no signs of Chinese Communist participation in planning that conflict, nor, until the summer of 1950, any preparation for possible participation in it.[9] The Russians alone had been involved in building up the North Korean Army and in unleashing it. However, the unexpected U.S. intervention in support of the defenders, and the unexpected U.S. success in crushing the North Korean forces (autumn, 1950), led to what General MacArthur termed, with some justice, "an entirely new war." The Chinese entered the contest.

The Sino-Soviet military relationship also entered a new phase, for the Chinese had to be entrusted with waging a war begun without them. It is likely that the Russians had been planning that the Chinese acquire jet fighters—apart from the Korean War. But under the exigencies of the war, MiG fighters appeared in Manchuria in late October, and entered combat against U.S. aircraft along the Yalu on November 1, 1950.[10] By December, 1951, the Chinese Communists had about 700 MiG-15 fighters and 200 Tu-2 piston light bombers, mostly concentrated in North China, and claimed a total air strength of 2,480 aircraft of all types.[11] By 1952, they had Il-28 jet light bombers, though these were not used in combat.[12] Later, at about the end of the war, a token number of Tu-4's (B-29 type piston medium bombers) were transferred to Communist China.

Military expenditures represented 48 per cent of the Chinese budget by 1951.[13] The Soviet military-aid program became and remained extensive, but it also was expensive. The Chinese were compelled to *purchase* all this matériel, and they incurred heavy debts in the process. From 1950 to 1957, the value of such aid approximated $2 billion, of which perhaps half was covered by Soviet credits.[14] Even school children were canvassed for funds to be spent on Soviet tanks and aircraft in 1953.[15] Early in 1957, during a period of relative freedom of expression in China, General Lung Yun, a former dissident Nationalist, but then a member of the Revolutionary Military Committee of the C.P.R. and a vice chairman of the National Defense Committee, publicly declared that it was "totally unfair for the People's Republic of China to bear all the expenses of the Korean War." [16] He noted that the United States had forgiven Allied debts in World Wars I and II, while the Soviet Union had not. Finally, he recalled that the Soviet Army had dismantled and taken away Manchurian industry in 1946.

Finally, in 1965, the Chinese Communists succeeded in repaying in full the heavy debt imposed by the Soviet Union for military assistance in the Korean War.

Soviet assistance was essential to China; the Chinese had no choice but to accept Soviet terms. Modernization and mechanization of the Chinese military establishment required production, logistics, and communications systems that would have been impossible to obtain otherwise.

While building Chinese military power, Stalin kept it fully dependent on the Soviet Union. Weapons were supplied, but not assistance in creating military production. China was held on a short leash: The MiG's and Ilyushins, and the few obsolescent Soviet submarines and destroyers, would need to be replaced in a few years, and their replacement could come only from the U.S.S.R. The Russians could not directly prevent the Chinese Communists from building their own military industry, but they could withhold their assistance while arguing that it was more economical to buy Soviet-produced weapons. And, by saddling them with outlays as heavy as they could bear, the Russians further held back the Chinese from building an independent military establishment.

Stalin used the occasion of the Korean War to sell more modern weapons to China; he also pressed the Chinese in other ways. In September, 1952, he forced a modification of the 1950 Treaty extending indefinitely the Soviet occupation of Port Arthur on the Yellow Sea by deferring withdrawal until after a Japanese peace treaty was signed.[17]

The death of Stalin profoundly—though not immediately—affected Sino-Soviet relations. Soviet and Chinese interests converged in finishing the Korean War, but beyond this, both countries recognized the need for redefining their relationship. Accordingly, a high-level Soviet delegation visited Peking in October, 1954.

Symbolically, it was important that the review of Sino-Soviet relations took place in Peking rather than in Moscow. Khrushchev, Bulganin, Mikoyan, and Shvernik headed the delegation, reflecting the combined political, Party, economic, and military interests involved. Agreements were signed on October 11, 1954. One reversed the Stalin *diktat* of only two years earlier; the U.S.S.R. agreed to withdraw from Port Arthur by May 31, 1955, and to turn over the Soviet installations there without compensation. A scientific-technical agreement was also signed. The provision of the 1950 Treaty for joint exploitation of uranium resources in Sinkiang was revoked,[18] with full control reverting to China on January 1, 1955. No new military agreements were announced or, apparently, reached.

In May, 1955, the Chinese Communist Minister of Defense, Marshal P'eng Teh-huai, was invited to the ceremony founding the Warsaw Pact, and then spent June in Moscow in discussions with Soviet military representatives. But China did not become a member of the Warsaw Pact.

In 1955, the Russians withdrew from Port Arthur as promised, leaving the aircraft belonging to their units there to extend the impression of generosity. An additional agreement on cooperation in the peaceful applications of atomic energy was reached in 1955. The following year, China joined other Communist states in entering the cooperative "socialist" nonmilitary atomic research center at Dubna near Moscow (where the Russians, incidentally, could siphon off the work of the best East European and Chinese nuclear physicists). Chinese specialists at Dubna were finally all withdrawn in 1965.

The flow of Soviet modern weapons diminished during the late 1950's, not because the Russians decided to choke it off but because the short-term air force and naval strength levels had been reached. In retrospect, it seems clear that the Chinese demand that modern defense industry be built up in China was gaining acceptance. Progress had been made by the Chinese in conventional basic land armaments such as small arms and artillery; but now, with Soviet help, a beginning was also made in the partial construction and assembly of jet fighters, complete construction of light piston aircraft, and construction of tanks, submarines, and small patrol craft. By September, 1956, the first jet fighters of Chinese "manufacture" were flown—with some fanfare.[19] By the end of the 1950's, the Chinese Communist Air Force had hundreds of MiG-17's and some MiG-19's, as well as many older MiG-15's.

The Chinese Communist Army, by the late 1950's, had been substantially modernized into a force of reasonably well-equipped light infantry divisions.[20] Soviet training activities had been largely completed and phased out in the mid- and late-1950's, and the military mission in Peking turned to problems of production facilities in more modern armaments and to coordination of military activities.

It should be noted that, throughout both the Stalin and post-Stalin periods, there has been no indication of coordinated training exercises or maneuvers between the Soviet and Chinese Communist armies, navies, or air forces. Apart from the very limited direct Soviet support to the Chinese during the Korean War, there has been no real coordination of their military operations or training. In the Far East, there has been no bilateral equivalent of the Warsaw Pact to integrate air defenses and naval operations. Why? Political factors must have put a damper on the exercising of alliance privileges that would bring such military benefit. Political charges between the Soviet and Chinese Communist parties later revealed that a Soviet-proposed joint naval command in the Pacific foundered because of Chinese refusal to accept a subordinate role.[21] Chinese sensitivity over equality of roles probably also was responsible for failure to integrate an air defense system.

Ultimately, the growing political estrangement between the Russian and Chinese Communists more sharply affected military relationships, but, even when the political surface was placid and harmonious, there were severe limits on the nature and extent of military relationships.

During the period after 1954, there were important developments in military doctrine in the Soviet Union and Communist China. Both countries belatedly recognized the implications of nuclear war, though the implications for each were very different. The Russians had to adjust their concepts to weapons they had or were acquiring, while the Chinese military leaders were faced with the frustration of recognizing the decisive importance of weapons they did not possess.

In 1955, a number of Chinese military men began to stress the importance of nuclear weapons and of new military technology in general, and to state specifically that China needed and would acquire "a sufficient quantity of the most modern matériel to arm the Chinese People's Liberation Army."[22] However, some military leaders (especially in the General Staff) placed most emphasis on the immediate need for modern weapons, while those in the Ministry of Defense (and the political officers) continued to emphasize the basic political-morale factors of a people's army, in the Maoist tradition.[23] This divergence was in part over doctrine and in part over policy: Should Communist China acquire her own

70
Anniversary
1957

nuclear weapons or rely on the Soviet Union? By either approach, China would depend heavily on the U.S.S.R.—either for Soviet nuclear protection and support, or for Soviet assistance in developing Chinese capabilities.[24] In 1955, also, the Russians began to assist in the development of a modern Chinese military industry and a nonmilitary nuclear program.

On October 15, 1957, an important agreement with respect to "new technology for national defense" was concluded between the U.S.S.R. and Communist China. This agreement was secret, and was disclosed by the Chinese only in 1963, in protest over alleged Soviet perfidy in unilaterally "tearing it up" in June, 1959.[25] The Russians have not explicitly discussed the agreement, but they have implicitly acknowledged its existence by criticizing the Chinese for revealing joint defense secrets. The precise terms of the agreement are still not known, but it is likely that they were vague and general. The Chinese disclosure of the agreement did not specify its content, but stated that, in June, 1959, the Russians "tore up the agreement, *and* refused to supply a sample atomic bomb and technical data concerning its manufacture"; they did not state the supply of a sample nuclear weapon and technical data was promised in the agreement, which is extremely unlikely, but they imply that liberal interpretation of the spirit of the agreement *should* have extended to supply detailed data on nuclear weapons. It is clear that the Soviet leaders in the latter half of the 1950's were torn between wishing to improve relations with China and seeking to prevent Chinese acquisition of nuclear and other advanced weapons. As a consequence of these opposing motivations, their policies were not fully consistent. The Russians refused to assist in nuclear-weapons technology, but they did assist the Chinese in building a major gaseous diffusion facility for production of fissionable materials (U-235) useful for weapons as well as for other purposes. Thus, they assisted the Chinese Communist nuclear program until 1960—but reluctantly and incompletely.

On the fortieth anniversary of the Russian Revolution, November, 1957, Mao Tse-tung and a delegation of Chinese military leaders visited Moscow. The successful Soviet testing of an ICBM and launching of the first artificial earth satellite encouraged the Chinese almost more than it did the Russians, but it also underlined the gap between Chinese and Soviet capabilities. Later indications suggest that Mao sought a greater role for China in the Communist camp, and that he may have requested nuclear weapons for China and other far-reaching concrete actions not specified

in the new agreement.[26] Among Mao's colleagues visiting Moscow
were the Minister of Defense, Marshal P'eng Teh-huai, and the
two leading Army "modernizers," Marshal Yeh Chien-ying and
General Su Yu, the Chief of the General Staff.[27] Presumably, the
military mission was concerned with implementing the October
agreement. It is, however, possible that additional assistance on
nuclear weapons was requested—and denied. It is thus possible
that the nuclear issue became associated with the ideological-
political disagreements over the 1957 multi-Party declaration.

During the period from late 1957 until mid-1960, the Russians
continued to aid the Chinese in developing their own missiles and
aircraft, and probably in working toward construction of their own
fissionable materials production. But it is quite clear that, at some
point between November, 1957, and May, 1958, the Russians disclosed the "strings" that they placed on any disposition of nuclear
warheads: Soviet control in a joint enterprise. The Chinese have
since declared that: "In 1958 the leadership of the CPSU put forward unreasonable demands designed to bring China under Soviet
military control. These unreasonable demands were rightly and
firmly rejected by the Chinese Government." [28] The Russian proposals were for a joint Sino-Soviet naval command in the Far
East, for more closely integrated air defenses, and possibly also
concerned deployments of offensive Soviet nuclear weapons systems. The Secretary General of the Sino-Japanese Friendship
Association, Chang An-po, has said that these Soviet proposals
were made in April, 1958.[29]

At some point (or points) between October, 1957, and June,
1959, the Chinese pressed to get actual nuclear weapons. The
Russians themselves have acknowledged that they refused even to
consider Chinese requests for nuclear weapons. As Radio Moscow
has stated: "The Chinese leaders have been at great pains to obtain possession of nuclear weapons. They strenuously tried—this is
no secret—to get the Soviet Union to give them the atomic bomb.
The CPSU and the Soviet Government naturally could not consider this, since it might have led to the most serious consequences." [30]

As the facts of nuclear-missile warfare, and the implications of
Soviet refusal to provide nuclear weapons to China, sank more
deeply into the Chinese consciousness in 1958, significant policy
disputes led to new decisions. During the spring and summer of
1958, a debate over military doctrine erupted. The unrecon-
structed "modernizers" who stressed the urgent need for nuclear

weapons and other advanced military technology were pitted against the "conservatives" who stressed the importance of the basic political factors and massive military manpower and relied on eventual Chinese development of its own weapons needs.

As early as January, Marshal P'eng declared that the Chinese must "on the basis of *our national* industrialization systematically arm our army with new technical equipment. In the light of *our* industrial capacity, we can do so only gradually." [31] In May, Foreign Minister Marshal Ch'en Yi remarked in an interview that "At the moment China does not own atomic weapons, but we shall have them in the future." [32] And also in May, Air Force General Liu Ya-lou emphasized the need first to press priority economic build-up of the country, and then, on that basis, *"China's* working class and scientists will certainly be able to make the most up-to-date aircraft and atomic bombs in the not distant future." [33]

This new line combined the importance of nuclear weapons with a major *Chinese* effort to design and construct them (Chinese scientists, as well as workers and engineers, were referred to). But, faced with the Soviet refusal to supply nuclear weapons, the new line did not last long. It placed too much emphasis on the need for early Chinese acquisition of nuclear weapons—an impossibility, despite vigorous efforts. Doctrinal confusion over balancing the decisive importance of something that they did not have with assertions of *current* Chinese strength was too great. The military leaders may also have pressed Mao too hard. For these reasons, a major conference called by the Military Committee of the Party's Central Committee met from May 27 until July 22—two whole months of debate. Party leaders (including Mao) addressed the conference, which reportedly was attended by a thousand Chinese military officers. By the end of July, a new line had been adopted. Marshal Chu Teh spoke on July 31 of "defects" resulting from "tendencies toward an exclusive military viewpoint." [34] He said that the Chinese should study Soviet military experience, but by a "selective and creative" approach. The *Liberation Army Daily* on the next day explained that "a very few comrades" had "one-sidedly stressed the role of atomic weapons and modern military technology, and neglected the role of man." [35] Also on August 1, Marshal Ho Lung warned in *People's Daily* against relying on "outside aid" in solving China's military problems.[36] Yu Chao-li, in *Red Flag* on August 16, quoted Mao that "the atomic bomb is a paper tiger," a theme quickly picked up by others.[37] Finally, on September 6, 1958, the Central Committee of the Party adopted a resolution to mobilize the entire male population into a "people's militia," a development explicitly tied to Mao Tse-tung's "strategic thinking on the people's war." [38] In October, General Su Yu was removed as Chief of the General Staff.

The Chinese thus were forced gradually to build up advanced weapons capabilities with minimal Soviet assistance, while playing down the significance of these weapons that they did not yet have. There were ample signs of undercurrents of military dissatisfaction with this solution.[39]

The impotence of the Chinese, and Soviet refusal to back them in any risky situation of Chinese interest, was evident in the Quemoy crisis of August-September, 1958.[40] It is not clear to what extent the Russians approved Chinese plans to stir up a crisis in the Taiwan Straits by heavy artillery bombardment of Quemoy. Khrushchev met Mao in Peking at the end of July, 1958, probably to discuss both the recent Middle Eastern crisis and the Chinese plans with respect to Quemoy. In meeting the Middle Eastern crisis, which had been touched off by the revolution in Iraq on July 13, Khrushchev veered from one line to another, and the Chinese were probably troubled by his shift from bellicosity to proposing either a meeting of the U.N. Security Council or of the Big Five (with India)—both of which could have involved settlement of an Asian crisis with Communist China conspicuously absent, and either the Republic of China or India involved. Thus, by the time of Mao's meeting with Khrushchev, the Chinese leaders had doubts about the consistency of Soviet support.

Subsequent Soviet action in the course of the Quemoy crisis was hardly reassuring. Only when the Russians were sure that the Chinese would enter negotiations and not press the confrontation to the extent of a direct challenge to the United States did Khrushchev, on September 7, give a public pledge of Soviet assistance, and then only if China itself were attacked by the United States. Thus the Soviets attempted to deter the United States from expanding the crisis, but also failed to lend real support to Mao's offensive move against the offshore islands.*

At the time of Khrushchev's meeting with Mao, Marshals Malinovsky and P'eng Teh-huai were also present. Soon thereafter, "leaks" in Warsaw allegedly disclosed Soviet-Chinese accords on increased economic and military assistance. These reports suggested that the Russians had even agreed to supply the Chinese

* See Chapter 7 for a detailed analysis of the Quemoy crisis.

with nuclear warheads.[41] On the basis of later information, it is clear that nuclear warheads were neither promised nor supplied, and neither the Russians nor the Chinese have ever referred to such an agreement.

During 1958 and 1959, the Chinese continued to stress their determination to get nuclear weapons. At first, in 1958, the Chinese supported the idea of a nuclear-free zone in the Far East, but when Khrushchev proposed this in a speech on January 27, 1959, Chinese reaction was cool.[42] Rather, the Chinese seized an East German statement of January 26, that, if West Germany got nuclear missiles, they too would "request" them from *their* allies. The Chinese (alone of the other Communist states) commented this would be "not only fully justified, but also necessary." [43] On January 21, 1960, the National People's Congress passed a resolution stressing that China would not be bound by any disarmament agreement except with its express consent, and that it would accept no disarmament agreement unless it had participated in its negotiation. The Russians were not being trusted to look out for Chinese politico-military interests.

Two startling developments in over-all Sino-Soviet relations occured in mid-1959. From April 24 to June 13, 1959, Minister of Defense P'eng Teh-huai visited Eastern Europe, and was in Albania at the time of Khrushchev's visit. Marshal P'eng had not been one of the ardent "modernizers" in the mid-1950's, but he was well aware of the crucial importance of modern weapons. If he again asked for increased Soviet assistance, there is no evidence that he achieved anything. (In June, W. Averell Harriman was told by Khrushchev that the Soviet Union had sent missiles—he did not say with nuclear warheads—to protect Communist China against Taiwan, but this may have been an overstatement.) [44]

Suddenly, on September 17, 1959, the dismissal of Marshal P'eng Teh-huai and four vice-ministers was announced. P'eng was charged with heading an "anti-Party group." And, indeed, he had directly challenged Mao at the Lushan Central Committee plenum in August, 1959.[45] Moreover, P'eng had apparently written a letter to the Soviet Communist Party attacking Chinese Communist policies. (In an unpublished speech at Bucharest in June, 1960, Khrushchev criticized the Chinese Communist removal of P'eng for having communicated his views to the CPSU.) [46] Pe'ng may have been disturbed that the growing breach with the U.S.S.R. jeopardized Soviet arms aid. Meanwhile, another sign of the growing estrangement between the two Communist powers was the rehabilitation, in April, 1959, of former General Lung Yun who, in 1957, had openly criticized Soviet military assistance.[47]

Details are not known of the Russians' alleged repudiation of the 1957 agreement on June 20, 1959, and of their refusal to supply data on nuclear weapons technology. Perhaps Chinese Defense Minister P'eng Teh-huai had requested such aid during his visit to Moscow, and a Soviet reply on June 20 canceled the 1957 arrangements. If so, the Russians may have contributed to P'eng's downfall on his return to China. Be that as it may, such a Soviet move in June, 1959, fits both the trend of the deteriorating relationship between the two countries and the pattern of *détente* being built between the U.S.S.R. and the United States at that time.

The deterioration of Sino-Soviet relations over the next year was rapid, and finally erupted in April, 1960, with the publication by the Chinese of an ideological attack on the Russians. In July and August, 1960, the Russians withdrew their 1,300 economic and military advisers and technicians. This action was drastic, sudden, and virtually complete.

Since the sudden virtual cessation of Soviet military and economic assistance, there has been almost no Sino-Soviet military relationship. The effects, even in the short run, have been significant for the Chinese. Continued, though declining, Soviet export of petroleum products to China has been the chief form of indirect aid. On the other hand, clashes on the Sinkiang border have been reported in recent years.

After 1960, the Chinese Communist armed forces actually *decreased* in net capability. In the few years immediately ahead, the Chinese will undoubtedly develop their own capacity to build jet fighters, defensive surface-to-air missiles, radar, small warships, and short-range rockets. It is also to be expected that they will develop their nuclear devices into deliverable bombs and warheads, and will probably develop medium-range missiles. But all these developments were seriously delayed and are still hindered by the sharp slow-down of Soviet military and economic assistance of mid-1960, its complete cessation by 1963, and declining overall trade since that time. For several years, the Chinese had to postpone their production of jet fighters and submarines; also postponed have been whatever plans they may have had for producing jet medium bombers. The numbers, and still more the proficiency, of the air forces have declined from attrition of matériel and from shortage of fuel for proficiency training. The ground forces have been much less affected, but they, too, are short of modern heavy ordnance.

At present, the Chinese Communist army numbers about 2.5 million men, with about 110 infantry, about 4 armored, and about 2 airborne, divisions.[48] The Air Forces total about 2,300 aircraft of all types, including about 2,000 combat aircraft, mainly jet fighters (mostly older model MiG-15's and MiG-17's, with several hundred MiG-19's and from 25 to 35 MiG-21's), and about 275 Il-28 jet light bombers. Apart from about a dozen Tu-4 piston medium bombers, not new when given to the Chinese in the mid-1950's, and one or two Tu-16 medium jet bombers, the Chinese have no long-range air forces.[49] The Navy has 4 destroyers, 4 destroyer escorts, about 30 conventional attack submarines, and a modest number of patrol craft. By the end of 1965, the Chinese were probably beginning to produce jet fighter aircraft and submarines, including one missile-launching submarine (though not yet equipped with missiles).[50] Within a few years, the Chinese will probably have a small operational capability with 1,000 n.m. range MRBM's.[51]

The end of Soviet aid—apart from its material effects on the Chinese—placed the military alliance commitment in question. Soviet spokesman S. Titarenko, in a celebrated article in August, 1960, mentioned China directly in regard to the economic and military vulnerability of a socialist state that had strayed outside the socialist camp, was "isolated," and no longer engaged in "mutual cooperation." By the same token, he implied that Soviet support to China in case of war was conditional.[52] Marshal Malinovsky, in January, 1962, noted that Soviet strength would protect only "those socialist states *friendly* to us"—a very blunt warning indeed.* [53] *Pravda,* in January, 1963 bitterly remarked that "those who criticized the U.S.S.R." for the Cuban missile venture couldn't hold off the imperialists without the U.S.S.R.[54]

The Soviet Government statement of September 21, 1963, carried further the earlier indications of a more careful and controlled Soviet interpretation of alliance commitments to China. On the one hand, the statement nullifies any Chinese Communist requirement for nuclear weapons of its own by pledging the protection of

* Malinovsky's restrictive statement about protecting socialist states "friendly" to the Soviet Union has been repeated on various occasions since, including Marshal Malinovsky's address to the Twenty-third Congress of the CPSU (*Krasnaya zvezda, [Red Star]*, April 2, 1966).

the Soviet nuclear deterrent to the whole socialist camp; but on the other hand, it criticizes Chinese Communist pursuit of "special aims and interests" which go *beyond* the legitimate interests of the socialist camp and "which *cannot* be supported by the military power of the socialist camp." [55] Thus, it made clear that Soviet alliance commitments do *not* extend to such situations and that Moscow will make the ultimate decision on what it regards as the legitimate interests of China (or Cuba, or any other socialist state), and, therefore, on its own course of action if China becomes embroiled with the United States.

The Chinese, in turn, have had to recognize (as Li Fu-Ch'un put it—coincidentally on the same day Titarenko's article was published in August, 1960) that China must "mainly rely on our own efforts" in the future.[56] And again, when Malinovsky was threatening the Chinese in 1962, Marshal Ch'en Yi was saying that all the Chinese problems including *"national* defense" could be solved by self-reliance.[57]

Unfettered by considerations of the Chinese reaction, the Russians opened new military assistance programs with more modern armament to Indonesia and the Middle East. Thanks to the U.S.S.R., Indonesia had a cruiser, Tu-16 jet medium bombers, and air-defense and short-range missiles by the mid-1960's, while the Chinese did not. Tu-16's were also provided to several other neutrals. In a move particularly galling to the Chinese, the Russians promised to provide India with a factory to produce MiG-21's. The Russians have more recently tried, with some success, to bribe the North Koreans toward their side in the dispute within the Communist Bloc with modern military aid. (Both the U.S.S.R. and China signed separate military defense pacts with North Korea in July, 1961.) Some Chinese military men may hanker for military cooperation with the U.S.S.R., but they probably exert no influence on the political controversy.

One or two paramount features of the decline in Sino-Soviet military relations may help in understanding, if not in predicting, future developments.

As the Soviet Union became increasingly concerned with avoiding risks of a nuclear war, and saw advantage in cultivating a *détente* with the United States, the Chinese Communists became increasingly assertive in urging more active confrontation of the imperialists.

The Russians have not wished to lessen fundamental Chinese dependence on the U.S.S.R., to give the Chinese Communists a fulcrum for bargaining power vis-à-vis the Russians, to raise Chinese prestige in the Communist movement or the world at large, or to increase the risks they themselves would run if the Chinese had capabilities that might tempt them to risk a conflict with the West. The Russians recognize the dilemma they would then face of supporting China at unacceptable costs to the Soviet Union, or of seeing Communist China destroyed at irreparable cost to Communism. Intensifying these concerns is the Chinese Communist pressure for stronger support of revolutionary activity by Communists elsewhere, as well as for more vigorous support of immediate Chinese aims. The Soviets define their policy in terms of their own interests.

Consequently, it is not surprising that in pursuing *their* objectives the Chinese have been dissatisfied with Soviet policy. The Russians may want a nuclear-free zone in the Far East to disarm both the United States and Communist China; the Chinese are unwilling to give up their aspirations to nuclear-great power status, even if their "security" were otherwise ensured. The Soviet efforts in the mid-1950's to give up the most imperialistic of Stalin's extortions vis-à-vis China, such as the Port Arthur base, were not sufficient; neither was the grudging support given from 1958 to mid-1960 to the production of aircraft and the creation of Chinese missiles.

Lobbying *within* the opposing countries is another point of interest in respect to the present and future. Chinese leaders, by indirection discussing Soviet internal affairs, made a fairly open bid to the Soviet *military* to oppose Khrushchev. In his interview with foreign reporters on October 28, 1963, Foreign Minister Ch'en Yi stated: ". . . the CPSU, the Soviet people, *and the Red Army* will not readily give up their friendship toward China," despite the Khrushchev policies.[58] With equal pointedness, the Chinese, on November 19, 1963, declared that, while the Red Army remains "a great force safeguarding world peace . . . Khrushchev's whole set of military theories runs completely counter to Marxist-Leninist teachings on war and the army. To follow his wrong theories will necessarily involve disintegrating the Army." [59] The situation has not basically changed since Khrushchev's ouster. Similarly, the Russians have continued to bid indirectly for the support of the Chinese Communist military leaders by such flattering references as the following: ". . . the mass heroism of its fighters and commanders turned the People's Liberation Army into an integral factor of victory of the Chinese Revolution." [60]

The broader political causes of the Sino-Soviet dispute, and the

widening split since 1959, have intensified further military disassociation from the never-intimate relationship of the 1950's.
These developments burden and delay, but do not completely for-
close, Chinese military modernization. The course of Sino-Soviet
military relations will depend upon the political relations of the
two powers.

If the conflict continues to deepen, and either side feels vitally
threatened by the other, even the possibility of Sino-Soviet military
hostilities cannot be entirely excluded from the consideration of
both parties. The release of secret Chinese Communist People's
Liberation Army papers by the U.S. Department of State has disclosed a Military Affairs Committee directive of early 1961 on the
need to preserve security of the Southwest and *Northwest* (i.e.,
Sino-Soviet) frontiers of China.[61] On the tenth anniversary of the
founding of the Sinkiang Uighur Autonomous Region, the official
report of the Chinese National Committee, and the concomitant
press accounts, stressed that the peoples of Sinkiang "completely
smashed the large-scale subversive activities and sabotage carried
out by the Khrushchev revisionist group." [62] Vice Premier (and
former Marshal) Ho Lung stated more specifically: "In 1962, the
people in the Sinkiang-Uighur Autonomous Region resolutely
smashed the subversion and destruction frenziedly carried out by
the Khrushchev revisionist clique in Sinkiang . . . and safeguarded the northwest frontier of the motherland." [63]

There have been reports since 1963 of tightening of the Soviet
frontier defenses, and of strengthening of both army and Border
Guard units along the Sino-Soviet frontiers. Soviet military exercises in the Far East have involved mock repulse of a Chinese
attack into the Maritime Province.[64] In early 1966, the Central
Committee of the CPSU, in a secret letter sent to all Party organizations in the Soviet Union and to all fraternal Communist Parties,
stated that the Chinese (Communist) Government was spreading
false allegations "that the Soviet Union unlawfully holds Chinese
territory in the Far East," and that "the Chinese side is provoking
border conflicts. Such conflicts have again increased in recent
months." [65] In a statement by Foreign Minister Ch'en Yi, the Chinese replied to the effect that the Russians have carried out "un-
bridled subversive activities in China's border areas. . . . They
have deployed their troops on the Sino-Soviet border and carried
out continual military maneuvers on the border, which presupposes
China as the enemy." [66]

The same secret CPSU letter also raised two other new politico-military issues. One arises from the polemical dispute over whether the Soviet Union is giving sufficient assistance to the Democratic Republic of Viet-Nam (North Viet-Nam). After asserting that "military aid is being rendered to the extent that the Vietnamese leadership itself considers necessary," despite the fact that the Chinese refuse to permit Soviet aircraft transporting weapons to overfly China, and have raised obstacles to rail shipment, the Russians conclude that: "There is every reason to assert that it is one of the goals of the policy of the Chinese leadership on the Vietnamese question to originate a military conflict between the U.S.S.R. and the United States. They want a clash between the U.S.S.R. and the United States in order that they may, as they themselves say, 'sit on the mountain and watch the battle of the tigers.' " [67] Finally, as though that were not enough, the Soviet leaders' letter also states: "The C.P.R. leadership ever more obstinately propagates the thesis of potential military clashes between China and the Soviet Union." [68] As an example, the letter cites Chinese Foreign Minister Ch'en Yi's reference at his press conference on September 29, 1965, to "a possible 'coordination' of Soviet actions in north China with an aggressive war by the United States against the C.P.R."; it termed this charge "utterly false." [69]

Complete reconciliation, with broad and deep alliance ties in all aspects of military preparation and planning—which would go far beyond anything achieved in the 1950's—seems as remote and unlikely as open conflict. The outlook is for a continuation of relative mutual military isolation, politico-military rivalry and indirect conflict, and, at best, conditional alliance commitments.

6. The Eruption of Sino-Soviet Politico-Military Problems, 1957-60

By HAROLD P. FORD

Highly significant in the polemical fall-out of recent years has been the increasing indication that modern weapons questions lie near the heart of Sino-Soviet estrangement. Whether or not it is true, as the Chinese Communists charge, that the Russians later reneged on a 1957 "advanced technology" commitment, Soviet and Chinese behavior since 1957 testify to considerable Russian long-range concern over a nuclear-armed China, Russian reluctance to assist China to gain nuclear capability quickly, and accumulating Chinese anger at such uncomradely behavior. The unique ingredient in more recent polemical exchanges has been increased explicitness on the modern weapons issues; the issues have existed all along. This is not to say that the Sino-Soviet schism is not the product, as well, of competing revolutionary strategies, national interests, ideological pretensions, and struggle for supreme Communist authority. Underlying these antagonisms and contributing to them, however, have been continuing, deep-seated differences over modern weapons—central to the initiation and aggravation of Sino-Soviet estrangement.

The aggravation of Sino-Soviet estrangement—an estrangement that may be said to have been inherent in the relations established between Moscow and Peking in 1949—dates from early 1958. At the time of the November, 1957, Moscow Conference of Communist Parties, the Chinese appear to have had high hopes of acquiring Soviet nuclear weapons assistance. These hopes were dashed in early 1958, at the very time that the Chinese were becoming acutely uneasy over the Soviet Union's sudden interest in exploring ways to lessen military tensions with the West. These events ap-

100

parently precipitated the beginnings of a *de facto* separation between China and the Soviet Union in the spring of 1958, that is, three to four months before the launching of the Chinese Communist radical move to create "communes."

In late 1957, China still emphasized the supposedly indestructible unity of the Sino-Soviet partnership. In Moscow, Mao Tse-tung himself assured the Russians that "there is no force on earth that can separate us." But two elements that were part of China's emphasis on so-called indestructible unity were to undergo considerable change in the weeks to come. One element was the insistence that China's duty lay in persistently learning from the Soviet Union's advanced military knowledge, technology, and experience, or, in other words, the acknowledgment of China's profound military and strategic dependence on the Soviet Union. The second element was the Chinese expectation of increased assistance, in the near future, from the Soviet Union in the field of modern weapons. These pervading elements can be seen in several Chinese statements made on the eve of the Moscow conference:

Today the Soviet Army has become a highly modernized army, and possesses the most modern combat weapons, including the intercontinental ballistic missile. The superiority of socialism over capitalism has been demonstrated. As indicated by Chairman Mao Tse-tung, the Chinese Army, in its work of modernization, will learn from all Soviet advanced experience. [Marshal Lin Po-ch'eng, October 30] [1]

[Soviet military achievements] . . . have enriched Marxist-Leninist military theory and become priceless assets of all the countries of the socialist camp. [Marshal Yeh Chien-ying, October 30] [2]

. . . the Soviet armed forces . . . are the great example for the modernization of the Chinese armed forces . . . [by learning from the U.S.S.R. and other bloc countries and by persisting in "correct" study attitudes] . . . the modernization of our Army may thus be accomplished with a reduction of roundabout ways. [Defense Minister Marshal P'eng Teh-huai, November 4] [3]

The Soviet Union has consistently done its utmost to render tremendous generous assistance to its brother countries. Facts prove that such mutual assistance and cooperation between the socialist countries is the most reliable guarantee for the prosperity and strength of the great socialist family. [Marshal Chu Teh, November 7] [4]

The Chinese apparently had some basis for their great expectations. Considerable modernization of China's armed forces had already taken place with the help of the Soviet Union. By late 1957, the Army and the Air Force had made at least some preparations against the contingency of nuclear war.[5] In addition, the commanders of certain army divisions and headquarters had coupled study of Mao's military writings with "the combat plans of the respective units as well as the potentials of powerful weapons they could possibly obtain." [6] The most telling, and the last, indication that China was expecting modern weapons was the promulgation of a new training program for the Army in January, 1958, which stated that:

> Beginning from this year, all branches of the Army will carry out a new program of combat training. . . . The new program, which is in the form of a draft program, has already been issued to all forces. It will be finally approved after June of this year. . . . The new program of combat training is based on our strategic policy, the peculiarities of our terrain, the glorious traditions of our Army, the experience of training practice of the past few years, *and the development of modern military techniques and military science. Soviet advanced experience in this field is also incorporated.* The new program comments briefly on the patterns of modern warfare and expounds in greater detail the direction that should be taken in the training of our Army. It points out that the object of training in the future should be to continue improving modern military techniques, and to learn the coordination of the various branches of the Army *in combat under the modern conditions of atom bombs, chemical warfare, and guided missiles,* as well as in other complicated situations, so that the Army may be ready at all times to deal with any emergency [italics added].[7]

Change came, suddenly and profoundly. The new training program was not approved; in fact, it was never heard of again. After an interim between January and April, 1958, marked by some winds of change, high officials and elite publications proclaimed an entirely new military line, much of which represented a 180-degree switch from that which had prevailed only a few weeks previously. Paraphrased, the themes of the new line were:

(1) It is despicable to rely on foreign countries, foreign military experts, and foreign military textbooks, and to despise one's own national military heritage.

(2) Men are what count, not weapons. Revolutionizing an army is more important than modernizing it. Politics and the incli-

nation of people's hearts, not military technique, are what decides victory or defeat in war.

(3) Slavish reliance on the Soviet Union (by name) has had a very harmful effect on Chinese military modernization, and has caused defects and detours.

(4) The nation in arms, a vast militia, organized in communes, is the best form of mobilizing for total war.

(5) Mao's military thinking ("People's" guerrilla war) is still valid, even for modern war. Some military cadres, "especially senior cadres," are "grossly in error" in overlooking this.

(6) "Dogmatism" is the blind following of foreign experience. Such fetters should be broken off, and combat tactics made to conform with actual conditions in China.

(7) Such "poisonous" dogmatism has "a deep ideological source." If one recognizes dogmatism and the "purely military viewpoint" as the antithesis of the correct line, then the correct military line of the Party and Mao can be better comprehended.[8]

At this time, various Chinese statements began to affirm that China would soon start to develop its own nuclear weapons and rockets. However, the inference that China must build such a capability largely on its own is inescapable. Such statements as those below, all made in 1958, testify to a lack of expectation of much Soviet support in the field of modern weapons:

> Chairman Mao drew a general conclusion in his writings—to defeat our better-equipped enemy with inferior weapons was the basic experience of the long revolutionary warfare in our country. In case a "motherland-defense" war were to break out in the future, the equipment of our armed forces would be inferior to that of the imperialist forces within a certain period. The principle of defeating a better-equipped enemy with inferior weapons, therefore, would still apply to future war which would utilize atomic bombs, missiles, and chemical weapons. [*Liberation Army Daily*, March 16][9]

> We tried to solve our problem purely from the military point of view, and hoped for outside aid instead of relying on mobilization of the masses. [Marshal Ho Lung, August 1][10]

> We should and absolutely can master, in not too long a time, the newest technology concerning *atomic energy in all fields*. . . . There are people who think that as long as we receive assistance from the Soviet Union and other fraternal countries, there is no need for us to carry out more complicated research ourselves. This way of thinking is wrong. . . . Because of the natural conditions of China

and the characteristics of her construction work, *there is in fact no possibility for us to make wholesale use of the existing experiences of other countries* [italics added]. [Marshal Nieh Jung-chen, August 2] [11]

It is true that many comrades wish we could speed up the modernization of our armed forces. But the result is not promoting but holding back the reconstruction of our armed forces . . . if only we can do away with our mono-military viewpoint, break down dogmatism, and give all priority to political activities, we will immediately achieve a big leap forward. [*Liberation Army Daily*, August 17] [12]

[Soviet military tactics are proper for war in Eastern Europe, but the thought of frontal, traditional warfare in China], . . . under atomic warfare conditions . . . is extraordinarily erroneous. [*Liberation Army Daily*, August 31] [13]

Some are of the opinion that although mechanically copying foreign technology may not fit into the present situation in our country, it may fit into the picture in the course of the future development of our armed forces. This view is also mistaken. If we do not base ourselves on reality today and form a habit of subjective thinking, if our warriors and cadres are turned into dummies, we cannot expect that we will be able to apply foreign technology discriminately at a given place and under given conditions in the future. . . . *If only we can rely on the masses and base everything on reality, we will surely work out something which is suitable for our armed forces* [italics added]. [*Liberation Army Daily*, September 20] [14]

The evident shortcomings in Soviet assistance with respect to modern weapons was not the only acute setback that the Chinese were to suffer. At this very same time (from late 1957 to early 1958), Khrushchev took a number of initiatives seeking to explore a lessening of military tensions with the West. Whatever the Soviet motives, the Chinese apparently read a serious intent into them, probably more serious than was, in fact, the case, and considered the Soviet moves a threat to China's military and foreign policy interests.

The unease of China's leaders, still anxious to take control of Formosa, can be appreciated. Khrushchev told the Supreme Soviet on December 21 that "we say to the representatives of the Western countries, and especially the United States . . . let us recognize the *status quo* . . . [and] renounce any attempt to alter the existing situation by force." [15] The Soviet Union campaigned for pacts against surprise attack and the military use of outer space, an increase in U.S.–Soviet commercial and cultural ties, and the convening of a U.S.–Soviet summit peace conference—one from which the Soviet Union apparently intended to exclude China but not India; *Pravda* stated that the "Communist parties" were now prepared to cooperate with Socialist, Catholic, and Liberal political parties everywhere to end "sectarianism" and to achieve a reduction of armaments and a ban on the testing and use of nuclear weapons.[16] On March 31, 1958, the Soviet Union unilaterally ceased testing nuclear weapons and, on April 4, dispatched to the United States and China a note, which included this caution:

> Today only three powers—the U.S.S.R., the U.S.A., and Great Britain—possess nuclear weapons; therefore, agreement on the discontinuance of nuclear weapons tests can be achieved relatively easily. If the tests are not stopped now, within a certain time other countries may have nuclear weapons, and in such a situation it would, of course, be much more difficult to obtain an agreement.[17]

Whatever country the Soviet Government had in mind—France or some other—it took Peking ten days to respond officially to this note. The effects of such Soviet military and diplomatic behavior, and China's angry responses, were immediately felt in a number of areas, in every case detrimental to Sino-Soviet cooperation.

The conclusion is inescapable that China's leaders judged that significant Soviet military equipment and aid could not be counted upon. "Traditional" Chinese Communist military doctrine was reasserted to tide China through the years when she might be without much in the way of modern weapons or equipment. On May 23, General Liu Ya-lou, the chief of the Air Force, proposed that nation-wide campaigns be undertaken at once to rid the armed forces of "doctrinaire" dependence on foreign countries and to make the study of Mao's military writings compulsory. Mao's "Ten Principles" of warfare—maxims of guerrilla fighting, retreat, dispersion, and encirclement, developed during earlier civil war days—were reissued in June amid fanfare that they were now China's "Ten Commandments" for modernizing her armed forces. A "new upsurge" of study of these works took place among Army personnel, from generals down to the rank and file. New military textbooks were compiled.

Nonsensical programs were undertaken to "make everyone a soldier" and to make this vast new militia an integral part of the communes. All citizens between the ages of fifteen and fifty—except for landlords, the crippled and sick, and "wicked" (counterrevolutionary) persons—were termed eligible for the new militia. Tens of millions joined and, by October, 1958, Peking claimed that all those eligible to join had done so. These warriors were set to doing drill, guarding installations and coastlines, and participating in numerous ambitious labor enterprises. The militia undertaking was termed "an important content of Comrade Mao Tse-tung's strategical thinking on the people's war and also a component part of his thinking on the people's communes"—a new phenomenon of "profound political and strategic significance." [18]

A major contributory cause of the frenetic "Great Leap Forward," officially launched in May, 1958, was the need to build up rapidly an economic base to support China's military needs. According to Peking, national construction had to be carried out at "top speed" if China's security was to be fully guaranteed; the building of modern industries would be a "prerequisite for modernizing our national defense," and all sense of inferiority or of "depending on other people" would have to be done away with, for any "lack of confidence in the nation is tantamount to the lack of confidence in the capacity of the 600,000,000 people for innovation." [19]

Resistance to the new military path among the leaders of the Army probably contributed to P'eng Teh-huai's later downfall. Chinese media in the months following May, 1958, are full of condemnation of those Army leaders who still stood for the "mechanical application of foreign experience," or "one-sidedly stressed the part of atomic weapons and modern military techniques and neglected the role of the people," or looked down on the militia program, or felt that effective military command would be impeded by "collective leadership of Party committee [which] is not adapted to the requirements of modernization and regularization." [20] It does not appear to have been a coincidence that, by mid-October, 1958, some 10,000 officers, including more than 70 generals, had gone off to serve temporarily in the ranks. Whether or not the Russians, a year later, were in contact with Marshal P'eng Teh-huai and involved in his fall, public charges were made at the time that "persons unknown" in the Chinese leadership were overly receptive to outside influence in opposing certain Chinese programs:

> Enemy elements hostile to the socialist cause of our country, both within our country and without, have seized the opportunity to slander us in an attempt to influence certain unstable elements

within our ranks. [*From the Resolution adopted by the Lushan Plenum of the Central Committee, August 16, 1959*] [21]

We definitely cannot adopt an attitude of compromise in dealing with the various thoughts, trends, and feelings which are opposed to the thought of Mao Tse-tung, no matter where such reactionary thoughts, trends, and feelings come from or who the people are that hold them, or on whatever front they are found—whether it be political, economic, cultural, or military—and whatever forms they take—overt or covert. [*Political Studies,* No. 19, October 12, 1959] [22]

The now familiar Chinese arguments for a more aggressive Communist Bloc foreign policy, reflecting less concern for the risks of war, were born in those same spring months of 1958. Previously, the Chinese had voiced no criticism of Khrushchev's tactics of peaceful coexistence as such; Chinese displeasure had been limited, in 1956–57, to certain consequences Russian moves might have for domestic Chinese and intra-Bloc affairs. Then, in April, May, and June, 1958, a Chinese Communist Party Central Committee session (not publicly announced until a month later), a Party National Congress, and a series of special meetings of an "enlarged" Politburo of the Party (not publicly announced until August), were accompanied by a series of sharp Chinese criticisms of "Yugoslav revisionist" foreign policy. Ch'en Yun told a Warsaw Pact meeting, in late May, that the bloc now had "absolute superiority" over the West, that U.S. "imperialism" was a "paper tiger" only outwardly strong, and that fear of American power—which he called "U.S.–phobia"—was entirely groundless and "extremely erroneous." [23] At that same time, it will be recalled, Peking and Moscow both made a number of criticisms—over a broad range of political, economic, and strategic questions—of Yugoslav revisionism. Both sides were, in fact, criticizing not only Tito, but one another, and with many of the very arguments that have become more explicit since 1960.[24] A sudden sharp rise of Chinese ideological pretension also took place at this time. Perhaps the most outspoken example of such pretension in military matters was that expressed by General Liu Ya-lou, May 23, 1958:

Chairman Mao's writings on military affairs are the most valuable models for the building and operation of all revolutionary armies and are models of Marxist-Leninist science. When I was in Moscow in 1939, one day several old comrades of the Communist Parties of foreign countries who worked for the Communist International

talked about Chairman Mao's works . . . and said, "No one has
ever dwelt on the military theories and problems of war as rationally
and penetratingly as Comrade Mao Tse-tung!" [25]

The estrangement over modern weapons appears to have been a
major contributory cause of the Chinese Communist offshore islands probe of August and September, 1958. Peking's precise
motives in undertaking the offshore islands venture remain undis-
closed. But Chinese and Russian actions in the weeks preceding
the heavy Chinese Communist bombardment of Quemoy, on
August 23, do make it clear that the undertaking was neither a coordinated ploy designed to divert U.S. strength and attention from
simultaneous Communist pressures in Iraq and Lebanon, nor a
step taken primarily to unify the China mainland population behind the regime's newly launched "Great Leap Forward" and
commune programs.

There had been little Sino-Soviet cooperation in those weeks.
Immediately following the close of the National Congress of the
Chinese Communist Party on May 23 (and accompanying the sudden new Chinese military emphases and the polemics against
revisionist foreign policies) Peking convened a high-level military
conference, which remained in session until late July. Then, at a
time when China and the U.S.S.R. had begun to argue, also, about
optimum Bloc policy in the Middle East, Khrushchev suddenly
flew to Peking. Three weeks later, with Sino-Soviet differences still
further expanded by the advent of the communes, Quemoy was
bombarded.

The Chinese Communists seem to have undertaken the offshore
islands venture in an effort, first, to show Moscow the correctness
of their thesis that the United States was precluded, by recognition
of the Communist Bloc's superior power, from forcefully responding to aggressive Communist thrusts,[26] and, second, as a somewhat desperate, unilateral effort to compensate for their many frus-
trations at Moscow's hands in the preceding months. They may
even have hoped that the Soviet Union, against its will, might have
to bail them out militarily.

However, as the Formosa Strait crisis developed, the Soviet restraint, by clear implication, suggests that the Russians had no
intention of permitting the crisis to expand—whatever Peking's
initial motives.*

Chinese Communist anger grew, in those latter weeks of 1958,

* See Chapter 7 for a detailed analysis of the Quemoy crisis and Sino-
Soviet relations.

over what the Chinese apparently considered to be Soviet indifference to China's interests. Let China's mounting temper speak for itself:

> . . . since the end of the Second World War, the age of appeasement of the aggressors has gone forever. . . . It would be better for Washington to cast aside, before it is too late, any illusion it may have about U.S. aggression being appeased by others. [*People's Daily*, September 15] [27]

> We shall definitely liberate Formosa, Penghu [the Pescadores] and the offshore islands in order to unify the mother country. The war provocations and military extortions of the American imperialists frighten only neurotics, and do not frighten the Chinese people who have arisen. [Kiangsu *Ch'un-chung*, October 1] [28]

> [Some people] have been scared out of their wits by imperialists and reactionaries . . . they have even advised us to "face sufferings," and to "entreat" imperialists and reactionaries [to show mercy]. . . . If we say that such frightened people speak for imperialists and reactionaries, this would seem harsh and unpleasant to hear. Some of them even call themselves "defenders of peace." [*People's Daily*, November 1] [29]

> Some people are of the opinion that we had better not offend the U.S. imperialists and that if they are offended, they will become more frenzied and this will not be in the interests of world peace. [*People's Daily*, November 12] [30]

> [Some people] still entertain their fear of imperialism, especially the imperialism of America. They have underestimated the revolutionary power of the people. Because of this, they will not dare to carry on any decided fight against the enemies. They will not dare to try to win the victory. These people are the right-wing-tending opportunists. If they are left to guide the revolution, there will be failure. [*Cheng-chih Hsueh-hsi*, December] [31]

Such Chinese anger was warranted. Moscow's backing was halfhearted despite the various Soviet warnings given Washington in those weeks. The fact remains that the United States had given the Republic of China considerable military assistance; the U.S.S.R., apparently, gave Peking none. The Chinese Communist Air Force was humiliated even before the appearance of the U.S. Sidewinder air-to-air missiles on Nationalist aircraft; no offsetting Soviet arms were made available.

Most important of all was the attenuation of Soviet commit-

ments during the crisis. Soviet warnings to the United States finally
warmed to a declaration, on September 7, that Moscow would
consider an attack on Communist China to be an attack on the Soviet Union, but this "guarantee" came the day after Premier Chou
En-lai had publicly indicated that Communist China was ready to
resume ambassadorial talks with the United States. The last straw
appears to have come on October 5, when Khrushchev defined
away the Soviet "guarantee" of China by stating that the Formosa
Strait affair was an internal matter for the Chinese people, and that
the Soviet Union had no intention of interfering in this "civil
war." [32] This statement must have been a shock to the Chinese
Communists, who, as late as September 27, had been given some
reason for believing that a more generous Soviet protection could
be counted upon. Witness two Soviet statements made in Peking
on that day:

> The Chinese people are powerful and strong and they have their
> loyal and devoted friends and brothers who will come to their help
> in a moment of such necessity. [*D. V. Efremov*, Deputy Director of
> the Administration for Utilization of Atomic Energy of the Soviet
> Union] [33]

> The Chinese people have the full right to take back their own
> territory and can rest assured that the statement that the Soviet
> people support China is firm and dependable. We have no doubts
> that the Chinese people will triumphantly deal with *all* the tasks
> concerning the Formosa area. [Italics added.] [*Soviet Chargé S. F.
> Antonov*] [34]

Khrushchev's looser definition of Soviet support, on October 5,
was almost certainly a corrective to the overenthusiastic statements
of the two lesser officials. And it seems more than coincidence that
the Chinese Communists chose the next day, October 6, to break
the crisis by suddenly suspending their bombardments for a week.
(By the end of the month, they had settled upon the curious, face-
saving expedient of alternate-day shellings.) That the "some cautious people," whom the Chinese had begun to castigate, were
Russian is made clear in certain further remarks by Khrushchev on
November 14:

> Any predatory aspirations are alien to us. . . . We proceed from
> the fact that there are no countries which have not been settled;
> hence *the conquest of any country or territory* means the enslave-
> ment of people and the exploitation of them, and their wealth. It

would radically contradict our ideology, the great teaching of Marxism-Leninism and the policy of the Soviet Union *and of all other socialist countries.* We know our strength well. . . . But we must not leave out of our reckoning the strength of the imperialist camp. [Italics added.] [35]

A relevant postscript to the offshore islands episode was Khrushchev's call, in his opening address to the Twenty-first Congress of the CPSU on January 27, 1959, for an atom-free zone for the Far East, so that war there, "particularly atomic war," could be averted. Peking made no official comment on this proposal for three weeks thereafter.

A number of political, economic, and military developments deepened the chasm between Moscow and Peking. Of special importance for military and strategic discord, in addition to the offshore islands crisis, were Khrushchev's experiments, in 1959 and early 1960, with the "Camp David spirit" of peaceful coexistence, and Soviet efforts to freeze the Chinese out of nuclear weapons status and to preclude China from initiating nuclear hostilities.

The Formosa Strait crisis not only added a new dimension of bitterness to the Sino-Soviet discord, but became the basis for much of the subsequent debate—couched in ideological terms—between Peking and Moscow on the ripeness of the world revolutionary situation, the efficacy of "peaceful coexistence," and the degree to which the West should be pushed. The overriding external ambition of the Chinese Communist regime has remained that of destroying the Republic of China and pushing American power out of the Formosa area, and this pragmatic national interest has remained near the core of Peking's acute displeasure with any Soviet "peaceful" tactics that do not especially further the Chinese Communist ambition. Indeed, satisfaction of this desire appears to be the prerequisite of a change in the Chinese Communist attitude toward "peaceful coexistence." As authoritatively expressed by Peking in 1959, the Chinese position holds that:

> Without the slightest excuse the U.S. aggressor has been building military bases right and left abroad, seizing and occupying other people's territories at this point and at that, trying to prolong his unwelcome stay. If there is going to be a "thaw" and coexistence, then these military bases must first of all be withdrawn and the occupation of other people's territories ended. There is no reason at all for the United States to hold on to all these places which it

occupies and which are not a part of the United States. It must get out, and that's all there is to it.[36]

The high points of Khrushchev's line during 1959 and early 1960 were that a definite thaw had occurred in East-West relations, that President Eisenhower was a man of peace, and that those who disagreed with these evaluations were ostriches, Trotskyists, or madmen. Khrushchev affirmed that "serious negotiations" with the West were to take place to lessen the dangers of war. On returning home from his trip to America he announced that the American President and he had "touched upon" the subject of China in their talks. Further, visiting Peking in late September, 1959, on the return trip from the United States (at a time when the Chinese Communist Party had just purged Defense Minister Marshal P'eng Teh-huai, apparently suspecting him of having been in covert contact with the Russians), Khrushchev went so far as to tell his audience that, although President Eisenhower wanted peace, cold war exponents (unnamed) were pushing the world toward a new world war. He warned that "those who ignite it will be the first to be consumed in its fire," and that the Communist camp, while strong, must *not* "test the stability of the capitalist system by force" because "the peoples would not understand and would never support those who took it into their hands to act in such a way." [37] This broad suggestion that the Soviet Union would not support Chinese Communist military adventurism was followed by noticeably growing Sino-Soviet coolness, culminating in Khrushchev's blistering condemnation, in his report to the Supreme Soviet on January 14, 1960, of "madmen" who imperiled world peace. On this occasion, he reached a new peak in only thinly veiled criticism of the Chinese:

> [Hitler said] "We must discard all sentimentality—be hard. One fine day, when I give the order for war, I shall not hesitate to send ten million young people to their death." Hitler regarded other nations and peoples as fertilizer and slaves for the chosen Aryan race that was to hold sway over all people. To camouflage these criminal aims, Hitler called his party National Socialist. The fascist leader adopted the word "Socialism," which was so popular with the peoples, in order to attract a greater number of naive and inexperienced people.[38]

These remarks were made in the context of an address that emphasized the horror of nuclear war, the impossibility of insuring victory in such a war through surprise attack, and the danger that some "madmen" might use rocket and nuclear weapons before total and universal disarmament had been achieved. Coming on top of the accumulating Chinese grievances against Moscow, this address may well have been the direct and immediate cause of Peking's apparent decision to bring its grievances before world Communism by publishing the historic *Red Flag* tirade against "modern revisionism" in April, 1960. It should be noted that much emphasis in these *Red Flag* remarks was given specifically to questions of nuclear weapons, nuclear war, and the significance thereof for Communist policy.

It seems clear that the Russians had discovered, during their November, 1957, meetings with Chairman Mao Tse-tung in Moscow, that the Chinese at the time greatly overestimated the immediate significance, for the relative standing of the Soviet Union in the world balance of power, of the then recently developed Soviet Sputnik and ICBM. As a result, the Chinese were eager to push the West more vigorously and seemed to underestimate the risks involved. Soviet policy could not accept any situation in which the Soviet Union might become involved in nuclear hostilities in the Far East. Thus, every precaution had to be taken, whatever China expected in the way of support with nuclear weapons, to deny or delay Chinese acquisition of the ability to precipitate such a situation.

Subsequent Soviet efforts to this end have included denial to the Chinese of Soviet nuclear weapons or advanced delivery systems; efforts to impose Soviet foreign policy decisions on the Chinese and, failing their compliance, to isolate Peking within the world Communist movement; numerous public warnings of Chinese adventurism and of China's military isolation from the Soviet Union; and, finally, the nuclear test ban. Public airing of these issues was veiled until the 1960's, but the issues themselves had become serious in the late 1950's.

7. The Limits of Alliance: The Quemoy Crisis of 1958

By JOHN R. THOMAS

One of the most rewarding insights into the substance—and the limits—of the Sino-Soviet alliance may be derived from an examination of the workings of the alliance in crises affecting the vital interests of either China or Russia. Two useful examples to consider are the 1955 and 1958 crises over the offshore islands.

Retrospectively, in each crisis the lack of effective Soviet support of the Chinese People's Republic (C.P.R.) is evident. But the display of Soviet caution in 1958 is more significant, for it is the more recent example and occurred in circumstances radically different from the earlier probe. In 1955, the Soviet Union was, by a wide margin, militarily inferior to the United States (the launching of the Sputnik and the first ICBM still lay ahead); hence, the Soviet Union could not have been expected to commit its prestige to the support of Peking's ambitions. By the summer of 1958, however, Soviet military-technological advances seemed to many to have redressed the balance of power. By then, a C.P.R. challenge of the United States should have received bolder Soviet backing. That it did not provided one of the first concrete signs that the oft-proclaimed unity of the two allies was thin and brittle, and, seemingly, growing more brittle as Soviet power increased. To Chinese eyes, the Russians had shown themselves faint-hearted in promoting the Communist cause, a major factor in current Sino-Soviet differences. Given the recent widening of these differences, Soviet reluctance to back future Chinese Communist ventures has increased even more, particularly if Chinese probes of U.S. strength were launched against Soviet advice or without consultation, as would be likely.

114

On August 23, 1958, Communist Chinese batteries commenced a heavy bombardment of Quemoy. That assault was followed by a rapid U.S. military build-up to a capability not only of silencing the C.P.R. coastal batteries, but also of countering any Communist Chinese action that went beyond the shelling of the offshore islands. With the exception, however, of a few small-scale engagements between Chinese Nationalist and C.P.R. naval and air forces, military action was confined to the shelling of Quemoy. The C.P.R. did not challenge the U.S. forces in combat. Furthermore, since the C.P.R. failed in its original aim of "starving" Quemoy into submission by a total interdiction of supplies, the United States was not confronted with the necessity of taking any military action against Communist China.

On the political side, the crisis produced several C.P.R., Soviet, and U.S. declarations and counterdeclarations that raised the conflict beyond the contest over the offshore islands to the level of a possible U.S.–Sino-Soviet military confrontation. The "war of words" included a sweeping Soviet declaration that an attack on the C.P.R. would be an attack on the Soviet Union, as well as a U.S.–Soviet exchange of threats to employ nuclear weapons in an armed conflict between the two sides. On October 6, the C.P.R. announced that it had halted the shelling of the offshore islands. For all practical purposes, the military phase of the crisis had ended.* Promptly, the Americans and the Russians ceased to exchange "deterrence" declarations.

On the Sino-Soviet side, only the C.P.R. engaged in military action, while the Soviet Union confined itself to verbal threats. The timing and phrasing of its declarations suggest that the Soviet Union acted with extreme caution (undoubtedly, in C.P.R. eyes, with overcaution), and thus contributed to Communist China's humiliation in failing to attain its implied objective, namely, to seize the offshore islands as a prelude to "liberating" Taiwan.

Soviet conduct is likely to have been prompted by certain *positive* considerations, which evoked Soviet acquiescence to a limited Chinese probe, and *negative* considerations, which constrained the Russians from giving more than verbal support carefully hedged to safeguard them against direct military involvement with the United States.

* On October 13, the C.P.R. extended the cease-fire for another two weeks. Shelling was resumed later—but only on alternate days, indicating its use for nuisance value only.

With regard to positive considerations, the defensive attitude of the United States was probably the greatest single factor in Soviet acquiescence in a new Chinese testing of U.S. intentions in the Formosa Strait area. By 1958, the Russians had some reason to believe that the United States would, at worst, only defend the *status quo* in the Far East and, at best, yield areas such as the off-shore islands in the face of controlled politico-military pressure. Soviet calculations that the United States military was not prepared to alter the *status quo* by rolling back Chinese power were undoubtedly buttressed by the fact that the "unleashing" of Chiang Kai-shek in 1953 produced no visible challenge to Red China's domination of the mainland. On the contrary, as far as the Russians could see, the United States, in the face of Chinese Communist aggressiveness, became even more timid about possible military action by Chiang's forces on the mainland. Thus, after the first C.P.R. probe in the Formosa Strait area in 1954, the United States went so far as to dissuade Chiang from bombing Red China or even flying his bombers over the mainland.[1] By 1958, also, it was evident to the Russians that the United States had once again "released" Chiang despite his strong desire, expressed on numerous occasions, to the obvious embarrassment of the United States, to return to the mainland. This U.S. embarrassment did not go unnoticed by the Russians.

The Russians interpreted the foregoing developments as indicating that the United States, by 1958, had acceded to the reality of a changed strategic situation. As they saw it, if the Americans had been unwilling to risk action on the China mainland earlier when the United States still had a nuclear monopoly, they were less likely to do so after losing that monopoly; indeed, the growth of Soviet power in the 1950's seriously hampered the ability of the United States to act in an unlimited fashion in the Far East.[2] Therefore, at worst, a carefully controlled test of U.S. intentions by Communist China would elicit a limited defensive response, insufficient to involve the Soviet Union. However, the Russians could hope for an even better outcome. The 1954–55 Communist Chinese probe had been followed, after U.S. prodding, by a Chinese Nationalist withdrawal from the Tachens; applying pressure in 1958 might similarly produce a retreat from Quemoy, particularly in the face of strong Soviet declaratory support, absent in the earlier venture.* At the same time, in view of the "defense-

* The Soviet Union had reason to believe that the growth of its military power since 1955 would magnify the impact of its declarations and induce the United States to yield even more readily by persuading Chiang to with-

mindedness" the United States displayed by 1958, the Russians could hope that such support, confined to verbal threats, would not provoke full-scale U.S. action against either Communist China or the Soviet Union.

Another positive consideration governing Soviet behavior during the crisis related to the offshore islands issue *per se*. The Soviet Union could expect that military action limited to Quemoy would focus on the offshore islands and play down the broader question of Taiwan; such an effect would produce maximum political pressure on the United States from the non-Communist world and evoke minimum U.S. military reaction. Thus, politically, the United States would be put on the defensive in the eyes of many of its allies and much of the non-Soviet world. Unlike Taiwan, separated by 90 miles of water and patrolled by the strongest fleet in the world, the offshore islands, only several miles from the mainland, were to many non-Soviet observers strategically indefensible, even if the islands, under different circumstances, should have remained in Chinese Nationalist hands.* For other non-Soviet observers favoring a two-China solution, the islands seemed a natural adjunct of the mainland.† Therefore, a probe limited to the islands could be labeled more easily by the Russians as a civil war action—a label that would appeal to those in the non-Soviet world who were against any involvement in Chinese internal affairs.‡ Consequently, the Russians probably considered that action limited to Quemoy would maximize political pressure on the United States to modify its position in the area. Such pressure would also

---

draw from Quemoy. This belief seemed to motivate Soviet statements to the effect that in view of the new relationship of forces in the world as well as in the Far East, the United States would not allow Chiang to drag it into dangerous ventures but, on the contrary, would bring him to his senses. (*Krasnaya zvezda* [*Red Star*], September 3, 1958.)

* John F. Kennedy's views were representative of how highly held was the belief on this score. In a TV debate with Vice President Nixon during the 1960 Presidential campaign, the President-to-be said that Quemoy and Matsu were "not strategically defensible, not essential to the defense of Formosa."

† This view was given its strongest airing by the British. For example, a government spokesman reiterated, in the House of Commons, that Britain considered the offshore islands part of Communist China. (*Los Angeles Times*, February 23, 1961.)

‡ Expanding the issue to include Taiwan would have presented more of a problem for Soviet political exploitation since there was less agreement in the non-Soviet world on whether Taiwan belonged to the mainland. Undoubtedly, this explains Soviet restraint during the crisis in not lumping together the question of the islands and Taiwan.

serve to restrain the United States from a military overreaction that might ultimately involve the Soviet Union.

Repeated Soviet stress, during the crisis, on the isolation of U.S. policymakers from allied, world, and even domestic opinion seemed to reflect advance Soviet calculations that the United States would hesitate to "go it alone." Such a consideration seemed to be involved in the Soviet decision to support the C.P.R. venture by issuing menacing threats. These threats could be undertaken with relative safety, since the Russians could count on factors other than direct Soviet deterrence statements to moderate U.S. reaction.

Militarily, the Russians could favorably consider a C.P.R. operation confined solely to the offshore islands and to artillery shelling as ideal in testing the firmness of the American position in the Far East. In such a test, the United States would not be confronted with the pressing necessity of responding at a level that might have risked Soviet involvement. For one thing, there were no U.S. forces, except for a few advisers, on the islands; therefore, there was no risk that major forces might be attacked, accidentally or otherwise, provoking a possible U.S. overreaction. (Such a possibility might well have been turned into a certainty if a C.P.R. attack had been mounted in the Strait or on Taiwan.) Furthermore, restricting the military action primarily to limited-range artillery fire again reduced the risk that U.S. forces would be hit; only widespread air strikes could have really affected the U.S. ships and planes positioned in the Strait.*

Lastly, military action limited to Quemoy would, from the Soviet viewpoint, maintain the fiction of the civil war, since C.P.R. guns would fire on Chinese Nationalist troops—not on U.S. forces. Khrushchev's clarification, on October 5, that only a U.S. attack on the C.P.R. would bring the Soviet Union into the fray indicated Soviet interest in maintaining a civil war façade in order to forestall internationalization of the crisis. It seems reasonable that, within

---

* The few air sorties flown by the C.P.R. Air Force in the Strait area during the crisis never involved U.S. ships or planes. No air strikes were made on Quemoy itself, doubtless out of fear of hitting the U.S. ships escorting the Chinese Nationalist supply ships. This restrained behavior may well have reflected Soviet considerations, since the C.P.R. was dependent on the Russians for both planes and fuel. There were also no submarine attacks on the U.S. 7th Fleet, despite the fact that the Communist Chinese had, at the time, the fourth largest submarine fleet in the world, according to an estimate made by Vice Admiral John S. Thach, U.S. antisubmarine forces commander in the Pacific [*Los Angeles Times,* February 19, 1961]. Inasmuch as the submarines had been supplied by the Russians, it may be that the Soviet Union had some voice in determining the restraint displayed during the crisis in the operations of the C.P.R. undersea fleet.

the limits of sanctioning any C.P.R. probe, the Russians assented
to action confined solely to shelling of the offshore islands because
this action came closest to meeting the "civil war" requirement.

At the same time that the favorable considerations discussed
above may have induced Soviet acquiescence in a limited Chinese
probe, the Russians appeared to have been constrained by other,
negative considerations from rendering more than ambiguous
declaratory support. The 1950 Sino-Soviet pact of mutual assistance was one such negative consideration. In any U.S.–Chinese
military showdown, the pact could have become a serious liability
for the Russians. As a record of explicit and implicit obligations, it
undoubtedly was more valuable to Communist China—the
weaker member of the alliance—as a possible means of interpos-
ing Soviet power between itself and the United States. If the pact
were invoked by the C.P.R., the Soviet Union could not shirk its
obligations lightly without severely straining or even rupturing the
Sino-Soviet alliance. The Soviet Union, therefore, had to consider
the possibility that Communist China, in an encounter with the
United States, might invoke the pact in a situation in which the
Russians, considering their own self-interest, might not be willing
to consider the pact operative. Consequently, the Russians had to
tailor their support in a manner that would make it clear that they
reserved to themselves the exclusive right to determine the pact's
applicability. From the Soviet viewpoint, the "safest" crisis involving the C.P.R. was one in which the pact did not figure at all. This
had been the case in the 1954–55 crisis, when the pact was ignored entirely. On that occasion, it can be conjectured, the Russians made it clear to the C.P.R. that a U.S. reaction to a probe
could not serve to bring the pact into operation. In 1958, the
Russians were prepared, or had been persuaded by the C.P.R., to
let the pact play a role in their declaratory support; for the first
time, they referred to the pact in a crisis situation. However, as
will be indicated later, the timing of the citation, and the care with
which the pact's possible applicability was obscured, continued to
indicate extreme Soviet caution. Since they did not exploit the pact
fully and unambiguously, it can be assumed that the Russians desired to guard against the possibility of being drawn, against their
better judgment, into an armed struggle with the United States.
Moreover, the cautious Soviet reference to the pact let the C.P.R.
know, in still another way, that the Communist Chinese could not
automatically count on Soviet aid and should, therefore, guide
themselves accordingly.

Another consideration inducing caution on the part of the Soviet

Union was its awarness that, in any probe involving the Chinese, it would not have absolute control over the situation on the Communist side. This condition was not one the Russians would face in some other power plays. In a Berlin crisis, for example, the East Germans could make no moves without Soviet foreknowledge and approval. Soviet troops and advisers on the spot would assure the U.S.S.R. direct control over a developing situation and guarantee that blunders, if any, would be of Soviet making. In a venture involving the C.P.R., the Russians could only restrain, rather than control, their partner, since they had no highly placed advisers in Peking to "guide" the Chinese leadership, nor did they have military forces on Chinese soil to exert direct influence.* Therefore, the Russians could have no advance assurance that the C.P.R. might not push a probe beyond the limits they considered safe. This possibility could have recurred during the crisis as the unintentional result of differing Soviet and Chinese estimates of the risks involved, and of the importance of the probe's objectives. Or, the C.P.R. might have deliberately attempted to promote a Soviet conflict with the United States. Because of the great importance of the C.P.R. in the Communist world, once the probe got under way, the Chinese could readily—intentionally or otherwise—have placed the Soviet Union in the difficult position of becoming involved in a C.P.R.–U.S. conflict, or of refusing to do so at great price to Soviet power and prestige. Apprehension on this score seemed to govern Soviet behavior in the crisis.

Another factor inducing caution was the Soviet reading of the East-West strategic power balance. In 1958, the Russians did not believe that the preponderance of power was on their side. In fact, they stated only that a major shift toward the Soviet Bloc had taken place as a result of Soviet missile and space achievements in 1957. They carefully avoided claiming that the scales had tipped

---

* One of the earlier causes of Sino-Soviet friction was the Soviet desire to place military installations on Chinese territory under Soviet control and the C.P.R.'s refusal to meet Soviet wishes. Thus, the C.P.R. apparently balked at the establishment on Soviet terms of a unified Sino-Soviet military command in the Pacific; reportedly, the Russians reconsidered the scheme out of fear that they would be unable to exercise sufficient control in the proposed command to forestall possible C.P.R. efforts to drag the Soviet Union into a war over Taiwan. (Cited by Edward Crankshaw in *The Observer,* London, February 12, 1961.) Indeed, the C.P.R. apparently had done more than simply resist Soviet efforts to arrive at "cooperative" arrangements. There were reports that the C.P.R., instead of permitting Soviet personnel in China to "advise" had tried to "convert" them to Chinese views on the Sino-Soviet ideological differences then emerging into the open.

absolutely in their favor. Indeed, their behavior during the crisis seemed to reflect the belief that, since they lacked the lead in strategic capabilities over the United States, they could not count on deterring a fairly high level U.S. military response (e.g., the employment of tactical nuclear weapons), if the C.P.R. pushed too hard.*

Adding to the Russian lack of confidence in the Soviet Union's ability to deter the United States was an awareness that the United States had local superiority (in terms of air, sea, and nuclear power) in the Formosa Strait area.† Consequently, it could be assumed that Soviet caution in past crises in areas like Berlin, where the Russians had local military superiority, would be more than matched in an area like the Formosa Strait, where such an advantage was absent. Indeed, the relative inactivity of the Chinese Communist Air Force in the crisis may have reflected Soviet intentions of reducing the risk that the C.P.R. would offer a full-scale challenge to U.S. power over Quemoy.‡

It is possible, of course, that, before the crisis, the Russians might have been persuaded that the United States "rationally" would not overreact to a C.P.R. probe (e.g., by employing nuclear weapons) because of political considerations. Thus, the Russians might have believed that the United States would not risk the negative impact of such an action on world opinion, particularly in Asia—indeed, that the United States would be additionally restrained by considerations of the political liabilities it would reap if it used nuclear weapons against a nonwhite people for the second time. Nevertheless, the Soviet Union could not discount the possibility that the United States might act "irrationally" by allowing military advantages to override political considerations.§

* Even before the crisis began, the Russians were discussing the possibility that the United States might use nuclear weapons in the Formosa Strait. Major General N. Talensky, a major Soviet commentator on military strategy, indicated that his reading of Western strategy foresaw the use of nuclear weapons in the Formosa Strait. This area, according to his interpretation of Western views, was one of a number suited to limited nuclear war. *Mezhdunarodnaya zhizn'* [*International Affairs*], No. 2, February, 1958, p. 26.)

† This awareness was reflected before and during the crisis by the sizeable Soviet commentary on the capabilities of U.S. forces in the Formosa Strait.

‡ Since the C.P.R. Air Force was dependent on the Russians for jet fuel to fly its Soviet-built MiGs, it may have been unable to engage in large numbers of sorties during the crisis because of Soviet withholding of the necessary supplies.

§ On the eve of the Quemoy crisis, the Russians had an example of politically "irrational" U.S. behavior in Lebanon. Here, the United States

As a result, the Soviet Union, in weighing its role in the crisis, had to consider the possibility that an unexpected, high-level U.S. response might draw it into a conflict at a time when the Russians did not have overwhelming strategic power to insure victory if the crisis escalated to a general war. As will be indicated later, the Soviet Union's declaratory loopholes seemed to indicate a readiness to avoid involvement if confronted by a U.S. overreaction to a C.P.R. probe.

Finally, one other major consideration on the negative side seemed to govern the cautious behavior of the Russians. To them, the offshore islands were of marginal interest, not worth a war with the United States. Moreover, such involvement would have jeopardized objectives of higher priority and of more immediate and direct Soviet interest.* By contrast, the offshore islands were undoubtedly of great importance to the C.P.R., since they represented a foothold of a rival regime, and could serve as a rallying point for opposition to the Communist Chinese. Hence, the C.P.R. undoubtedly had been willing all along to run higher risks in dislodging the Nationalist forces than the Russians considered wise.†

Although it can be assumed that the Soviet Union was as interested as the C.P.R. in forcing a withdrawal of U.S. power from the

---

had resorted to troops at the expense of incurring additional political disfavor in the Arab world, and elsewhere. During the Quemoy crisis, the United States again gave the Russians reason to believe that it might act "irrationally"; it seriously considered the use of nuclear weapons out of fear that its conventional power in the area would be unable to cope with a large scale C.P.R. assault on the offshore islands. (See James Reston, *The New York Times,* February 26, 1961.) In the face of a heavy nuclear build-up, Soviet commentators scoffed at claims that the U.S. was deploying power necessary only for the defense of the offshore islands. The Soviet stress on the magnitude of U.S. nuclear power, and the absence of matching conventional power, seemed to betray genuine concern that the nuclear threshold might be reached sooner than the Chinese and the Russians anticipated.

* For example, the 1958–59 Berlin crisis was in the offing when the Quemoy venture was launched. Walter Ulbricht left East Germany for his "vacation" in the U.S.S.R. on August 1. It is probable that he met Khrushchev after the latter returned from his meeting with Mao in early August. A number of East German pronouncements shortly thereafter hinted at developments that culminated in Khrushchev's November 11 declaration on "the solution" of the West Berlin problem.

† It is highly probable that some of the Sino-Soviet differences stem from the lack of Soviet eagerness to help the C.P.R. eliminate a rival regime. From the Chinese Communists' viewpoint, the Russians undoubtedly would display less caution if they had to contend with a rival regime well situated just outside of Soviet borders, having its own armed forces, and receiving the same support given the Chinese Nationalists by the U.S.

Far East, the Russians could not expect the Chinese Communists to achieve this objective with their own limited power. And, again, although the Soviet Union might have been happy to see the United States bogged down in a limited conflict over the offshore islands without Soviet involvement, it could have no guarantee that a probing operation mishandled by the C.P.R. might not involve the Soviet Union in the "wrong conflict, at the wrong place, and the wrong time." The Russian behavior clearly indicated that the Soviet Union was not prepared to risk such an eventuality. At the time of the crisis, the Russians implied a determination to avoid a U.S.–Soviet armed struggle.* A year later, Soviet sentiments remained unchanged, but, that time, the Russians addressed the C.P.R. more directly. While in Peking, in September, 1959, Khrushchev openly declared that the capitalist system must not be challenged by force.† If that were the Soviet view in 1959, it can be assumed to have conditioned Soviet behavior even more in 1958, when the Soviet Union was weaker and, therefore, had still greater reason to be restrained in its support of the C.P.R.

The precise terms in which Khrushchev spelled out his views, with the foregoing considerations in mind, at his meeting with Mao in Peking from July 31 to August 3, may never be known. But it can be assumed that the Soviet Union's *military* considerations—among others—were conveyed to the Chinese in some detail, since Khrushchev brought along his Defense Minister, Marshal Malinovsky, undoubtedly to present the Soviet military assessment of the risks involved.‡

Up to a point, the Russians were undoubtedly prepared to support a C.P.R. effort to force a withdrawal from Quemoy or, if this failed, to deter the United States from inflicting a disproportionate defeat on the C.P.R. But this course presented a dilemma. On the

* In a comment on the crisis, a top Party publication implied that Soviet support for the C.P.R. was not being rendered at the cost of risking war; it bluntly declared, "The Soviet Union does not want military conflict." (*Kommunist,* No. 12, August, 1958, p. 81.) This statement came at a time when the C.P.R. was proclaiming that it was not afraid to face the possibility of war. *Red Flag,* on August 16, stressed U.S. weakness, a line that was not pushed by the Russians during the crisis.

† *Sovetskii flot* (*Soviet Fleet*), October 1, 1959. This particular declaration met with stony Chinese silence, even as other Khrushchev statements received high approval ranging from "applause" to "lengthy and stormy applause," according to the notations appearing in the Soviet press.

‡ The apparently negative attitude of the Soviet military toward the C.P.R. probe will be detailed later.

one hand, the Russians, in order to deter the United States from vigorous counteraction, had to impress the United States with the dread risk of "escalation," i.e., the likelihood that a conflict over Quemoy would trigger general nuclear war. On the other hand, by strongly injecting themselves into the dispute, the Russians increased the possibility that the local conflict would bring about a general war. To make their threats credible, the Russians had to profess their staunch commitment to the defense of the C.P.R. Yet, to do so risked involvement all the more. For, if Soviet threats failed to deter the United States from taking strong action against the C.P.R., the Russians had either to honor their commitment or to stand by passively in the face of a C.P.R. defeat. A Chinese Communist defeat would not only have shaken the Sino-Soviet alliance, but would also have marred the image of power that the Russians sought for future political use (as, for example, in the 1958–59 Berlin crisis, which was shortly to follow the Quemoy gambit.)

The Russians did not resolve their Quemoy dilemma. Their failure contributed to China's fiasco. The lesson of Quemoy strengthened the conviction of the Chinese Communist leaders that their Soviet colleagues lacked the courage forcefully to advance the Communist cause. The rift over Quemoy looms as a major factor in the Sino-Soviet dispute.

In the early phase of the crisis, i.e., before September 6, 1958, the C.P.R. carried on the heaviest, and most sustained, bombardment of Quemoy. (The C.P.R. made the first move to ease tension when, on September 6, it offered to resume negotiations with the U.S., and the U.S. promptly accepted.) During this period, the Russians played down the seriousness of the crisis. They did not express overt approval of the C.P.R. action, nor did they go on record, formally or officially, with a pledge of aid. They indicated, possibly for Chinese Communist consumption, the limits of their support: the Soviet Union was not prepared to back a C.P.R. venture that might lead to actual conflict with the U.S. The Russians avoided creating the atmosphere of acute tension that has characterized their crisis strategy elsewhere. Thus, Khrushchev, on August 24—one day after the C.P.R. initiated the heavy bombardment of the offshore islands—declared that, looking at the international scene, he saw no developments that could lead to war in the immediate future:

> Many ask will there be a war or not. Of course, one cannot vouch for the madmen who exist in the imperialist world; but *at the pres-*

ent time, it seems to me, *there is no cloud from which thunder could roll.* The imperialists are circling the fence around the socialist countries like hungry wolves around a sheephouse; but our fence is solid and there is a reliable defense.*

As if to emphasize Khrushchev's views that there was, indeed, no crisis in the making, the Russians initially played down the wider implications of the Quemoy developments. Although they briefly noted Communist China's shelling of Quemoy in the days immediately following the initiation of the action, they did not suggest that this action was a prelude to more serious developments in the Formosa Strait area. Indeed, the first citations were on the order of numerous other reports of small-scale Red Chinese military action against intrusions by the Nationalists, reported by the Russians over the years after the Communist Chinese take-over in 1949. On August 27, the Soviet press cited TASS (the Soviet news agency) dispatches from London referring vaguely to action by the C.P.R. shore batteries.[3] A day later, the action was noted merely as a punitive retaliation by Chinese Communist batteries against Chinese Nationalist ships trying to land supplies on Quemoy.[4] The first direct Soviet comments were couched in guarded terms. Some Soviet commentary did not even mention the Quemoy shelling and referred only vaguely to "suspicious maneuvering by the 7th Fleet." [5]

The Soviet press, even after it had begun to report the seriousness of Quemoy developments, exercised more than usual restraint. Before September 6, the Russians downgraded the notion that U.S. actions in the Formosa Strait would lead to a world war.† After upgrading the crisis, they contented themselves with a hint: a possible conflict might not be confined to the Formosa Strait area.[6] In thus de-emphasizing the seriousness of the situation, the Russians revealed their anxiety to avoid involvement. A

---

* *Pravda,* August 24, 1958 (italics added). It should be noted that Khrushchev spoke on August 13. An eleven-day delay in publication is not unique, although it is not the usual Soviet practice. If Khrushchev actually delivered this speech on August 13—ten days after his meeting with Mao—he did so with full knowledge of the impending C.P.R. probe. By publishing Khrushchev's views after the probe got underway, the Russians may have intended to cool down the ardor of the Chinese. Since Khrushchev did not see any current danger of war initiated by "imperialist madmen," it would seem that only the C.P.R. could have provoked a conflict.

† Exaggerated claims that Western moves would lead to war were made by the Russians very early in other crises. For example, in the Lebanese crisis immediately preceding Quemoy developments, the Russians asserted, two days after the U.S. landing, that the move could result in world war.

world war, as they had made so clear on other occasions, could not take place without Soviet participation. The Russians voiced explicitly the possibility of a world war arising from the Quemoy crisis only *after* the crisis had entered the political phase—and the way had been opened for C.P.R.–U.S. negotiations.

Soviet de-emphasis of Quemoy developments in the military phase of the crisis reflected Soviet interest in dampening C.P.R. ardor and, at the same time, in forestalling U.S. preparations for a full-scale showdown. Soviet concern increased as the United States assumed a firm position.

On September 4, after conferring with President Eisenhower, Secretary of State Dulles stated, in the President's name, that the United States was prepared, if necessary, to use its armed forces to defend the offshore islands.[7] Dulles spoke against the background of a sizeable U.S. military build-up in the Far East. The Russians had no reason to doubt that the United States not only had the capability to thwart a Chinese Communist probe at a level higher than the shelling of the offshore islands, but also intended to use this capability if required.* Dulles stated flatly that the offshore islands were connected with U.S. security interests. Secretary Dulles' declaration established, as Khrushchev put it in his letter to President Eisenhower on September 7, "the sphere of [U.S.] operations . . . on the territory of China." [8] In effect, the United States, in Soviet eyes, declared that an attack which threatened to overwhelm Quemoy and Matsu would be an attack on the United States.† Whether the United States would now deem itself challenged seemed to depend primarily on the C.P.R. and, to a lesser degree, on the Soviet Union—through its ability to influence the C.P.R.

The C.P.R., possibly under Soviet pressure, backed away from the challenge. The Chinese Communist declaration of September 4, laying claim to twelve miles as the limit of its territorial waters, seemed to concede that the C.P.R. was now prepared to scale down its attempt to liberate Taiwan and the offshore islands. The

* Dulles indicated that the C.P.R. use of force against Quemoy would "forecast widespread use of force in the Far East."

† The Russians earlier viewed Madame Chiang's plea (at a Los Angeles press conference) for the defense of Quemoy and Matsu—"the eyes of Taiwan"—against the C.P.R. as a demand that the U.S. consider any C.P.R. attempt "to liberate" the islands an attack on the U.S. (*Krasnaya zvezda,* September 3, 1958).

C.P.R. now spoke vaguely of its right to "liberate" these territories at "any suitable time," although, an earlier declaration (directed at the Quemoy garrison on August 27) had announced the imminent invasion of Quemoy.[9] Instead of relying on the use of force, the C.P.R. now examined the possibility of solving the crisis by political means. As if to underscore their readiness to back away from a military resolution, the Chinese Communist batteries ceased shelling Quemoy, and the C.P.R. made the first conciliatory move of the crisis: the offer of September 6 to resume negotiations with the United States.

The Russians had achieved their aim of reducing the possibility of a C.P.R.–U.S. military confrontation.* The C.P.R., undoubtedly, was less than happy, for it was being forced to sue for negotiations, without having made any tangible gains.

It is unlikely that the C.P.R., unhampered by Soviet pressures, would have made the first conciliatory move when it did. In the face of a strong U.S. stand, the C.P.R. might have resumed negotiations at a later date, guided by its own convictions. As matters stood, the Russians induced the C.P.R. to resume negotiations before the Chinese Communists were ready. The C.P.R. timetable originally may have called for a prolonged interdiction effort. More likely than not, thirty to sixty days of intensive shelling would have reduced Quemoy to a starvation level. In that case, the C.P.R. might have extracted some concessions from the United States.† It is not far-fetched to assume that the Soviet Union, concerned with the hardening of the U.S. position, may have persuaded the C.P.R. to make the first conciliatory move. The C.P.R. probably would have preferred to await a more opportune time before offering to resume negotiations. In making its offer less than forty-eight hours after the U.S. declaration, the C.P.R. appeared to be yielding to U.S. pressure.‡ This admission of weakness could be expected to affect its bargaining position. Since it seems unlikely

* As a Polish broadcast on September 10 put it, the C.P.R. move pointed the way to shifting the crisis from "the military to the political and diplomatic field." A Moscow Radio broadcast on September 9 described the C.P.R. conciliatory gesture in more euphemistic terms as an initiative to achieve "a normalization of the situation in the Far East."

† It was estimated that Quemoy had enough supplies on hand to enable it to hold out sixty days even if the blockade were total (*The New York Times*, September 8, 1958).

‡ A White House statement on the C.P.R. offer tactfully labeled the move as an apparent peace overture (*The New York Times*, September 7, 1958).

that the C.P.R. chose freely to weaken its hand thus, it would not be surprising if the C.P.R. held the Russians largely responsible for Chinese Communist humiliation.*

Soviet acclaim of the C.P.R. offer to negotiate, as an opportunity for a peaceful resolution, seemed to reflect Soviet satisfaction at having interested the C.P.R. in such a move. In contrast, the C.P.R. stressed that its offer should not be interpreted as weakening its will to liberate the offshore islands and Taiwan.† Apparently, the C.P.R. was trying hard to dispel the impression that it was about to negotiate from a position of weakness and that its offer was meant as a gesture to ease tension. After its September 6 offer, the C.P.R., by its unyielding declaratory stand, seemed determined to give the United States no additional cause to believe (despite Soviet hints to the contrary) that it was anxious to let the crisis peter out without conflict.‡

The Russians may have given the C.P.R. still another cause for dissatisfaction. Any clear indication that the Soviet Union was anxious to end the crisis without conflict laid to rest the specter of a Soviet Union ominously poised to back the C.P.R. to the point of war, and lessened the pressure on the United States. Understandably, the C.P.R. was grieved.

Anxious to avoid a C.P.R.–U.S. clash, the Russians pushed aside considerations of how their move would affect the C.P.R.'s position vis-à-vis the United States. Even after initiating their subsequent campaign of threats, the Russians apparently wanted it understood that they preferred the crisis to end in negotiations, not war. They publicized the following interpretation of the blustering letter that Khrushchev dispatched to President Eisenhower on September 7:

* The Chinese Communists appear to believe that the Russians overestimate U.S. power. As has been suggested elsewhere (see Donald S. Zagoria, *The Sino-Soviet Conflict 1956–1961,* [Princeton, N.J., 1962], pp. 202–3), the C.P.R. felt that, in the Lebanese crisis, the Soviets had retreated too readily in the face of a show of U.S. power. C.P.R. irritation at Soviet timidity in the Quemoy crisis was probably even greater, since it was displayed at the expense of direct C.P.R. interests.

† *Jen-min Jih-pao* (People's Daily) declared that the C.P.R. move should not be considered "empty noise."

‡ Though Soviet characterization of the C.P.R.'s move as a peaceful gesture may have been good propaganda to influence world opinion, to the United States the move was a C.P.R. retreat. Since the C.P.R. probably was more interested in impressing the United States than world opinion, it could not have been happy with a Soviet line that reinforced the image of the C.P.R.'s weakness.

The Moscow AP correspondent follows up his summary of N. S. Khrushchev's message with a story reporting that, although Krushchev's words *may sound harsh* to the West, the message is viewed as restrained by Western diplomats in Moscow.

Khrushchev's letter, remarks the correspondent, which *was sent after Chou En-lai agreed to the resumption of talks* on the ambassadorial level is aimed at *reducing the immediate threat of war for the sake of Taiwan.* The correspondent notes that, together with an energetic warning that in case of an attack against China, it will not be alone, the message of the head of the Soviet Government contains a frank appeal: *talk instead of war* [italics added].[10]

In sum, the Russians did not propose to go to war with the United States over C.P.R. interests.*

Apparently, as added insurance that the crisis would be directed into political channels, the Russians took measures of their own. With the opening of the U.N. General Assembly on September 17 in the offing, the Russians signified their interest in shifting the crisis from the Formosa Strait to the comparatively less perilous environment of the U.N.† The Russians suggested that the U.N.'s attention should be focused, above all else, on the admission of the C.P.R. to membership.[11] When the General Assembly opened on September 17, the Russians argued forcefully for the admission of the C.P.R.; this insistence assured that developments in the Formosa Strait would receive a thorough airing.‡ The Russians could

---

* *Kommunist,* the central party organ, in commenting on Khrushchev's September 7, 1958, declaration, implied that Soviet support of the C.P.R. was not being rendered at the risk of war. It stated bluntly that the Soviet position was based on a "persistent" policy: "The U.S.S.R. does not want military conflicts." (*Kommunist,* No. 12, August, 1958, p. 81. A delay in publication suggests the dilemma the Russians faced in making clear the limits of their support without openly undercutting the C.P.R.'s position. This issue was not distributed until after mid-September.)

† Similarly, the Russians tried frantically to divert the Lebanon crisis into political channels. They attempted to convoke, first, a summit meeting and, then, a U.N. special session. They sought to avoid the choice between challenging the United States or backing down at the cost of considerable political embarrassment.

‡ The C.P.R. insisted that the crisis was part of a civil war, which brooked no external interference. In C.P.R. eyes, the crisis had arisen, in the first place, because the United States had meddled in internal Chinese affairs. To circumvent the C.P.R.'s avowed opposition to U.N. intervention in the Quemoy crisis, the Russians appear to have resorted to the issue of C.P.R. membership as a roundabout way of introducing the crisis into U.N. deliberations. If the C.P.R. had chided the Russians for taking the Lebanese crisis to the U.N., it can be assumed that the Chinese Communists felt even more strongly about Soviet efforts to be "helpful" in the Quemoy affair.

hardly have expected that the Quemoy crisis would be conducive to favorable U.N. action on the C.P.R.'s admission. But their vocal sponsorship of Communist China might have been prompted by another motive: U.N. discussion of the China question might generate sufficient political pressure on the United States—the one side to the controversy most susceptible to political pressure—to ease the Quemoy crisis.

Extreme caution distinguished Soviet reaction to a number of C.P.R. "offensive" declarations, which, by their nature, might have transformed the Quemoy crisis into more than a limited test of U.S. intentions. The C.P.R., on September 4, officially proclaimed the extension of its territorial waters to twelve miles. The U.S. refusal to recognize this claim created a real possibility that the C.P.R. and U.S. forces might clash. The U.S. Navy, in escorting Chinese Nationalist supply ships to within three miles of the coast of Quemoy, came within range of the C.P.R. coastal batteries; by firing on U.S. ships in defense of its "territorial sovereignty," intentionally or otherwise, the C.P.R. might have provoked a strong U.S. riposte. To intimidate the United States, the Soviet Union could have pledged itself to defend the inviolability of Chinese Communist territory. The Russians refrained, pointedly, from giving such a pledge.

Even further, the Russians declined publicly to approve the C.P.R.'s twelve-mile declaration. On this score, their marked indifference to the stated interests of their major ally was especially revealing. The Russians had waged a vigorous campaign at the 1958 Geneva Conference to secure for themselves international recognition of the twelve-mile limit. In fact, they had shot down planes that they claimed had violated the twelve-mile limit beyond the Soviet coast.*

The Soviet Union, it seems, had some advance information of Communist China's proclamation. The Soviet press, several weeks before the C.P.R. stated its claim to the twelve-mile limit, reported specifically that U.S. ships and planes were operating twelve miles from the Communist Chinese shore, [12] and, in at least one instance, even claimed that U.S. forces were operating a good deal closer to the Chinese shore.[13]

* On the occasion of the RB-47 incident of July, 1960, the Russians contended that the U.S. plane was downed because it had violated Soviet territory twenty-two kilometers from the Soviet land mass, or just over the twelve-mile limit. (*Pravda,* July 12, 1960.)

Despite its apparent foreknowledge, the Soviet Union responded to the C.P.R. twelve-mile declaration at first ambiguously, then noncommittally. While the crisis passed through the military phase, the Russians stated, somewhat lamely, that the C.P.R. declaration "would find full understanding of the Soviet public," and "would receive wide support among *other states* [italics added]."* The obvious hesitation of the Soviet leadership to commit itself, at that time, seemed to be confirmed by the fact that official Soviet reaction was withheld until the crisis passed into the political stage. Even then, the Russians clung to caution. A Foreign Ministry note, issued on September 9, was worded in stiffly diplomatic terms unrelated to the crisis. It stated that the Soviet Union took "note" of the C.P.R. twelve-mile declaration and "would fully respect" it, and that "appropriate Soviet organizations have been given orders about strict observance of the provisions" of the C.P.R. declaration.† There was no indication of whether or not the Soviet Government actually supported the claim.

Although the Russians denounced U.S. violations of the C.P.R. twelve-mile limit as bordering on aggression,‡ they did not offer to aid the C.P.R. in repelling U.S. forces. It would appear that the Russians were anxious not to give the C.P.R. any declaratory handle for invoking aid. The Russians' silence spoke louder than their words: they would not challenge the United States, even at the price of some political embarrassment.§

* *Izvestiya,* September 6, 1958. This was the only major Soviet comment on the C.P.R. declaration before the Soviet Government responded officially on September 9. The weakness of the initial Soviet response was reflected by the absence of indications of the Soviet *Government's* backing of Communist China's position. Such support would have been more authoritative and, therefore, more menacing. Indeed, the fact that the Russians subsequently had to issue a separate declaration of the government's view suggests how weak the Russians believed their earlier statements were.

† The Soviet Foreign Ministry note was published in the Soviet press on September 10. The Soviet agreement to respect the C.P.R. twelve-mile claim seemed to be strictly academic, since no Soviet ships or planes were in the Formosa Strait. Moreover, the C.P.R. would certainly not have construed the movement of Soviet ships as violating its sovereignty.

‡ *Krasnaya zvezda* on September 9, 1958, stated that "U.S. adventurists" had embarked upon "open action" when the 7th Fleet "invaded C.P.R. territorial waters" in the region of Quemoy, through the escorting of Nationalist supply ships initiated on September 7.

§ Secretary of State Dulles discounted the risk that the twelve-mile limit declaration would lead to war. (*The New York Times,* September 8, 1958.) Nevertheless, he made it clear that the U.S. Navy would reply if its ships

The Soviet attitude toward the C.P.R.'s proclaimed objective of seizing the offshore islands and liberating Taiwan is a study in half-heartedness. No other conclusion can be drawn than that the U.S.S.R. acquiesced in an initiative confined to testing both U.S. and Chinese Nationalist resolution by bombardment of the offshore islands; the Russians would not support an invasion of the offshore islands, let alone an attack on Taiwan.

Even before the initiation of the crisis the Russians de-emphasized the "liberate Taiwan" slogan. On several occasions they reported the C.P.R. aims *as proclaimed by C.P.R. spokesmen;* in their own comments, they ignored carefully the Taiwan issue. The silence on the Taiwan question of the Mao-Khrushchev communiqué in early August anticipated subsequent Soviet reticence.

After the crisis flared on August 23, Soviet silence on a C.P.R. take-over of the offshore islands and Taiwan could no longer be mistaken for a lapse of memory. On August 27, the C.P.R. proclaimed: "The Chinese People's Liberation Army has determined to liberate Taiwan, a territory of the fatherland, as well as the offshore islands, and the landing on Quemoy is imminent." [14] It warned the Quemoy garrison of the destruction that would follow "the joint assault of our modern army and air force." [15] The Russians completely ignored this declaration.

Silence on Red China's threat to invade Quemoy seemed clearly to reflect the Soviet Union's lack of confidence in its ability to deter the United States from opposing a C.P.R. attempt to make good the threat. If, indeed, the C.P.R. really intended to invade Quemoy, the Soviet attitude restrained it from doing so; obviously, the C.P.R. was unwilling to face the United States alone. The fact that the C.P.R. called a halt even before the United States declared, on September 4, its intention to help Chiang defend the islands, suggests that the C.P.R. was not backing down in the face of U.S. pressure. Rather, it seems that the Russians played a key role in this retreat.

When the crisis shifted to the political plane, the C.P.R. once more asserted its right to liberate Taiwan and the offshore islands, "including resort to war," as the Chinese Communist ambassador

---

were deliberately hit (*The New York Times,* September 10, 1958). Confronted by this possibility, the Russians apparently decided not to make any commitment, since the United States might be unable to distinguish between deliberate and accidental C.P.R. shells fired at U.S. ships coming within three miles of the offshore islands.

in Albania put it, on September 30.[16] Again, the Russians were silent.*

The Russians threatened the United States least when the risk of military conflict was greatest. In the first week of the crisis, they pointedly abstained from threats. And, until the tension-easing developments on September 6, they exercised great restraint. Thus, the initial warnings were not made in the name of the government or uttered by leaders whose official position would have implied a commitment of the Soviet Government.†

Before September 6, the most forthright dare was voiced by *Pravda* on August 31, in an article signed by "Observer." It warned the United States that a threat of an attack on the C.P.R. would be a threat to the Soviet Union; in that case the Soviet Union would render every kind of "moral and material aid." This statement contained a number of significant reservations. Its tone was not as unconditional as that of subsequent Soviet threats—for example, Khrushchev's letter of September 7 to Eisenhower, which stated in seemingly unequivocal terms that an attack on the C.P.R. would be not just a threat to, but an attack on, the Soviet Union. Incidentally, the Russians did not speak of one crucial factor of aid to the C.P.R., namely, men. The Russians hedged on whether their soldiers would fight alongside their Chinese comrades-in-arms. Peking undoubtedly recalled that, in the Korean War, Soviet equipment—but not Soviet personnel—was involved in the conflict; the Chinese paid for their involvement with heavy human losses. The manner in which the Russians were now pledging their support conveyed to the Chinese a painful impression: in case of conflict with the United States, the Chinese would again spill their

---

* The Russians' taciturnity *during* the crisis is particularly revealing, when compared with their loquaciousness in times of relaxed tensions. In an interview with Averell Harriman *after* the crisis (June, 1959), Khrushchev declaimed vigorously that he backed the C.P.R.'s claims, and that, if the question had to be answered by the use of force, the Russians would contribute their share (*Life,* July 13, 1959).

† In this regard, the Russians have always observed the niceties of diplomatic convention. International custom bids nations to take formal declarations of policy made in the name of the government more seriously than extemporaneous remarks made on informal occasions. The Russians cleave to international custom. For example, on numerous occasions, Khrushchev's broadly worded statements uttered at embassy cocktail parties and receptions, or in interviews with journalists, were either eliminated or sharply toned down in subsequent official Soviet Government notes.

own blood while the Russians remained on the sidelines, giving "moral" aid.*

The August 31 threat, restrained as it was, constituted the only major warning delivered by the U.S.S.R. before the United States declared its intention, on September 4, to defend Quemoy. Since the United States apparently did not as yet consider the crisis serious,† the Russians were relatively safe in going on record with a comparatively mild declaration to test its effect on the United States. They may have calculated that an initial declaration of support might produce a "bloodless" victory: the United States, since it had not yet adopted a position from which it could not retreat easily, might yield on Quemoy, if confronted with a hint of possible Soviet intervention.

Only after the September 6 moves to ease tension were under way did the Russians raise the pitch of their threats. They seemed to view the prompt acceptance by the United States of the Communist Chinese offer of negotiations as a sign of Washington's fear of an armed conflict. Moscow's threats, therefore, could now be uttered with impunity.

The broadest threat of the crisis was contained in Khrushchev's letter of September 7 to President Eisenhower: "An attack on the Chinese People's Republic, which is a great ally, friend, and neighbor of our country, is an attack on the Soviet Union." [17] Khrushchev appeared to state, unequivocally, that an attack on the C.P.R. would *automatically* result in Soviet involvement. Since he did not spell out the source and level of attack, he seemed to imply that his threat covered action by either U.S. or Chinese Nationalist forces at *any* level, conventional or nuclear.

The Russians, however, began quickly to scale down Khrushchev's warning. He himself took the lead. In a speech at Stalingrad on September 11, he declared that the Soviet Union "would

* Soviet references to the vast millions of Chinese ready to take up arms against the United States seemed to reflect the Soviet feeling that the C.P.R. had plenty of manpower to spare and, hence, by implication, that the Soviet Union's involvement would not be required. More significantly, Soviet reference to the unlimited Chinese manpower seemed subtly to underline that the Russians were not prepared to sacrifice themselves for C.P.R. interests.

† In the first days of the crisis, the State Department did not believe that a situation seriously bordering on war was in the making (*The New York Times,* August 31, 1958). Pentagon sources were also reported as not concerned about C.P.R. capabilities to act beyond the shelling of Quemoy (*The New York Times,* August 30, 1958).

consider" an attack on the C.P.R. as an attack on the Soviet Union.[18] This speech appeared to redefine the Soviet position as one in which considered judgment would determine the applicability of the Soviet commitment. A subsequent declaration that Soviet aid would be rendered "if this is necessary," [19] implied that a careful weighing of facts might find no need for Soviet involvement. The Russians further strengthened this implication by stressing C.P.R. capabilities and praising C.P.R. success in meeting U.S. aggression. They described the C.P.R. as having grown considerably stronger since the Korean War, and having "everything necessary to give a suitable rebuff" to any aggressor.

Moreover, lest anyone, including the C.P.R., might misunderstand, the Russians further narrowed their threats by "clarifying" declarations. Just a week after Khrushchev's sweeping threat was made public, the Russians hinted, unofficially, that their involvement would apply only to U.S. action. This hint served as a forerunner to Khrushchev's statement of October 5, in which he "clarified," officially, his original threat. He pointed out that, since the Chinese Nationalist–C.P.R. conflict was a civil war, only U.S. action against the C.P.R. would bring the Soviet Union into the conflict. By labeling all C.P.R.–Kuomintang engagements as part of a civil war and proclaiming his intention not to interfere in such an "internal" matter, he staked out a position enabling him to beg off in a number of contingencies. The most important of these contingencies was a premeditated C.P.R. or Nationalist action designed to involve the United States and the Soviet Union.

According to Soviet sources, Chiang Kai-shek planned to use planes with C.P.R. markings to bomb U.S. ships.[20] The United States could be expected to retaliate against such an attack,* thereby increasing the chances of Soviet involvement. In noting the possibility of premeditated action by the Nationalists, the Russians appeared to be warning the United States to keep a tight rein on Chiang's forces, and to forestall him from triggering a U.S.–C.P.R. conflict, which, in turn, might escalate into a U.S.–Soviet conflict.

The Soviet position on the Chinese civil war, combined with Soviet views on possible Nationalist ruses noted above, could have given the U.S.S.R. an excuse, if one were needed, to avoid involvement in the event of limited U.S. action, such as an air strike

---

* Secretary of State Dulles declared explicitly that the 7th Fleet would react if its ships were hit by the C.P.R. (*The New York Times,* September 9, 1958).

against the C.P.R. coastal batteries shelling Quemoy. The U.S.S.R. could have maintained that the U.S. planes carrying out the attack on C.P.R. batteries, or other coastal installations, were actually Chiang's planes using U.S. markings. (Indeed, since the Nationalists were equipped almost exclusively with U.S. war matériel, the C.P.R. might well have found it difficult to disprove such a contention.) The Russians might well have taken this way out, in view of their undisguised aversion to letting themselves be pushed into an open conflict by possible C.P.R. indiscretion or premeditation.*

Khrushchev's seemingly unequivocal declaration of September 7, in addition to being modified by subsequent "clarifications," contained a number of implicit reservations, the most important of which related to the Sino-Soviet Pact. In his message, Khrushchev referred to the C.P.R. as an "ally," whom the Soviet Union would aid in case of attack. He refrained, however, from citing the Pact by name and from declaring it operative in case of a C.P.R.–U.S. conflict.†

A glance at the key sentence of the Pact may suggest the reason for Khrushchev's omission, and account for the fact that the Russians scrupulously avoided any reference to the treaty during the military phase of the crisis. The Pact obligates each party to respond *automatically*. It states that if one of the signatory parties is subjected to attack—and is thereby in a state of war—then the other signatory party "shall immediately render military and other assistance by all means at its disposal." ‡ As noted earlier, Khrushchev's sweeping statement that an attack on the C.P.R. would be an attack on the Soviet Union was subsequently "clarified" to tone down this categorical undertaking. Hence, the cautious handling of the Pact by the Russians appeared to betray their concern lest a

* The Chinese Communists apparently had attempted, on at least one occasion, to provoke an incident involving U.S. forces. It was reported that they had transmitted false radio signals in an attempt to draw U.S. planes over the mainland, but had not succeeded. J. R. Beal, *John Foster Dulles: 1888–1959* (New York: 1959), p. 337.

† The 1950 Sino-Soviet Pact calls for mutual defense in case of an attack on the Soviet Union or the C.P.R. by Japan or any nation allied with it.

‡ The text of the Pact is given in Appendix B. The Pact appears to call for a more automatic military response than, for example, the NATO agreement. The latter stipulates that each member will assist the party attacked by taking "such action *as it deems necessary,* including the use of armed force." The operative clause of the SEATO agreements is even weaker; it calls for consultations "*in order to agree* on measures which should be taken." (Italics added.)

formally recorded Soviet commitment be lightly invoked by the C.P.R.

The U.S.S.R. did not resort to the threat value of the Pact until it was relatively safe to do so. Khrushchev, speaking as head of the Soviet Government, referred to the Pact in his letter to President Eisenhower of September 19. His warning, however, was carefully hedged by the manner of its timing. He cited the Pact *after* political developments—the resumption of C.P.R.–U.S. negotiations and the opening of the U.N. General Assembly—had lessened the possibility of a C.P.R.–U.S. clash. The Russians were now convinced that the danger of war had passed. As they put it, "American strategists decisively miscalculated the strength of the C.P.R. forces and determination of the Chinese people to defend its rights." [21] Evidently, the Russians had reached an understanding with the C.P.R. that the Chinese would begin to call off the Quemoy venture.

Soviet caution reached its apogee in the campaign of nuclear threats. The Russians did not rattle the nuclear bomb until the crisis had entered safely into the political phrase. At the height of the critical situation, the Russians did not speak a word about intervening with their nuclear might in the Far East. Khrushchev's seemingly unequivocal declaration of September 7 was the most glaring example of Soviet caution on this score. Even as he assailed U.S. use of "nuclear blackmail" against the C.P.R., Khrushchev refused to invoke the Soviet nuclear shield in support of the Chinese Communists. Instead, he proclaimed his confidence in the courage of the C.P.R. to face the nuclear danger posed by the United States. [22] In remaining silent on Soviet nuclear backing for the C.P.R., in case of a U.S. nuclear attack, Khrushchev, it would appear, implied that the C.P.R. would have to rely on its own resources. Hence, even though his declaration was addressed to the United States, it seemed to be warning the Chinese Communists not to push the crisis to a point at which the United States might have to react with nuclear weapons.

Khrushchev's initial restraint might have been due to his belief that, despite the forthcoming C.P.R.–U.S. negotiations, the making of nuclear threats against the United States was still dangerous. In the days immediately following September 6, there was still a real possibility that, if the Russians had made any nuclear commitments, they might have had to act on them, or refuse to do so at obvious political costs.

In the immediate period following Khrushchev's September 7 declaration, the United States was still uncertain that Quemoy could be supplied without taking action to silence the C.P.R. batteries. The United States indicated that it was prepared to take such action. Since conventional ammunition was reported to be short, the United States might have had to resort to nuclear weapons. The use of nuclear weapons, of course, could have escalated the crisis into a U.S.–Soviet confrontation. In an apparent effort to avoid having to face such a possibility, the Russians continued to maintain complete silence on their nuclear intentions—notwithstanding the fact that they decried the alleged intentions of the United States to use nuclear weapons against the C.P.R.*

By the time the Russians went on record with a nuclear retaliatory threat, the United States had sharply revised its estimate of the military situation. By September 19, the chances that the United States would have to join actively in the defense of Quemoy had greatly diminished. But even in the unlikely event of U.S. military action, it appeared from U.S. estimates that there would be no need to resort to nuclear weapons.

Only at this point did the Russians invoke their nuclear power in support of the C.P.R. Khrushchev declared, on September 19, that:

> atomic blackmail directed at the C.P.R. will scare neither *us* nor the Chinese People's Republic. Those who carry out plans of atomic attack on the C.P.R. should not forget that not only the U.S. but the other side possesses not only atomic but hydrogen weapons and also the corresponding means of delivery, and should such an attack be delivered on the C.P.R., then the aggressor will receive a fitting rebuff by the same means. [Italics added.] [23]

Khrushchev's new threat seemed more ominous than his earlier one, since it specifically injected the Soviet Union into the conflict. Whereas, on September 7 Khrushchev had carefully restricted himself to pointing up the C.P.R.'s courage in facing U.S. nuclear threats, he now declared that the Russians would join the C.P.R. in standing up to U.S. brinksmanship. Since only the Soviet Union had atomic and hydrogen weapons on "the other side," Khrushchev's reference tended to convey the impression that the U.S.S.R. would carry out the nuclear retaliatory blows.

---

* The statements by Dulles and Eisenhower on September 9 and 12, respectively, indicating U.S. determination to defend Quemoy against a C.P.R. assault, were labeled open threats to use nuclear weapons against China "at any moment." (*Sovetskaya Rossiya*, September 16, 1958.)

But, even as he made the nuclear threat, Khrushchev carefully outlined the limits of its applicability. In noting that a U.S. attack on the C.P.R. would be met "by the same means," Khrushchev seemed to imply that, in the event of a U.S. nuclear blow against the C.P.R. the response would be measured: if the United States resorted to local limited use of small-size weapons (the major nuclear contingency seriously considered by the United States), it would, at worst, be subject to local retaliation at the same level. Thus, despite his contention elsewhere that the initiation of the use of nuclear weapons would result in a world war, Khrushchev seemed prepared to limit a nuclear exchange—assuming, of course, that he would let developments reach even that point in the first place.

Khrushchev did not declare explicitly that the Soviet Union itself would employ nuclear weapons against the United States. It is possible that, had he intended to act at all on his nuclear commitment, he would have contented himself with supplying the C.P.R. with a token nuclear capability in order to avoid direct involvement.* But it is very doubtful, particularly in the light of subsequent events, that the Russians intended to do even that much.

In any case, despite Khrushchev's nuclear threat, the Russians seemed bent on avoiding a situation in which they had to choose between nuclear involvement or embarrassing abstention. As it became apparent that nuclear threats, instead of deterring the United States, actually stiffened its position, they hurriedly backed down. President Eisenhower brusquely rejected Khrushchev's letter of September 21; Secretary of State Dulles intimated, on September 25, that the United States was prepared to risk war over Quemoy; the Secretary of the Air Force declared, on September 27, with specific State Department approval, that the United States was prepared to use nuclear weapons in defense of Quemoy. The Soviet press, which had keynoted Khrushchev's nuclear threat immediately after its delivery, now began omitting references to Soviet nuclear retaliation. For example, at the inauguration in Peking, on September 27, of the first experimental nuclear reactor (a reactor that had been built with Soviet aid), C.P.R. speakers declared that the United States was threatening the C.P.R. with nuclear war.

* On several occasions prior to, and during, the crisis, Soviet and other Communist Bloc sources hinted that the C.P.R. already had nuclear capabilities, which, of course, would have involved Soviet assistance, but could also have served to mask Soviet involvement if the Russians had provided a limited capabilty to the Chinese after U.S. use of such weapons.

After boldly proclaiming that the C.P.R. was not afraid to face such a possibility, one high spokesman said it was relying on "the support of the socialist camp headed by the Soviet Union." The Soviet speakers did not pick up the cue; declining to restate Khrushchev's threat, they confined their comments to congratulating the C.P.R. on its scientific achievement, represented by the acquisition of a nuclear reactor.[24] Even more revealing was Khrushchev's behavior. On September 30, only ten days after he had threatened the United States with nuclear retaliation, Khrushchev passed over the subject completely in his message of congratulations to Mao Tse-tung on the occasion of the C.P.R.'s ninth anniversary.[25] In fact, he omitted any reference to the Quemoy crisis and Soviet support of the C.P.R., even as other Soviet sources continued to note the acute and dangerous state of the crisis.

Still another portent was the Soviet reaction to the Sidewinder incident. In an air engagement on September 24, an outnumbered Nationalist unit inflicted heavy C.P.R. losses by the use of the U.S.–furnished Sidewinder air-to-air missiles. The C.P.R. brought the incident into the open on September 29, several days after Air Force Secretary James H. Douglas had announced U.S. nuclear intentions. The C.P.R. declared that the world was in danger of war as a result of the Sidewinder incident, in which *"American* imperialism" had used "guided missiles and atomic weapons [italics added]."* By equating the use of Sidewinders with the employment of nuclear weapons, the C.P.R. may have been trying to invoke the Soviet nuclear support pledged by Khrushchev on September 19. Furthermore, by ascribing the attack to the United States, the C.P.R. apparently sought to head off the possible Soviet excuse that, since the Nationalist forces had used the Sidewinders, the attack constituted a civil war action in which the Russians could not interfere. But the Russians carefully sidestepped the implication of the C.P.R.'s position. In their own commentary on the Sidewinder incident, they eliminated specific reference to nuclear weapons, by charging that the "people of the world had been put under threat of war with the use of *newest weapons,"* [26] and pointedly cited the *potential* danger involved: "Today the Nationalists are using U.S. guided missiles and *tomorrow* they may decide to use the same missiles *with atomic warheads* [italics added]." [27]

The Russians, thus, seemed intent on frustrating C.P.R. efforts

* *Sovetskii flot,* October 1, 1958. The Russians here repeated verbatim a charge contained in an editorial of the C.P.R. daily, *Jen-min Jih-pao,* which implied that Sidewinders had been armed with nuclear warheads.

to force them to act on their pledge to aid the C.P.R. For even as they assailed the Chinese Nationalists for their use of Sidewinders, the Russians promised no help in remedying the Chinese Communists' weakness exposed by the Sidewinder incident.* Indeed, the Russians compounded the frustration of the C.P.R. by stressing its ability to take care of itself. They featured prominently the C.P.R. Defense Ministry's statement that *its* forces would inflict retaliatory blows "no matter what weapons the United States might give to the Chinese Air Force." [28]

One more development indicated how far the Soviet Union had backed away from the threat to use its nuclear strength in the C.P.R.'s behalf. On October 3, the Soviet Union announced that, in view of continuing U.S. and British testing, it had resumed nuclear testing because its "security interests" required it. The C.P.R. attempted to exploit this development by linking it to the crisis. Satellite spokesmen also interpreted the move as strengthening the Soviet deterrent posture in support of the C.P.R. The U.S.S.R., however, carefully avoided even the slightest hint of such a link.

The Soviet retreat, which began with the muting of nuclear threats, culminated in Khrushchev's "clarification" on October 5. He now declared that only a U.S. attack on the C.P.R. would result in Soviet involvement; the Russians, he said, intended to stay out of any Nationalist–C.P.R. armed conflict. Such a conflict constituted a continuation of the Chinese civil war. The Russians had pledged themselves to a policy of noninterference in Chinese internal affairs. This statement was in stark contrast with earlier Soviet warnings that an attack from any source would trigger a Soviet military response. Khrushchev's "clarification" was accompanied by Soviet charges that the U.S. was instigating the Nationalists to attack the C.P.R., but, a Nationalist attack would not trigger Soviet involvement under Khrushchev's new threat, now confined only to U.S. action.† Since it was clear that the Russians were disengaging from the crisis, the C.P.R. had little choice but to call off the probe completely: a day after Khrushchev's clarification, the C.P.R. issued its first cease-fire order.

---

* The Russians did not supply air-to-air missiles to the C.P.R. during the crisis.

† Earlier, the Russians maintained that the U.S., itself, was preparing to attack the C.P.R. Seemingly anxious to rule out entirely the possibility of their involvement, they now hinted that it would be unnecessary since the United States, by instigating Chiang, no longer appeared interested in acting against the C.P.R.

The Soviet leaders' obvious unwillingness to be drawn into any new imbroglio in the Far East, in the fall of 1958, was demonstrated further by the complete absence of the boastful display of military power that had become standard Soviet behavior in crisis situations.

During the crisis, the Russians did not take steps to heighten the readiness of their armed forces. There were no indications that the Soviet strategic air force had been placed on alert, or that large-scale movements of Soviet ground forces were carried out, either in the Soviet Far East or elsewhere in the Soviet Union. Nor were there public announcements about activities of the Soviet armed forces, designed to increase apprehension in the West about Soviet intentions.*

The closest the U.S.S.R. came to saber-rattling was an announcement on September 21, that the Soviet Northern Fleet, based in Murmansk, was going to engage in maneuvers of a month's duration "with different types of modern weapons." [29] (This euphemism was, at that time, often employed by the Russians to refer to nuclear weapons.) All shipping was warned to stay away from a geographically defined area of the Arctic Ocean. This announcement, however, lost much of its significance because of its "safe" timing: political developments, by then, had eased the tension. Moreover, in the context of the Quemoy crisis, a similar announcement pertaining to the Soviet Pacific Fleet—the fleet operating closest to C.P.R. shores, and the one logically suited to assist the C.P.R.—would have indicated greater Soviet willingness to engage in a war of nerves for the sake of the C.P.R.

Then, too, the Russians pointedly refrained from exploiting the annual demobilization of their armed forces personnel who completed their term of service (normally carried out in early September). In fact, since they initiated the demobilization at the height of the crisis, they did not appear interested in suggesting that Russian forces might become involved in the crisis.†

* For example, the Russians could have announced that troops of their Far East and Trans-Baikal military districts bordering on the C.P.R. were going on maneuvers, and that top Soviet military commanders were being sent to take charge of the maneuvers. They had used this device at the height of the Lebanese crisis, a few months earlier, when they announced that several marshals were being dispatched from Moscow to take charge of maneuvers to be carried out by Soviet military units in districts bordering on the Middle East.

† Soviet behavior on this occasion is particularly revealing in contrast to that of other times. Thus, in the 1961 Berlin crisis, Khrushchev announced,

The one reference that hinted, even remotely, at possible participation by Soviet armed forces occurred apparently with "safe" timing in mind, in the political phase of the crisis. The Russians, professing their readiness to aid the C.P.R., reminded the public that their pilots had flown as "volunteers" on the Chinese side against Japan in 1937–38.[30] That they spoke of volunteers, rather than of their regular forces, suggests that they had intended to limit their involvement, if any, so as not to engage the U.S.S.R. directly, since such aid was unlikely to provoke a full-scale U.S. reaction against the Soviet Union itself. In this connection, the Russians might have drawn some instructive lessons from U.S. behavior in Korea; even a mass influx of Chinese "volunteers" did not evoke a U.S. reaction against the C.P.R. proper. And the United States had exercised this restraint in the days of a virtual U.S. nuclear monopoly. By 1958, the Russians might have expected that the United States, in the face of greater Soviet power, would be even more inhibited from acting directly against them in the event that they decided on limited involvement through "volunteers" on Chinese soil. However, since they pointedly spoke of giving this aid "if needed," the chances that the Russians would have done so were slight. The timing of their threat made it unlikely that the volunteers would be needed.

In contrast with the verbal campaign waged by Soviet political leaders and press, the top Soviet military leaders maintained almost total silence during the Quemoy crisis. The only ranking officer even to take note of Quemoy developments was Marshal P. A. Rotmistrov of the Tank Troops. In an article devoted to the anniversary of the Soviet armored forces, he mentioned, in passing, that the Soviet armed forces were "vigilantly" watching the situation in the Far East. Rotmistrov said nothing about Soviet support for the C.P.R.[31] Other high-ranking military leaders abstained completely from recording their position, even when the occasion seemed to call for comment. At the height of the crisis, Soviet Defense Minister Marshal Malinovsky, in addressing the graduates of the military engineering academy in Moscow, con-

---

on July 8, that he was suspending the planned reduction of the Soviet armed forces proclaimed by him in January, 1960. On August 7, he said that he might have to mobilize reserves, and move additional forces to the border dividing East and West Germany. On August 29, the Russians announced that they were holding up the scheduled demobilization of men whose active service would end in 1961 "until the conclusion of a peace treaty with Germany."

spicuously refrained from giving his views on the crisis.[32] It was left to a junior officer—a major—to note that the graduating class was joining the Soviet forces "at a time of tense international setting when the imperialist aggressors headed by the United States try to kindle a new focus on war in the Far East." However, even he carefully avoided referring to Soviet support of the C.P.R. by noting only that: "We, the young military engineers, assure the Central Committee of our party, that we shall honorably justify the confidence shown us and shall, in case of need, rise to defense of *our* homeland's interest at the first call." [33]

Even more pointed was the silence of Marshal I. S. Konev, then Warsaw Pact Commander, at the occasion of ceremonies on October 10, in Warsaw, commemorating the fifteenth anniversary of the Polish Army. Konev not only did not pledge support to the C.P.R., but did not even refer to the crisis—an omission all the more striking since the Polish Chief of State, "taking the opportunity of the presence of the delegation of the C.P.R. Army," denounced U.S. aggression and extended Polish "sympathy and solidarity." [34]

The reticence of the Soviet military leadership was significant, especially when compared with its behavior in other crises. Particularly conspicuous was Malinovsky's silence. Of all Soviet marshals, he should have been outspoken on aid to the C.P.R., since he had participated in the Mao-Khrushchev meeting in early August. Certainly, Malinovsky had not been reluctant, on other occasions, to echo, or even enlarge upon, Khrushchev's blustering statements.

This restraint by the Soviet top military leadership was reflected, also, in the military press treatment of the threats uttered by Soviet political leaders in support of the C.P.R. Unlike the political press, the military papers either toned down, or omitted entirely, some important portions of Khrushchev's sweeping declarations.* The

---

* On the day after Khrushchev's September 7 letter was made public, the political press headlined stiff editorial warnings to the U.S., keyed to Khrushchev's sweeping threat that an attack on the C.P.R. would be an attack on the Soviet Union. In contrast, *Sovetskaya aviatsiya,* for example, did not repeat this threat in describing Soviet support for the C.P.R. It confined its comments to noting that the statements of Soviet leaders were "crystal clear." While the political organs followed up Khrushchev's September 19 declaration with front page editorials, the principal military papers, such as *Krasnaya zvezda* and *Sovetskii flot,* made no editorial comment on Khrushchev's nuclear threats. The lesser organs that took editorial note of Khrushchev's declaration omitted references to key elements. *Voennyi vestnik,* a Soviet military

military, it seems, had some reservations about the scope of Khrushchev's threat. None of the military commentators interpreted it as a Soviet commitment to act in behalf of the Chinese Communists in the event of an attack on the C.P.R. "in whatever form it might take." * The military press actually downgraded the menacing implications of Khrushchev's declaration. Khrushchev's September 7 threat implied that an attack on the C.P.R. would result in automatic Soviet involvement; the military press interpreted his statement more cautiously by declaring that an attack on China would be "evaluated" as an attack on the Soviet Union.[35]

In addition to toning down Khrushchev's threats, the Soviet military press tended to mute the theme, carried by the political journals after September 6, that the Quemoy crisis might lead to a world war. Apparently, the military deemed it inexpedient to repeat claims by Soviet political leaders that an armed conflict over Quemoy could not be contained.† The sober-minded Soviet military leaders appeared to believe that a limited war need not escalate, given the mutual restraint of the great powers, into a general war. In the context of Quemoy, the Soviet Union, in particular, would have to exercise restraint, since only the Soviet Union, and no other power, could expand a local conflict in the Formosa Strait.‡

The Soviet military, it seems, were apprehensive lest Soviet intransigence in the crisis would alert the U.S.—to the detriment of Soviet objectives elsewhere. A United States aroused by the possibility of conflict with the U.S.S.R. over Quemoy might more vig-

---

monthly, failed to threaten nuclear retaliation even as it charged that "American generals and admirals boldly threatened to use atomic weapons against the C.P.R." It apparently also had reservations about the C.P.R.'s offensive operations, since it failed to cite Khrushchev's warning that, if the United States did not get out of the Formosa Strait, the C.P.R. would have no alternative but to expel the United States. Of equal significance was *Voennyi vestnik's* omission of any reference to the 1950 Sino-Soviet pact of mutual aid, which Khrushchev explicitly cited in his warning of September 19.

* An interpretation of Khrushchev's September 7 "attack" statement made by *Sovetskaya Rossiya*, September 10, 1958.

† Before the crisis, as noted earlier, the leading Soviet military strategist, Major General N. Talensky, stated that the United States considered this locale as one of the areas "suitable" to fighting a local war, even with the employment of tactical nuclear weapons. (*Mezhdunarodnaya zhizn'* No. 2, 1958.)

‡ The C.P.R. had no nuclear weapons or intercontinental missiles and bombers to wage general war against the United States; the latter, because of its local superiority, could have dealt with any C.P.R. assault on the offshore islands and Taiwan without resorting to all-out war.

orously resist pressure applied to areas of more immediate Soviet interest, for example, Berlin.

Finally, the silence of the Soviet marshals may have been called for by the expressed Soviet interest in keeping the crisis "under control." Had the military spokesmen matched Khrushchev's blustering, they would have enhanced the image of the vast Soviet military machine standing poised to execute Khrushchev's threats. But their discretion gave additional proof of Soviet reluctance to stoke the Quemoy crisis with fuel more inflammable than the propagandistic declarations of the political leaders and press. That the U.S.S.R. chose not to exploit the military in an issue involving C.P.R. interests is particularly revealing, when contrasted with the lack of restraint on matters involving direct Soviet interests. (For instance, Soviet Defense Minister Malinovsky was permitted to voice dire threats in the Berlin crises, in 1959 and 1961, and assisted ostentatiously when Khrushchev broke up the 1960 summit meeting in Paris.)

Altogether, cautious behavior of the Soviet military during the Quemoy crisis softened the impact of Soviet threats. It undoubtedly heightened the dissatisfaction of Red China with Soviet support, which had been pledged in such equivocal terms.

All of the evidence suggests that extreme caution governed Soviet conduct throughout the Quemoy crisis. The Russians spoke softly when the danger of conflict was greatest, i.e., in the military phase before September 6. It seems clear that, during this period, the U.S.S.R. was not eager to join the C.P.R. in testing U.S. intentions. At that time, Russian warnings appear to have been made for the record, to guard against possible Chinese Communist charges that the Russians had not given fraternal support nor fulfilled their obligations under the Sino-soviet Pact. The Russians indulged in the most menacing threats only, after the C.P.R. was persuaded to make the first move to ease tension; their restraint betrayed concern that any bellicose statements issued before the C.P.R. agreed to halt hostilities might have exacerbated the conflict and tended to commit the U.S.S.R. Soviet threats grew more strident as the crisis shifted into a political phase, and were made primarily for political effect. During this period, the possibility of a C.P.R.–U.S. conflict was steadily decreasing, as it became progressively clearer that the C.P.R. would be unable to "starve" Quemoy into submission by interdiction and the United States would not have to break the blockade by direct action. This situation, in turn, decreased the likelihood that the Soviet Union would be faced with the need to make good its threats.

That the Russians were aware of their lack of support of the C.P.R. in the Quemoy crisis may be deduced from the initial modesty of their claims. In the aftermath of other crises, the Russians stated, categorically, that their "timely" warnings had saved the countries involved from conquest by the West. Thus, the Russians boasted, after the Suez crisis, that their efforts saved Nasser from being overthrown by Britain and France; they asserted that it was their stand that had saved Syria from being overwhelmed by Turkey in the autumn of 1957; and they claimed that their warnings had deterred the United States from marching on Iraq in 1958. However, in the early period after the Quemoy crisis, the Soviet Union carefully refrained from making similar claims, possibly anticipating that the C.P.R. might deflate them in the same way that, upon the cooling of Soviet-Egyptian relations, Nasser ridiculed Soviet claims to the star role in the Suez crisis.* The modesty of the Soviet claims after the Quemoy crisis is illustrated by the remarks of Anastas I. Mikoyan on the forty-first anniversary of the Bolshevik Revolution; in his speech, Mikoyan gave credit to the C.P.R. for its success "in not allowing the outbreak of conflict in the region of Taiwan." [36]

The Soviet military exhibited even greater humility. *Red Star,* the Soviet Ministry of Defense organ, in an editorial marking the anniversary of the Sino-Soviet Pact, said only that the efforts of the C.P.R. and "peace-loving forces" halted U.S. aggression during the Quemoy crisis.[37] It did not refer to the Soviet role directly.

With the subsequent widening of Sino-Soviet differences—but at a time when there was still mutual interest in veiling the differences from open scrutiny by the outside world—the Russians retreated into complete silence on their role in the Quemoy crisis. At the Bucharest Conference of Communist Parties, in June 1960, Khrushchev arrogantly described how Soviet strength had foiled imperialist war plans in the Suez, Syrian, and Lebanese crises.† He observed, in particular, that the Soviet threats proved effective against "the most powerful imperialist government—the U.S.A."

* The C.P.R., being privy to better inside information than Nasser, could have done an even better job of knocking down exaggerated Soviet claims.
† See *Pravda,* June 22, 1960. Khrushchev boasted, for example, that the Suez war ended in "literally 22 hours" after the Soviet Union had warned Britain, France and Israel; they "at once put their tails between their legs . . . the war was stopped."

But, for all his braggadocio, he passed over the Soviet role in the Quemoy crisis. This policy of modesty was, essentially, continued until Sino-Soviet differences were allowed openly to surface. Even then, Soviet claims were more in the nature of a defensive move in the polemics.

In summing up, it can be said that the Quemoy crisis of 1958 stands as a very significant concrete instance in which Sino-Soviet unity has been tested under fire. Unity was found wanting as the crisis revealed a major cleavage, stemming from differing appraisals of U.S. power, over the strategy and tactics to be followed in advancing the Communist cause against U.S. opposition. The cautious behavior of the Russians reflected their belief that the United States should not be challenged by a head-on confrontation.* The limits they set on how far they were willing to risk Soviet power in Communist China's behalf proved so narrow as to give rise to C.P.R. bitterness, which subsequently infused the ideological dispute about the nature of Western imperialism and the inevitabliity of war. But the ideological controversy cannot obscure the additional fact that Sino-Soviet alliance did not display its vaunted solidarity in circumstances involving, predominantly, the national interests of one of the allies. In the Quemoy crisis, the Russians, for their part, clearly indicated that their own interests and welfare came first. The C.P.R. paid a humiliating price in learning this lesson. And Soviet unwillingness to back its ally had played a large role in that humiliation.

Nor have the Chinese Communists forgotten or forgiven. In their blistering Government Statement of September 1, 1963, they stressed that it is "especially ridiculous" to give credit to the U.S.S.R. and to Soviet nuclear weapons "for the Chinese people's victory in smashing the armed provocations of U.S. imperialism in the Taiwan [Formosa] Strait in 1958." The Statement then continues:

> What are the facts? In August and September of 1958, the situation in the Taiwan [Formosa] Strait was indeed very tense as a result of the aggression and provocations by the U.S. imperialists. The Soviet leaders expressed their support for China on September 7 and 19 respectively. Although at that time the situation in the Taiwan Strait was tense, there was no possibility that a nuclear

---

* Khrushchev made this explicit a year later during his visit to Peking when he warned against testing "imperialist" strength by force (*Sovetskii flot*, October 1, 1959).

war would break out and no need for the Soviet Union to support China with its nuclear weapons. It was only when they were clear that this was the situation that the Soviet leaders expressed their support for China.* [88]

* See Appendix C for the full Chinese Government Statement.

8. The Sino-Soviet
Nuclear Dialogue: 1963*

By ALICE LANGLEY HSIEH

In the course of 1963, as the Sino-Soviet relationship further dete-
riorated and conflict was increasingly reflected on the state level,
the recriminatory exchanges between Peking and Moscow probed,
step by step, the origins and evolution of the dispute, and included
a series of disclosures on the nature of the Sino-Soviet military relationship since 1957. Much of what was then revealed as to the
key issues and turning points in the dispute had already been inferred by close readers of the earlier, more ideologically oriented
exchanges, and by students of Chinese military literature and behavior. The exchanges of 1963, however, were marked by a speci-
ficity that allows one both to test his past hypotheses and to advance his analysis of the motivations underlying the behavior of
the two parties. In particular, certain of the disclosures provide
important insights into the progress of China's military development and the degree of Soviet assistance, or lack thereof, to China
in her military aspirations. This chapter will focus on those issues
in the 1963 exchanges that have direct military implications for
the West, namely, the question of war and peace, China's acquisition of nuclear weapons versus reliance on the Soviet nuclear deterrent, and the role of Soviet military support and assistance.

Before considering these several issues, it should, perhaps, be
noted that this phase in the Sino-Soviet polemic appears to date
from the Cuban episode, during which Soviet miscalculation led
Peking to accuse Moscow of both adventurism and capitulation,
and following which Khrushchev appeared more willing to see a

* The reader's attention is called to the fact that this essay was written in
December, 1963, and published in the June, 1964, issue of *The Journal of
Conflict Resolution*. The editor considers that the analysis is, nonetheless,
valid, and still timely.

reduction of tension with the West. The several congresses held by European Communist parties in late 1962 stimulated a new round of statements, and Khrushchev reminded the Chinese that the United States was a paper tiger with atomic teeth. In the spring of 1963, Peking and Moscow eventually agreed that delegations of the CCP and the CPSU would meet in Moscow in June (later postponed to mid-July) to exchange views. This confrontation, however, was preceded, on June 14, by the dispatch and publication by the Central Committee of the CCP of an open letter to the Central Committee of the CPSU. The letter represented a tightly argued brief for the Chinese case on a broad range of issues. The Central Committee of the CPSU brought into the open its side of the dispute in an open letter dated July 14.

The meeting of the two delegations apparently did little more than underscore the differences in the Chinese and Soviet positions and the unwillingness of either side to make even minor concessions in the interest of a limited *modus vivendi.* Meanwhile, at sharp variance with the cold reception accorded the Chinese delegates, the Russians warmly welcomed American and British negotiatory teams, and, along with them, in late July, initialed the agreement providing for a partial nuclear test ban.

This move brought Sino-Soviet relations to yet another climax, for on July 31 the Chinese Government issued a statement condemning the partial nuclear-test-ban agreement, and announcing determined resistance to the treaty. The rash of official statements and articles subsequently issued by both Peking and Moscow touched more closely than previous ones on the origins of the dispute and the motivations underlying the positions of the two parties.

However, in considering the military import of these statements, a few words of caution are required. First, as of the date of writing this chapter (December, 1963), the exchanges were still in process and the extent of the disclosures was probably far from complete. Second, it should be noted that neither side has hesitated to exaggerate, distort, or misrepresent the views of the other. Soviet statements have been designed to evoke an image of Communist China as a regime addicted to war, and to contrast this image with that of a Soviet Union dedicated to peace. In turn, Peking has sought to paint its position as one in consonance with the basic premises of Marxism-Leninism, and of principled opposition to imperialism.

It should be borne in mind, moreover, that the several issues to be discussed are not only extremely complicated but, in most cases, interrelated with one another as well as with other issues in the dispute. Finally, in a number of instances, the views expressed by both the Chinese and the Russians are internally inconsistent, contradictory to earlier public pronouncements, and at even greater variance with material given a more restricted distribution.

One of the most highly publicized issues in the Sino-Soviet nuclear dialogue centers on Khrushchev's charge that, in contrast with his policy of peaceful coexistence and avoidance of nuclear war, the Chinese do not believe in the possibility of preventing a new world war, are not fully aware of the destructiveness of nuclear weapons, and advocate "the creation of a thousand times higher civilization on the corpses of hundreds of millions of people." [1] To these charges, the Chinese have been particularly sensitive, and, on their part, have accused the Russians of "nuclear fetishism" and of "recklessly playing with nuclear weapons or . . . fawning before imperialist nuclear blackmail." [2]

More specifically, the Chinese have sought to explain and justify the paragraph in the April 19, 1960, editorial, "Long Live Leninism!," which concluded with the now notorious sentence: "On the debris of a dead imperialism, the victorious people would create with extreme rapidity a civilization thousands of times higher than the capitalist system and a truly beautiful future for themselves." Not only did the Chinese, in their September 1 statement, accuse the Russians of textual misrepresentation, but they also sought to counter Soviet charges that the Chinese advocated the advancement of Communism through a nuclear world war by referring, for the first time, to a statement made by Mao Tse-tung in Moscow in November, 1957. Mao was said to have then remarked on the "steadily growing possibility of preventing imperialism from launching a new world war." The September 1 statement summed up the Chinese position as follows: China wants peace, not war; it is the imperialists who want to fight a war; a world war can be prevented; but if imperialism imposes a war on people, the imperialist system, and not mankind, will perish.* [3]

Since the foregoing has a familiar ring to readers of Soviet pronouncements on war in the late 1950's, the question must be raised: to what extent is the inevitability or noninevitability of a world nuclear war a real issue separating the Chinese and the Russians? From a close reading of Chinese statements in both the present round of exchanges and in the past, the issue hardly seems

* See Appendix C for the full text of the Chinese Government statement of September 1, 1963.

to be a real one. In fact, both parties agree, and have agreed for some time, that a world war between the socialist and capitalist camps is not inevitable—that is, that the United States is deterred from an unprovoked attack on the socialist camp.

Nor, despite the attention given in the current exchanges to the question whether one-third, one-half, or all mankind would perish in a nuclear war, are the two parties far apart in their image of a nuclear world war or the losses that would ensue. In March, 1954, Malenkov had gone so far as to say that a future war "means the destruction of world civilization." But, in the latter part of that year, the Khrushchev line that a future war would mean the collapse of capitalism *only* was reasserted. This line remained the Soviet position until approximately 1960. Early that year, almost coinciding with the publication of "Long Live Leninism!," Khrushchev made one of his closest approaches to the Malenkov destruction-of-civilization heresy. In October of that year, Major General N. Talensky, a leading Soviet military theoretician, advanced, as a personal view, the probability of extensive destruction on both sides, no matter which got in the first strike. At that time, he estimated that the world's population would be reduced by one-half as a result of a new global war.[4] This position has gradually become the official Soviet view on the consequences of a nuclear war. In 1962 and 1963, Khrushchev, on a number of occasions, stated that a future war would destroy all the big cities and would "take a toll of 700 to 800 million human lives." [5]

To a considerable extent, the hardening of the Soviet political line in 1960, and thereafter, was a direct response to the Chinese position, which, while admitting that a world war could be prevented, insisted that nuclear war was not to be feared, and that exaggeration of the destructiveness of nuclear war demoralized the people of the socialist camp and played into the hands of U.S. nuclear blackmail.[6]

The Chinese, on their part, have preferred to adhere to the earlier Khrushchev line that, in a future war, only capitalism would be destroyed. Consequently, the Chinese castigate the "annihilation of mankind" thesis, although it is difficult to see a significant difference between Mao's alleged 1957 estimate that one-third to one-half of the world's population would die in the event of a nuclear war [7] and Soviet estimates of from 700 to 800 million.

If pressed to make some distinction between the present Soviet and Chinese positions on the consequences of a world nuclear war, one could say that the Russians regard nuclear war as a disaster from which there is no recovery, while the Chinese regard nuclear war as a disaster from which recovery is possible.

Implicit in Mao's estimate that from one-third to one-half of the world's population would die in the event of a world nuclear war is a recognition of the vast destructiveness of nuclear weapons. Though the Chinese continue to voice the line that a nuclear war should not be feared to the point of paralyzing the struggle against imperialism, they have recently been more restrained in their public depreciation of nuclear weapons. Moreover, the hypothesis that the Chinese, contrary to what Khrushchev has said, do understand the implications of nuclear weapons for modern military operations and strategy receives further confirmation in the views of China's military leaders now available in the twenty-nine issues of *Kung-tso T'ung-hsün* (*Work Correspondence*), a confidential publication of the General Political Department of the "People's Liberation Army," covering the period from January into August, 1961. An analysis of this material demonstrates that Chinese military policies and doctrine are based on a realistic assessment of Chinese capabilities and weaknesses, of U.S. capabilities and strengths, of the extent to which China can rely on Soviet assistance and support, and of the opportunities existing for gain.[8] China's military leaders admit their vast technological-military inferiority to the United States, their concern over a surprise nuclear attack, the vulnerability of their targets, the deficiencies in their air defense, and their intent to avoid the "strengths" of the enemy. The material underlines the caution that characterizes China's external military policies—a caution that was more than evident in the Quemoy incident in 1958, as well as in the 1962 operations on the Sino-Indian border. In sum, there is little in Chinese military doctrine, policy, or behavior to support the thesis that the Chinese are militarily reckless or adventurist.

Before considering the implications of what turn out to be very minor differences between the Chinese and the Russians over the meaning of warfare in the nuclear era, it is necessary to touch on one further point. General Talensky, in his October, 1960, article in *International Affairs,* also took the personal position that war as an instrument of policy has outlived itself, and that it was impossible to resort to war as a means of resolving political disputes. Though as late as the spring of 1962, Soviet military doctrine as stated in Marshal V. D. Sokolovsky's book continued to regard war as the continuation of politics,[9] it would appear safe to describe the official Soviet position, as it has gradually evolved, as follows: War is a political act, waged for political ends, and, thus, is a continuation of politics, but such an act may be senseless in view of its consequences, and, thus, fail to serve the intended political ends. The Chinese, on their part, have not shifted in their long-held position that war is a continuation of politics. They argue that a number of opportunities exist in which war is feasible and continues to serve important political ends.[10]

What, then, do these exchanges on the nature of war add up to? It is important to note that implicit in Chinese acceptance of the position that a world war can be prevented is the belief that Soviet nuclear power deters the United States from an unprovoked attack on the Chinese mainland. This hypothesis is given further support in the 1961 *Kung-tso T'ung-hsün* material. At that time, China's military leaders did not appear to consider the likelihood of war involving the United States as high. This view probably reflected a belief that Soviet nuclear power acted as a protective shield for China. It probably also reflected a confidence that, if China avoided provocation of the United States, a direct confrontation with U.S. forces could be avoided. As late as October, 1963, in an interview with the former Japanese Prime Minister, Tanzan Ishibashi, Chou En-lai said that the Chinese Communists had faith that the Soviet Union would come to their aid in the event of war. He also declared that the Sino-Soviet Treaty of Friendship, Alliance, and Mutual Assistance was "still very much alive." [11]

If that is the case, why then have the Chinese and Russians chosen to give so much attention to questions related to the meaning of war in the nuclear age? The Chinese themselves provide us with the answer when they say: "The crucial point is, what should be the policy in face of U.S. imperialist nuclear blackmail and threats—resistance or capitulation? We stand for resistance." [12] In other words, the question basically at issue between Peking and Moscow is how to deal with the United States, the priorities to be accorded foreign policy interests, the areas in which gains can possibly be made, and the assessment of the risks involved. According to the Chinese, talk about the annihilation of mankind in a nuclear war and insistence that war is no longer a continuation of politics play into the hands of U.S. nuclear blackmail and paralyze the revolutionary spirit of the people, particularly in the underdeveloped areas. We shall now turn to this last point and consider the implications of the divergent Chinese and Soviet positions on local war, escalation, and the support to be accorded national liberation movements.

Here, too, the current discussion between Peking and Moscow on the impact of nuclear weapons on local conflicts must be considered in a longer-term context. For some years, the Soviet Union has taken the public position that it is almost inevitable that local wars involving the nuclear powers will escalate into general war,[13] although some softening of the Soviet line has been indicated recently, possibly in response to Chinese attacks.[14]

The Chinese, for their part, while admitting the possibility of preventing a world war, insist that other types of war, such as national liberation wars and revolutionary civil wars, are inevitable. In particular, they have challenged the Soviet position that local wars are bound to escalate into general wars. However, the reasons given in support of their position have varied. In an April 1, 1960, *Hung Ch'i* (*Red Flag*) article, the Chinese admitted that it was possible that local wars would escalate into general war, but cited instances where U.S. "aggression" had been smashed—Korea, Egypt, Hungary, Lebanon, Jordan, Iraq, Cuba—and, from these instances, argued that "the great force for safeguarding world peace can put local wars started by imperialism to a prompt end, and thus thwart imperialist plans for enlarging local wars." [15] In context, it would appear that what the Chinese were saying, in 1960, was that the nuclear power of the Soviet Union could deter U.S. intervention in local wars, or, if the United States did intervene, this power could prevent escalation.

In its letter of June 14, 1963, to the Central Committee of the CPSU, the Central Committee of the CCP again referred to the fact that "recently, certain persons have been spreading the argument that a single spark from a war of national liberation or from a revolutionary people's war will lead to a world conflagration destroying the whole of mankind." [16] This charge was repeated in Peking's statement of September 1, at which time the Chinese also contended that it was the Soviet belief that the emergence of nuclear weapons had changed everything, that this was a nuclear epoch, and that war was no longer the continuation of politics. But more important, the Chinese, at this time, argued that the United States did not dare to use nuclear weapons to stop national liberation movements—not because the Soviet Union possessed nuclear weapons, but because of the political costs and military inappropriateness of such use. Explaining the nonuse of nuclear weapons in Korea, Viet-Nam, Algeria, and Cuba, the Chinese argued that "politically, recourse to this kind of weapons would place U.S. imperialism in a position of extreme isolation, and militarily, the massive destructiveness of nuclear weapons limits their use, for in civil wars and wars of national independence, where the lines zigzag and the fighting is at close range, the use of nuclear weapons of mass destruction would inflict damage on both belligerents." [17]

Moreover, in response to the contention, in the Soviet statement of August 21, that the military might of the Soviet Union had stayed the hand of the aggressor in the cases of Suez, Syria, and Iraq, and at the time of the 1958 Formosa Strait crisis,[18] the Chinese ridiculed the Soviet position that Soviet nuclear weapons had played the decisive role in these situations, and insisted that the defeat of the imperialists had resulted from the struggle of the peoples concerned.[19] The Chinese were particularly indignant at the Russians for taking credit for the outcome of the 1958 Quemoy incident—a point to which we will return later.

The position of the Chinese in 1963 was hardly consistent with that taken in 1960. Nor was it consistent with the views revealed in the more restricted *Kung-tso T'ung-hsün* material. Implicit in statements by China's military leaders in 1961 was the concern that local conflicts or limited political-military activities might escalate into larger war if the United States chose to intervene. Training manuals included instructions on defense against tactical nuclear weapons.

That the Chinese are not as sanguine about the nonuse by the United States of tactical nuclear weapons in local conflicts as they made out in their September 1, 1963, statement is also suggested by their emphatic condemnation of the partial nuclear test ban for its so-called legalization of underground testing. This, they allege, permits the United States to develop tactical nuclear weapons. According to the Chinese, the United States "intends to use tactical nuclear weapons in local wars in order to deal with nonnuclear socialist and other peace-loving countries and people." [20]

The internal contradictions in the Chinese position are matched by those on the Soviet side. As already noted, the Russians argue that their military power prevents foreign intervention. At the same time, they take the position that, if deterrence fails, and the imperialists intervene, the local conflict is transformed into an interstate war with high probability of escalation. According to the Russians, "the threat of the employment of thermonuclear weapons in local wars is . . . quite real if countries possessing them or linked with nuclear powers by appropriate agreements of alliance are involved in these wars." [21]

As the Russians increasingly argue that the question of national liberation movements must be considered in connection with the task of averting a world thermonuclear war, the Chinese, in the course of the debate, seek to disassociate support of national liberation movements from the nuclear issue.

Again we must turn to the unspoken part of the dialogue to discern what the confusing public exchanges on local war and escalation mean for the revolutionary movements in underdeveloped areas. Both the Russians and the Chinese favor indirect military assistance to national liberation movements. Both are reluctant to participate overtly in internal crisis situations. It is in the degree of indirect assistance to be rendered, and in their attitude toward U.S. intervention, that their paths diverge. The Russians more quickly see a point where indirect assistance may bring about U.S. intervention, and are concerned about this. The Chinese may be downgrading the likelihood of U.S. responses to low-level probes, believing it possible to take greater risks, or, rather, possible for Moscow to take greater risks. Or, they may be saying that, within limits, it does not matter whether or not the United States intervenes, inasmuch as such involvement only serves to weaken the United States. In sum, what the jargon amounts to is a reiteration of a Soviet intention to avoid direct clashes with the United States in third areas, even though this means a de-emphasis of the role of armed struggle in national liberation movements. The Chinese, on their part, believe that Soviet policy—its support of peaceful coexistence, emphasis on the horrors of nuclear war, and downgrading of militancy in national liberation movements—paralyzes the revolutionary process and, consequently, the struggle against imperialism.

In turn, these divergent assessments of the risks and payoffs involved in fostering revolutionary activity reflect divergent foreign-policy priorities. The Chinese have one priority objective—to remove U.S. power and influence from the Western Pacific—and, in order to forward this goal, want to utilize whatever opportunities exist, in Asia, Latin America, or Africa, to keep the United States tied down, with the hope that eventually the United States will be compelled to reduce its commitments in the area of direct interest to China. The Russians appear more satisfied with a policy designed simply to neutralize the U.S. position in underdeveloped areas. Since its relationship with the United States is more complex, Moscow must look at revolutionary activities in underdeveloped areas in a broader context—one that involves the interaction of U.S. and Soviet military systems, defense budgets, etc., and the extent to which changes in the U.S. military posture, stimulated by local crisis situations, might affect Moscow's foreign policy priorities in Europe.

However, one important footnote to this discussion is required. In contrast to the positions in principle, which we have been describing, the Chinese, in practice, do not now feel it necessary to implement their stand on fostering revolutionary activities in such areas as Cambodia, Burma, and Nepal, where indirect pressures and ostensible Chinese friendship are having sufficient effect on local governments to satisfy Peking for the present.

Equally as interesting as, if not more interesting than, the confused exchanges on the question of war and peace is the light that the recent statements throw on China's intent to develop her own nuclear capabilities, Soviet reaction thereto, and the conflicting Chinese and Soviet interpretations of the role of the Soviet nuclear deterrent as far as China is concerned.

China's denunciation of the partial nuclear test ban underscored her intent to develop her own nuclear weapons. In the July 31 statement of the Chinese Government, the partial nuclear test ban was described as an attempt to consolidate the nuclear monopoly of the United States, Britain, and the Soviet Union; as a "big fraud"; as particularly advantageous to the United States because it did not prevent underground testing; as strengthening the position of the nuclear powers for nuclear blackmail; and as preventing "all the threatened peace-loving countries, including China, from increasing their defense capability." [22]

On August 15, Peking elaborated its charge that the Soviet Union was colluding with the United States to manacle China. It denounced the Soviet Union for unilaterally tearing up, on June 20, 1959, the agreement on "new technology for national defense" concluded between China and the Soviet Union on October 15, 1957, and for refusing to provide China with a sample of an atomic bomb and technical data concerning its manufacture.[23] We shall return to this point later when we attempt to assess the actual military assistance the Soviet Union has rendered China in recent years.

In response to these charges, Moscow was quick to point out that it was China's resentment at the Soviet Union's failure to give China atomic bombs that explained the attacks of the Chinese People's Republic (C.P.R.) on the U.S.S.R.'s foreign policy, and, especially, its attacks on the nuclear-test-ban treaty.[24] Moscow was no doubt right in saying that the opposition of the C.P.R.

leaders to the nuclear-test-ban treaty "showed their desire to possess their own atom bomb at any cost." One can also agree with Moscow's intimation that China wanted her own atomic bombs only because she had "developed some kind of special aims and interests that the socialist camp cannot support with its military force." [25]

Just as the exchanges have confirmed China's intent to develop her own nuclear weapons, so have they confirmed Moscow's reluctance to see Peking acquire an independent nuclear capability. The case for and against China's acquisition of nuclear weapons revolved around three main points: (1) the proliferation of nuclear weapons; (2) China's need to possess an independent defense potential; and (3) the alternative of reliance on the Soviet Union's nuclear deterrent.

On the question of the proliferation of nuclear weapons, the Russians revealed, in their August 21 statement, that, more than once, they had taken measures to convince the C.P.R. that prevention of the spread of nuclear weapons was in the interest of all socialist countries, including China. While arguing that the nuclear might of the Soviet Union stood guard over the world socialist commonwealth, and that the addition of one or more socialist countries to the number of nuclear states would make no material change in the defense potential of the socialist camp, the Russians did not disguise the fact that the key point in their opposition to proliferation was their concern over the possible nuclear arming of West Germany, and to a lesser extent, Japan.[26] They argued that "an increase in the number of socialist states possessing nuclear weapons would immediately give rise to a chain reaction in the camp of the imperialists, the atomic cancer would spread throughout the globe, and the threat of nuclear war would be increased manyfold." [27] While it is far from clear why such a chain reaction should necessarily occur, the Russians used this argument to charge that the Chinese do not care "how nuclear weapons are spread among the capitalist countries as long as the C.P.R. leaders can find out firsthand what a nuclear bomb is." [28]

In turn, the Chinese argued that nuclear weapons in the hands of socialist countries could not increase the danger of war and that such possession was a necessary defense against imperialist nuclear blackmail.[29] According to Liao Cheng-chih, Chairman of the Chinese Committee for Afro-Asian Solidarity and Vice Chairman of the China Peace Committee, until the United States was forced to destroy all its nuclear weapons, "the one and only way to counter the threat of a nuclear war is for more socialist and peace-loving countries to gain a nuclear self-defense capacity." [30] As to the question of West Germany, the Chinese complained that, while the Soviet Union was withholding nuclear weapons from China, the United States had given no assurance it would not arm West Germany with nuclear weapons. According to the Chinese, "the real point is that the Soviet leaders hold that China should not and must not manufacture nuclear weapons, and that only the few nuclear powers . . . are entitled to the continued production of nuclear weapons." [31]

More pertinent to the Chinese case was Peking's insistence that, "in fighting imperialist aggression and defending its security, each socialist country has to rely in the first place on its own defense capability, and then—and only then—on assistance from fraternal countries and the people of the world." [32]

The Russians countered this argument on several scores. On economic grounds, they argued that China, in its present state of development, was not yet prepared to produce nuclear arms in quantity, and that even the production of two or three bombs would bring exhaustion to the Chinese economy.[33] The Chinese, in turn, admitted their poverty and backwardness, but insisted that even if the Chinese people were unable to produce an atom bomb for a hundred years, they would neither crawl to the baton of the Soviet leaders, nor kneel before the nuclear blackmail of the U.S. imperialists.[34]

The Russians belittled the military significance of any nuclear weapons the Chinese might acquire. Granting that China, by over-straining its economy, could finally produce a few atomic bombs, the Russians asked: "How many bombs in this event would be aimed by the imperialists at the C.P.R.? Will the Chinese leaders feel any easier sitting on their own atomic bomb?" [35] On their part, the Chinese charged that such statements, in effect, instigated the imperialists to threaten China with atom bombs. They admitted that, were the U.S. imperialists to aim more atom and hydrogen bombs at China, this move would require vigilance, but that there was nothing terrifying about it, for "at this very moment the United States has many such bombs already poised against China. It will not make much difference if the United States listens to the Soviet leaders and adds a few more. The Chinese people will not tremble before U.S. nuclear threats." [36]

But the Russians did not limit themselves to depreciating a Chinese possession of a few atom bombs. An element of blackmail was present in the Soviet position. In their statement of August 21, the Russians asserted that "the attempt of any socialist country to rely on its own force in insuring its defenses—forces which, moreover, may not be sufficient in all countries—can prove to be a fatal mistake in the age of nuclear arms." And they added: "All the Socialist countries, including the C.P.R., no matter how its leaders try to prove the opposite, take into account when organizing their defenses the nuclear might of the Soviet Union." [37] In an article in *Krasnaya zvezda* (*Red Star*), Colonel I. Sidel'nikov suggested that if the Chinese chose, first, to rely on their own defense capability, it was possible that, in view of the nature of nuclear weapons, when they called for help it might be too late to be of much good to China. It is likely that he meant by this that China might be subjected to vast destruction before the Russians had the chance to intervene.[38]

In addition to the economic and military arguments against China's acquisition of nuclear weapons, the Russians questioned the underlying need for the Chinese to possess such weapons, pointing to the Soviet rocket-nuclear shield as insuring the independence and security of all the countries of the socialist camp. The Russians argued that the C.P.R. could now rely on the means of defense developed through the efforts of the socialist people, and that, consequently, China should devote her efforts to the development of her national economy, science, technology, and agriculture. The Russians went so far as to note that China was only free to criticize the Soviet Union because she enjoyed the protection of Soviet nuclear weapons.[39] Sidel'nikov made the point that strength lay in close military cooperation in advance of any conflict.[40] It was also asserted that China could not prove that her attempt to acquire atom bombs was in the interest of the defense of China and the entire socialist camp. Again the Soviet Union suggested that China's striving to acquire nuclear weapons raised "serious doubts as to the goals of the foreign policy of the C.P.R. leaders." [41]

In its statement of September 20, 1963, Moscow cited, as evidence supporting its case for Chinese reliance on the Soviet nuclear deterrent, the fact that Mao Tse-tung, in September, 1958, had admitted that, inasmuch as the Soviet Union had achieved great successes in the production of nuclear arms, China clearly need not organize the production of such weapons, especially considering their expense.[42]

No Chinese response is yet available to this assertion, the validity of which is open to serious question; nor have the Chinese, to date, replied to Soviet charges that Peking's special foreign-policy aims motivate its desire to possess nuclear weapons. Rather, the Chinese have preferred to question the purposes served by Soviet nuclear power, and the reliability of the Soviet Union as an ally. Peking has openly expressed doubt as to whether Soviet military power serves other purposes than the foreign policy interests and self-preservation of the Soviet Union.[43] Moreover, in an interview between Ch'en Yi and John Dixon, the Australian television producer, Dixon asked why Peking wanted to develop its own atomic weapons in view of Soviet assurances to defend China. Ch'en Yi countered with another question: ". . . what is this Soviet assurance worth? . . . This sort of promise is easy to make, but . . . worthless. Soviet protection is worth nothing to us." And Ch'en Yi added: "No outsiders can give us protection, in fact, because they always attach conditions and want to control us." [44]

In this reference to "conditions" and "control," Ch'en Yi may well have been reflecting Chinese resentment of Soviet policy and behavior at the time of the 1958 Quemoy crisis. That this issue remains a sore point in Peking's relations with Moscow is indicated in China's questioning of the Soviet position that the military might of the Soviet Union stayed the hand of the aggressor. The Russians, in their August 21 statement, had pointed out that the Chinese would remember how Soviet strength had served the C.P.R. in the period when tension flared up in the Formosa Strait. This and other Soviet contentions that the nuclear might of the Soviet Union had saved millions of Chinese from nuclear death, the Chinese described as ridiculous. According to the Chinese, although the situation in the Formosa Strait had been tense in August and September, 1958, "there was no possibility that a nuclear war would break out and no need for the Soviet Union to support China with nuclear weapons. It was only when they were clear that this was the situation that the Soviet leaders expressed their support for China." [45] The weakness of Moscow's response to this charge, its reliance on examples of Chinese gratitude following the Soviet letters of September and October, 1958, to President Eisenhower, does little to strengthen the Soviet case that its nuclear weapons played a decisive role in the 1958 Formosa Strait crisis. The Chinese version of the crisis tends to confirm earlier hypotheses that the Chinese, lacking any prior Soviet commitment, had intentionally restricted their activities to very limited probes of U.S. intentions; that they never regarded the likelihood of nuclear war as high, provided they kept to a very low level of violence; and that Soviet deterrent statements were made only at a time when the Russians had every reason to believe that any risk of involvement was at a minimum. Nor do these late-in-the-day revelations suggest that, at the time of the 1958 crisis, Chinese and Soviet policies were to any degree coordinated.*

Again, it is necessary to ask what are the real issues that underlie these mutual recriminations. What are the forces, despite the economic and military problems so bluntly pointed out by the Russians, that compel the Chinese to enter the nuclear arms race? Why is the Soviet Union driven even to the point of nuclear blackmail in its attempt to block China's acquisition of a nuclear capability?

Considering the latter question first, it is evident that the Russians are concerned about the development of any situation that might complicate their military relationship with the United States. Such complications could be created were a further proliferation of nuclear weapons to take place among capitalist countries. They could also be created by China's acquisition of nuclear weapons, particularly if the Chinese were to use their nuclear capability to heighten international tension, thereby increasing the risk of Soviet military involvement with the United States. At the very least, the Russians might well calculate that China's acquisition of nuclear weapons would give the United States reason to strengthen its military posture in the Far East, and to take an even firmer position in resisting Communist-inspired activities in the area.

The Chinese position is similarly related to its basic goals and foreign policy interests. Although Ch'en Yi, in his October, 1963, interview with Japanese correspondents, admitted that it might be several years before China could test atomic bombs and even more before mass production could be carried out, he underlined the reason why China would make every effort to acquire a nuclear delivery capability: "Atomic bombs, missiles and supersonic aircraft are reflections of the technical level of a nation's industry. China will have to resolve this issue within the next several years; otherwise, it will degenerate into a second-class or third-class nation." [46]

The Russians, on their part, have intimated that the reason why

---

* See Chapter 7 for a detailed analysis of the Quemoy crisis.

the Chinese want to develop their own nuclear weapons is in order to pursue special aims and interests that cannot be supported by the military forces of the socialist camp. This is a frank admission, which confirms the earlier interpretation of Soviet policy and behavior, at the time of the 1958 Quemoy crisis, that Moscow has no intention of supporting external military objectives of the Chinese if these aims seem likely to involve the Soviet Union in a war—not of its own timing and choosing—with the United States.

As noted earlier, the Chinese probably continue to believe that Soviet nuclear power deters an unprovoked attack on China. However, as long as China adheres to her basic foreign-policy objectives (or, as Moscow puts it, "special aims and interests")—the incorporation of Taiwan into Peking's domain, the achievement of hegemony in the Far East, and the removal of U.S. power and influence from the area—the Chinese have little alternative but to seek to rely on their own military potential and to develop their own nuclear weapons. Such self-reliance is necessary in order to make gains in areas where Soviet military support or assistance cannot be expected, or where Soviet aid would be subject to conditions and controls imposed by Moscow. This statement is not meant to suggest that the Chinese will be militarily reckless when they come into the possession of nuclear weapons. Rather, it is meant to suggest that, despite a continued awareness of their military inferiority to the United States, the Chinese envisage gains from the acquisition of nuclear weapons—if only from the political-propaganda use of such weapons, or from their use to back up low-level military operations.[47]

How long have the Russians been opposed to China's acquisition of nuclear weapons? How can the present Soviet position be reconciled with other evidence that, in the past, the Soviet Union may well have provided some nuclear and missile assistance to China?

Two important disclosures were made in the 1963 exchanges that must be taken into consideration in any attempt to trace the course of Soviet military assistance to China. First, there is the point already referred to—the Chinese assertion that, as of June 20, 1959, "the Soviet Government unilaterally tore up the agreement on new technology for national defense concluded between China and the Soviet Union on October 15, 1957, and refused to provide China with a sample of an atomic bomb and technical data concerning its manufacture."[48] Second, there is the Chinese complaint that "in 1958 the leadership of the CPSU put forward unreasonable demands designed to bring China under Soviet military control." According to the Chinese, "these unreasonable demands were rightly and firmly rejected by the Chinese Government." [49]

It is not unlikely that, as early as 1954–55, the Soviet Union made some scientific-technological gestures to China designed to assist the latter in beginning to create a basis for an indigenous nuclear-weapons-production program. At that time, Khrushchev may well have been seeking Chinese support in his internal struggle for power, for such gestures were accompanied by the initiation of Soviet assistance in aircraft and naval production and a number of other concessions to China. From what the Chinese have indicated, it would appear that some further arrangements were entered into in October, 1957. [50] Negotiations at that time may possibly have been affected by the 1956 turmoil in Eastern Europe and the 1957 struggle in the Soviet Party Presidium.

To date, the exchanges have not disclosed the details of the agreement or the extent and level of the nuclear technical data that was to be made available to the Chinese. Consequently, one can only speculate about the possible arrangements worked out at that time. In view of the phrasing of the Chinese charge, the agreement was probably general in tone. No doubt, it made some provision for Soviet assistance in the construction of facilities, but left the nuclear technical data to be made available to China at some unspecified time, and perhaps after further negotiations. Moreover, in view of Khrushchev's June, 1959, remark to Averell Harriman that Russia had shipped rockets to China, [51] and other reports that Moscow had provided China with short-range missiles, [52] it is probable that the agreement provided for some missiles to be made available to China for experimental purposes.

It is doubtful, however, if the agreement was fully satisfactory to either party. While the Russians, beginning in the mid-1950's, had given some assistance to the development of China's national defense industry, they had never gone out of their way to place this industry on a completely independent basis. There was little reason why they should do so in the case of China's development of nuclear weapons. In late 1957, Soviet proposals for a nuclear-free zone in Asia suggested signs of restlessness on the part of Moscow over the possibility of China's acquiring nuclear weapons. The Soviet gesture in October, 1957, may well have been a grudging one—a temporary price that had to be paid to maintain the façade of harmony in the Communist Bloc following the 1956 disturbances in Eastern Europe, to insure China's acceptance of Soviet leadership of the Bloc at the late 1957 Moscow Conference, and to guard against Chinese meddling in intra-CPSU politics.

For Peking, no nuclear warheads were forthcoming from Moscow. The development of a nuclear capability was still a long way off, and subject to possible Soviet rationing and stoppages at any time. Soviet military assistance was still inadequate for the achievement of Peking's basic objectives, especially Taiwan.

To what extent such matters as the implementation of the October, 1957, agreement were discussed by Mao Tse-tung and the Chinese military mission the following month in Moscow is still not known. However, China's continued acceptance of the premise that the only road to an independent nuclear weapons capability was by way of an indigenous program, even though such a program relied on some Soviet assistance, would tend to suggest that the question was discussed, but certainly not resolved to the satisfaction of the Chinese.

Whatever the specific terms of the agreement, it was soon to become clear that the Chinese were expected to pay a price for any nuclear-missile assistance Moscow chose to make available to Peking—and not only the usual financial one. At what point in 1958 the Soviet Union put forward "unreasonable demands" on China is still uncertain. In view of the recent revelations about Soviet aloofness in the 1958 Quemoy incident, it is possible to speculate that such demands may have been made during the Mao-Khrushchev meeting in Peking in late July and early August of 1958. In any event, it would appear that, some time in the course of 1958, Moscow sought to bring certain aspects of China's military establishment under Soviet control. Soviet proposals, as some commentators have suggested, may have been limited to a joint naval command in the Pacific, and integrated air defense arrangements.[53] Or they may have included a Soviet bid for bases in China, and joint Sino-Soviet control of nuclear weapons and advanced delivery systems on Chinese territory, or, even, for close military cooperation across the board. The Russians may well have been taking a bearish attitude not only toward China's activities in the Formosa Strait, but also toward China's intent to develop its own nuclear weapons. Whatever the Soviet proposals, it is clear that the Chinese were not willing to subordinate their search for an independent nuclear capability to arrangements that would place China's military policies under Soviet restraints. If such touchy military differences as these existed in 1958, the Soviet abrogation of the 1957 agreement in June, 1959, and the accompanying refusal to provide the Chinese with nuclear technical data would appear to have been only further steps contributing to Peking's growing resentment of Soviet military policies toward China. The existence of these 1958 differences would also suggest that, as far as the Russians were concerned, no irreversible implementation of the 1957 agreement had taken place, and that the Chinese, in furthering their nuclear production program, were very much on their own.

The *Kung-tso T'ung-hsün* materials leave little doubt that, at some point in 1958–59, the Chinese opted for a "go-it-alone" policy. China's willingness to choose military isolation, rather than accept Soviet demands for military controls as the price for Soviet nuclear assistance, apparently thwarted a Soviet calculation that Peking would accede to Moscow's requests. Peking's decision provides a significant key to Chinese behavior in the period thereafter. Having failed to work out some mutually acceptable arrangements with the Russians on an issue as important as the nuclear one, the Chinese no longer had anything to lose and, consequently, were free to challenge the Soviet Union on a broad range of issues which, in a different context, might have been subject to negotiation. As a result of China's attitude, the Russians lost, in the nuclear issue, their principal form of leverage on the Chinese.

Nevertheless, it should be noted that the decision to opt for a "go-it-alone" policy may not have been acceptable to all of China's military leaders. P'eng Teh-huai's differences with the regime no doubt included reservations about the military effect of certain domestic programs, such as the Great Leap Forward, the communes, the participation of the People's Liberation Army in economic activities, and the militia. It is also quite probable, in view of charges made against P'eng and Huang K'o-cheng in the *Kung-tso T'ung-hsün* material, that P'eng was tempted to make some concession to Soviet demands, or, at least, that he was anxious to avoid steps, in both the political and military spheres, that could result in China's being cut off from Soviet military assistance, and possibly from the protection of the Soviet nuclear shield. While it is questionable whether P'eng openly, or clandestinely, connived with the Russians, as has been suggested elsewhere,[54] it would not be incorrect to say that P'eng was far less sympathetic to a "go-it-alone" policy, and far more aware of the military implications of such a policy, than were China's top political leaders.

In the course of 1959, the broad range of differences between the Chinese and the Russians came increasingly into the open. According to the Chinese, the official abrogation of the 1957 agreement on new defense technology took place in June, 1959. During the year, cutbacks took place in Soviet deliveries of aircraft to China. In the Chinese leadership, differences on policy toward the Soviet Union were apparently brought to a head, for, in September, 1959, P'eng Teh-huai and Huang K'o-cheng were removed from their respective posts as Minister of National Defense and Chief of the General Staff. In mid-1960, the Russians withdrew their economic and military advisers and technicians from China.

Although the Chinese have continued to receive some petroleum products from the Soviet Union, by 1961, the *Kung-tso T'ung-hsün* material reveals, the Chinese were well aware that they could expect little military assistance or support from the Soviet Union, and had accepted a policy of self-reliance. China's armed forces in 1961 were clearly suffering, not only from the effects of the internal economic situation, but also from the lack of Soviet military assistance. This was evident in cutbacks in national defense industry, including aircraft and naval production, the attrition and cannibalization of Chinese aircraft, and shortages of fuel and other military matériel for the Chinese armed forces in general.

The Sino-Soviet military relationship has been both a victim of political conflicts and a key factor in exacerbating them. An analysis of the military issues provides important clues to the over-all foreign policy considerations that separate the Chinese and the Russians, and that, in turn, reflect divergent national interests. Without repeating what has already been said about the basic objectives of each party, it may be worth noting here that these divergent interests are likely to continue to color the Sino-Soviet military relationship in the future. At the moment, it is difficult to envisage even a partial restoration of military cooperation. In view of Soviet threats to exclude China from the coverage of its nuclear shield, it is easier to see a China confronted with military isolation, or with strictly conditional Soviet aid commitments.

Despite some recent signs of moderation in the Chinese position, this isolation—full or partial—may well be the short-term outcome. However, a number of important developments are bound to take place in China over the next decade: the death of Mao Tse-tung; indication as to whether or not the Chinese will be able to solve their economic problems over the long haul (not just the economic difficulties of the past few years); the restoration and maintenance of internal political dynamism, or, conversely, a growing apathy leading to instability. Although these developments are not likely to change China's basic objectives, they could affect the pattern of China's relationship with the Soviet Union and the timing of, as well as the means used to achieve, her basic objectives.

While it is questionable whether the death of Khrushchev would bring about any major change in Soviet policies,* the same may not necessarily be true of Chinese policies when Mao dies. At that time, a new fluidity may intrude upon the Chinese scene. If China has failed to resolve her economic problems, if apathy rather than dynamism characterizes the political process, if China has been faced with still further delays in developing nuclear weapons of her own, if her armed forces have not succeeded in pulling themselves up by their own boot straps, pressures may be revived among both economic and military leaders for some improvement in relations with the Soviet Union—if only on a basis of temporary expediency. Depending on the source of the succession, which may not be as smooth as is generally thought, elements dissatisfied with present policies may be in a position to use their support as leverage to notify some of the regime's extremist policies. This prediction is not meant to suggest that any regime in Peking is likely to subordinate its own objectives to Soviet national interests. It is simply meant to suggest that, at some time, Peking may be prepared to pursue its objectives through different channels—one of which could be that of a closer association with the Soviet Union.

* Since this chapter was originally written, Khrushchev was removed as the Soviet leader—and, indeed, there were no major changes in Soviet policies, at least not in those affecting Sino-Soviet relations. (Editor's Note—R.L.G.)

9. *Politico-Military Issues in the Sino-Soviet Debate, 1963-65*

By RAYMOND L. GARTHOFF

The main lines of dispute over military and politico-military issues had developed in the 1950's and early 1960's, and were vented in the open polemics of 1963. These themes, as they found expression in the articles, letters, and statements by Moscow and Peking in 1963 have been reviewed and analyzed in the preceding chapter. The present chapter serves two purposes: first, to examine one particularly significant additional source from 1963, and then, briefly, to review some of the main lines of continuing dispute on these issues from 1963 to 1966.

The public polemical articles are necessarily fashioned with an eye on the opponent's sensitivities, on the impact on other Communist parties, on the public at home, and on the rest of the world. This fact does not diminish their significance, but it does leave unanswered some questions. What, for instance, is the estimate of Chinese Communist military theory and politico-military strategy in an internal Soviet General Staff organ—in a discussion *not* intended to reach the average Soviet citizen, the Chinese Communists, or the "capitalist" world?

The Soviet General Staff theoretical journal *Voennaya mysl'* (*Military Thought*) in October, 1963, featured an article entitled: "The Peking Version of 'Total Strategy'." * This journal is marked: "For Generals, Admirals, and Officers of the Soviet Army and Navy Only." Some of its themes are also found in the public polemics, but it adds several others discussed more frankly than in any openly published articles. The author, I. Yermashev, is a writer who, for many years, had been concerned with politico-military matters.

* The full text of this article is printed as Appendix D.

The article opens with the statement that "The anti-Soviet campaign, conducted in China with extreme frenzy, has assumed unprecedented scale." [1] There is a defensive ring to the discussion, as well as a polemical thrust. Nonetheless, it is devoted to an analysis of Chinese Communist views on military theory and policy, and while it doubtless distorts the Chinese Communist position to some degree, it reveals a great deal about both the Chinese and Soviet conceptions.

Although the Chinese Communists claim their military science to be Marxist, says *Military Thought,* it is not. Rather, it is "an eclectic mixture." Moreover, in it there is a great deal that is "typically Chinese, preserved still from feudal times." [2] (In this connection, one is tempted to digress for a moment to note that while the ancient—fifth-century B.C.—Chinese classical military scholars Sun Tsu and ‚Wu Tsu were still worth highly favorable mention in the Soviet volume *Military Strategy* in its first edition in 1962, by the second edition in 1963, all reference to *any* Chinese military authority was deleted.) [3] The current Chinese Communist view of military science is, moreover, described as "facing the past, the Chinese past, not recognizing any experience other than the experience of China." This attitude, according to the Soviet critic, leads to another, and even more critical, fault of contemporary Chinese military science: ". . . it is simply obsolete. And it became obsolete not merely by itself but as a consequence of radical changes in many objective conditions, including the material base of war and, above all, of weaponry." [4]

What, specifically, do the Russians believe that the Chinese distort in substitution of a "subjectivist, Chinese" approach for an "objective, Marxist" one? Primarily, they exaggerate the significance of a political and ideological character of possible future war at the expense of evaluating realistically "the balance of real material forces"—that is, recognition of American military power.[5] The Chinese Communists are said to bank on a protracted war, and on winning such a protracted war "even if at a given time, that is, speaking plainly, at the present time, the enemy is stronger, because in the course of the struggle the relation of forces will change to the advantage of the weaker." [6] This expectation the Soviet writer finds unconvincing and (therefore?) un-Marxist. He cites Lenin and Engels, but his most telling comment is, in his own words: "It is absurd to suppose that a war of attrition will, as it were, favor the weak and harm the strong. In such a war, the weak will be exhausted before the strong." [7]

"Chinese Marxism" (here the quotation marks appear in *Military Thought*) is said to make of population a "decisive factor, along with political-morale factors, determining victory or defeat." [8] The Soviet critique notes that, along with population, a number of other material factors, above all weapons and underlying general economic strength, are crucial. The Soviet rebuttal not only notes the British conquest of India as an example in which size of population was no index of strength, but also pointedly recalls the defeat of China in 1895 by "little Japan," as another case discrediting Chinese stress on population resource in and of itself as a decisive factor.[9] Similarly, the Chinese example of the defeat of Japan in China in 1945 as an illustration of victory in a "protracted war"—the cornerstone case for Mao Tse-tung's theories— is rejected as "unconvincing." This rejection is based on the Chinese neglect to note that Japan was "tied down on many fronts in the Pacific Ocean," "the antifascist coalition took the war to the Japanese homeland" (both rare, if indirect, Soviet credits to the decisive wartime role of the United States in defeating Japan), and that "the Soviet Army dealt complete defeat to the Japanese Army in Northeastern and Northern China"—without all of which "the might of Japanese imperialism would not have been broken." [10] Both the historical role of the Chinese Communists, and the theoretical underpinning of their present military doctrine and politico-military strategy, are thus demolished by Moscow.

As the rift between the Russian and Chinese Communists grew in the early 1960's, the Chinese began to stress "reliance on one's own strength," seeking to make a virtue of the necessity imposed by the cessation of Soviet economic, technical, and military assistance. The Soviet criticism of the Chinese strategy attacks the slogan of self-reliance as "an anti-Leninist, anti-Marxist, nationalist slogan. . . . Such slogans of the Chinese splitters [of the Communist movement] are advantageous only to imperialism." [11] Lenin is cited on stressing the need for unity of the workers of the East with those of the West ("especially with the Soviet Union"). The slogan of "reliance on one's own strength" is said to be advanced by the Chinese for "the political and tactical aim of separating the peoples of the oppressed countries from the camp of socialism [i.e., the Soviet Bloc], sowing among them the seeds of nationalism and chauvinism" for Chinese ends.[12]

Military Thought refers to what must be one of the most grating examples of Chinese self-reliance: the development by Peking of its own nuclear weapons. Almost plaintively, the Russians say:

"After all, not a single socialist state except China considers it necessary to have its 'own' nuclear weapons, considering, entirely correctly, that the power of the Soviet nuclear forces reliably covers the entire socialist camp from attack. The leaders of the CCP do not believe in fraternal friendship with the other socialist countries and do not value this friendship, orienting themselves only on 'their own strength'." [13]

The main consideration in determining politico-military strategy, at least to the Russians, is the avoidance of world nuclear war. According to *Military Thought,* the Chinese Communists argue for —and attempt to force on others—a strategy based on the conclusion that the anti-imperialist struggle requires war.[14] One Chinese article in particular is cited: Lu Chih-ch'ao's "Examination of the Question of War Must Not Run Counter to the Marxist-Leninist Viewpoint of the Class Struggle," which appeared in *Hung Ch'i (Red Flag),* No. 16, August 15, 1963.[15] The discussion in *Military Thought* refers only obliquely to the main charge in the *Red Flag* article, namely that the Russians have substituted the non-Marxist viewpoint of judging the nature of war by the scope of its destructiveness in the nuclear age, rather than adhering strictly to the Marxist-Leninist viewpoint of the class nature of any war. The Soviet article does, however, deal with this charge by claiming that the *real* "class approach" is to consider the consequences of such a war, and, on that basis, one is led to the conclusion that "nuclear war must not be permitted." [16] The Chinese "psuedo-Marxist" belief in the inevitability of war is said to lead them to conclude that one must "act 'boldly,' why wait for war, not hesitating before the costs no matter how great." [17] *Military Thought* cites Mao Tsetung's now famous private remarks in Moscow, in November, 1957, to the effect that, if world nuclear war came, "only" half of the population of the world would die. And it comments: "All the subsequent development of this 'idea' [in Chinese Communist writings] bears witness to the fact that it was no chance remark, but a considered concept." [18]

Military Thought defends wars of national liberation as "just," but it qualified this support by reiterating the need for peaceful coexistence between states, and by challenging the alleged Chinese advocacy of revolutionary war *everywhere,* rather than selectively.[19] This point is a familiar one in the polemics between the two parties, and does not need further attention here. One interesting argument is advanced, however, which does not figure in the standard public arguments. After saying that "It would be erroneous to see in all that [Chinese Communist advocacy of revolutionary uprisings everywhere] something specifically Chinese, national; it is not hard to detect in it characteristics of the ideology of petty bourgeois revolutionism," [20] the Soviet journal, nonetheless, goes on to make a condescending, but slashing, critique of Communist China. The relevant paragraph is worth quoting:

> One must not forget that contemporary China is still just an enormous peasant country with a relatively small proportion of proletarian elements, with a young and not yet tempered working class, actually orginating only in the last quarter century; a country in which there are still strong and living remnants, not completely eliminated, of the old ideology of small and very small property owners of the recent past and even elements of feudal ideology in customs, the family, and interpersonal relations. One cannot completely exclude the influence of all these petty bourgeois social strata on the leaders, especially if these very leaders themselves also suffer from strokes of "extreme revolutionariness," especially in time of internal difficulties as a result of the adventurist course of the "speedup" [Great Leap Forward] to socialism by crude administrative measures—all this is well known.[21]

Thus, internal pressures and shortcomings are said to contribute to Chinese "petty bourgeois" and "anarchist" views on revolution everywhere. The Chinese callous indifference to what would be the enormous sacrifices of nuclear war is also said to contribute. The Soviet discussion argues that capitalism is, indeed, doomed but that the role of the socialist countries is to speed its fall, not through war, which would bring ruin to them, too, but through economic competition, for which peace is necessary.[22] Again, this is a familiar theme in the polemics of the past several years. On the basis of this Chinese readiness for nuclear war, which the Russians dialectically interpret as *desire* for nuclear war, the *Military Thought* article goes so far as specifically to accuse the Chinese Communist leaders of supporting genocide.[23]

In the Soviet view, these deficiencies in the Chinese Communist view on military science, policy, and strategy lead to several conclusions: the Chinese view on military science is "pure adventurism" [24]; the view of the West as a "paper tiger" is illogical and erroneous [25]; the result of a protracted *military* conflict would be defeat, not victory.[26] "The adventurist, 'total' strategy of the Peking style is pregnant with indescribable calamities for all peoples, including the Chinese people." [27] The Chinese Communist leaders (once, in the article, derisively referred to as "the Peking 'supermen' ") [28] are, in Soviet eyes, not only not genuine Marxist-Leninist, but they know they are not. "When one acquaints himself closely with the theories of the Peking leaders and their practical activity in the international arena it becomes clear that *they put in first place* not the interests of the peoples struggling for peace, socialism, and national liberation, but *their own great power aims* [italics added]." [29] In addition:

> They consider that world thermonuclear war is inevitable and, attempting to hurry it along, they evidently suppose that the Chinese people will have the best chance since they are the most populous people on the earth. In case of the destruction of the majority of the peoples of the world [sic] and their states, their culture (and this, in the language of the Peking political hysterics, is called 'the fall of imperialism') there would remain, in their opinion, the epoch of world domination by people of the yellow race. The Peking leaders have already come to terms with the idea of dividing people by race, by the color of their skin, rather than by class, social characteristics. Thus they have entered the path leading into the swamp of racism, with all of the consequences which flow from that.[30]

Finally, *Military Thought* concludes that:

> The propaganda war conducted with unheard of licentiousness in China against the Soviet Union, the CPSU, and other Marxist-Leninist parties is an integral part of this "strategy." By their hostile tone, malicious impertinence, and dirty insinuations, articles in the Chinese press could "grace" any anti-Soviet, superreactionary, even fascist press. . . . And all this is not the result of polemical venting, but on the contrary, a cold-blooded realization of the definite plan of the leaders of the CCP, descending the path of extreme chauvinism of a racist ilk.[31]

Such is the Peking version of "total strategy" as seen from Moscow, in a restricted organ of the Soviet General Staff.

The preceding discussion has shown the increasingly revealing (and bitter) Sino-Soviet polemics over politico-military strategic issues from the late 1950's through 1963.* The range of divergencies in Chinese and Russian Communist views on the relationship between war and "the revolution," and over the nature of Leninist doctrine on revolutions, particularly as they developed in exchanges from 1963 to 1966, have recently been comprehensively analyzed elsewhere.[32] Here it is only necessary to summarize a few of the main lines of divergence in the mid-1960's.

* See Chapters 6 and 8.

In the Soviet concept, the socialist states should support the march toward Communism of other peoples, but chiefly by the power of example of their own successful and productive societies —not by risking the socialist achievements of these countries in war. War, in the nuclear age, would benefit no one—not the socialist states, nor the workers of the capitalist states, nor the emerging and developing nations. Moreover, avoidance of war between states will, in fact, best facilitate the progress of the "world revolution." Finally, the Russians contend that the *fundamental* arena of the class struggle is *not* the struggle for national liberation in the developing areas, but the competition between the advanced socialist and advanced capitalist countries.

The Soviet position may be summarized in the following four interrelated tenets:

(1) *Peace* is necessary to preserve millions of lives and the achievements of world civilization, and to ensure the successful building of socialism and Communism.

(2) *Peaceful coexistence* between states with different social systems is necessary to preserve peace, does not mean cessation of the struggle of ideologies, and does not mean cessation, or even inhibition, of the national liberation movement and indigenous revolutions.

(3) *Peaceful competition* between the socialist and capitalist systems will be facilitated by the absence of war, and the superiorities of the socialist system will be demonstrated, leading other peoples to choose socialism.

(4) *Peaceful transition* from the capitalist to the socialist system is preferable to the use of force, and is made more feasible by global peaceful coexistence and competition. The Russians continue to recognize and support the possibility of violent revolution, but they regard it as appropriate only when the *bourgeoisie* and colonialists compel a resort to force. They stress both preference, and increased prospects for, "nonviolent revolution." [33]

The Chinese Communists, in contrast, hold that placing peace above revolution (as they characterize the Russian stand) is treason to true Marxism-Leninism. They similarly hold that war is not likely, even if the socialist states press their confrontation with the imperialists, and their direct support for the national liberation conflict. And, if war should come, they believe that socialism would, in any case, survive victorious, while capitalism would perish. They challenge all four of the Russian tenets enumerated above. In addition, they openly allege that the Russians really seek their own advancement and actually *oppose* "revolution," preferring collaboration and condominium of world rule with the United States.

The Chinese view of the Soviet position was summed up in mid-1965 in the following indictment:

> The question of how to deal with U.S. imperialism is a question as to whether the two-thirds of the world's population still living under the imperialist-capitalist system needs to make revolution and the remaining one-third already on the path of socialism needs to carry its revolution through to the end. The question is one that affects the destiny of the whole of mankind. It is a touchstone for everyone in the world. Everyone must make a choice and thereby show himself as a revolutionary, nonrevolutionary, or counter-revolutionary. It is on this momentous question that the Marxist-Leninists and the Khrushchev revisionists are following two diametrically opposed lines.
>
> The Khrushchev revisionists, cowed by the U.S. imperialist war blackmail, have succumbed to U.S. imperialist pressure. Thus, they are afflicted with incurable spinelessness. They are scared of revolution, shirk at sacrifice, dare not engage in a retaliatory struggle with U.S. imperialism, and even oppose the revolutionary cause of the people of all countries. They go out of their way to publicize the terrors of war and counterpose world revolution against the cause of safeguarding world peace. They complain that there are certain people who "assert that world revolution is more important than the preservation of peace." In order to beg for peace, they turn traitor to the revolution; instead of preferring death to slavery, they are willing to become slaves just to save their own skins. This is the renegade philosophy of Khrushchev revisionists.[34]

There have, subsequently, been many other Chinese attacks on the Soviet leaders. Perhaps the most authoritative and comprehensive is the celebrated treatise by Defense Minister Lin Piao, "Long Live the People's War!," in September, 1965. After an extensive recapitulation of the Marxist concept of a "people's war," and its application on a global scale (with the underdeveloped regions, as the world's "countryside," encircling the advanced capitalist countries, the world's "cities"), Lin Piao recalled Mao Tse-tung's "famous thesis that 'the imperialists and all reactionaries are paper tigers,'" and declared that "The spiritual atomic bomb which the revolutionary people possess is a far more powerful and useful weapon than the physical atomic bomb." [35] Following this exposition of the Chinese view of unremitting revolutionary war, Lin Piao launched into a frontal attack on the present Soviet leaders as "betrayers of people's war" who, themselves, "will be swept like dust from the stage of history by the mighty broom of the revolutionary people." It is, perhaps, useful to cite at some length the key passages pertaining to the Chinese evaluation of Soviet strategy:

The fundamental reason why the Khrushchev revisionists are opposed to people's war is that they have no faith in the masses and are afraid of U.S. imperialism, of war, and of revolution. Like all other opportunists, they are blind to the power of the masses and do not believe that the revolutionary people are capable of defeating imperialism. They submit to the nuclear blackmail of the U.S. imperialists and are afraid that, if the oppressed peoples and nations rise up to fight people's wars or the people of socialist countries repulse U.S. imperialist aggression, U.S. imperialism will become incensed, they themselves will become involved, and their fond dream of Soviet–U.S. cooperation to dominate the world will be spoiled. . . .

The Khrushchev revisionists insist that a nation without nuclear weapons is incapable of defeating an enemy with nuclear weapons, whatever methods of fighting it may adopt. This is tantamount to saying that anyone without nuclear weapons is destined to come to grief, destined to be bullied and annihilated, and must either capitulate to the enemy when confronted with his nuclear weapons or come under the "protection" of some other nuclear power and submit to its beck and call. Isn't this the jungle law of survival par excellence? Isn't this helping the imperialists in their nuclear blackmail? Isn't this openly forbidding people to make revolution?

The Khrushchev revisionists assert that nuclear weapons and strategic rocket units are decisive, while conventional forces are insignificant, and that a militia is just a heap of human flesh. For ridiculous reasons such as these, they oppose the mobilization of and reliance on the masses in the socialist countries to get prepared to use people's war against imperialist aggression. They have staked the whole future of their country on nuclear weapons and are engaged in a nuclear gamble wth U.S. imperialism, with which they are trying to strike a political deal. Their theory of military strategy is the theory that nuclear weapons decide everything. Their line in army building is the bourgeois line that ignores the human factor and sees only the material factor and that regards technology as everything and politics as nothing.

The Khrushchev revisionists maintain that a single spark in any part of the globe may touch off a world nuclear conflagration and bring destruction to mankind. If this were true, our planet world would have been destroyed time and time again. There have been wars of national liberation throughout the twenty years since World War II. But has any single one of them developed into a world war?

Isn't it true that the U.S. imperialists' plans for a world war have been upset precisely thanks to the wars of national liberation in Asia, Africa, and Latin America? By contrast, those who have done their utmost to stamp out the "sparks" of people's wars have in fact encouraged U.S. imperialism in its aggressions and wars.

The Khrushchev revisionists claim that, if their general line of "peaceful coexistence, peaceful transition, and peaceful competition" is followed, the oppressed will be liberated and "a world without weapons, without armed forces, and without wars" will come into being. But the inexorable fact is that imperialism and reaction headed by the United States are zealously priming their war machine and are daily engaged in sanguinary suppression of the revolutionary peoples and in the threat and use of armed force against independent countries. The kind of rubbish peddled by the Khrushchev revisionists has already taken a great toll of lives in a number of countries. Are these painful lessons, paid for in blood, still insufficient? The essence of the general line of the Khrushchev revisionists is nothing other than the demand that all the oppressed peoples and nations and all the countries which have won independence should lay down their arms and place themselves at the mercy of the U.S. imperialists and their lackeys who are armed to the teeth.

"While magistrates are allowed to burn down houses, the common people are forbidden even to light lamps." Such is the way of the imperialists and reactionaries. Subscribing to this imperialist philosophy, the Khrushchev revisionists shout at the Chinese people standing in the forefront of the fight for world peace: "You are bellicose!" Gentlemen, your abuse adds to our credit. It is this very "bellicosity" of ours that helps to prevent imperialism from unleashing a world war. The people are "bellicose" because they have to defend themselves and because the imperialists and reactionaries force them to be so. It is also the imperialists and reactionaries who have taught the people the arts of war. We are simply using revolutionary "bellicosity" to cope with counterrevolutionary bellicosity. How can it be argued that the imperialists and their lackeys may kill people everywhere, while the people must not strike back in self-defense or help one another? What kind of logic is this? The Khrushchev revisionists regard imperialists like Kennedy and Johnson as "sensible" and describe us, together with all those who dare to carry out armed defense against imperialist aggression, as "bellicose." This has revealed the Khrushchev revisionists in their true colors as the accomplices of imperialist gangsters.

We know that war brings destruction, sacrifice, and suffering to the people. But the destruction, sacrifice, and suffering will be much greater if no resistance is offered to imperialist armed aggression and the people become willing slaves. The sacrifice of a small number of people in revolutionary wars is repaid by security for whole nations, whole countries, and even the whole of mankind; temporary suffering is repaid by lasting or even perpetual peace and happiness. War can temper the people and push history forward. In this sense, war is a great school.

When discussing World War I, Lenin said: "The war has brought hunger to the most civilized countries, to those most culturally developed. On the other hand, the war, as a tremendous historical process, has accelerated social development to an unheard of degree." He added: "War has shaken up the masses, its untold horrors and suffering have awakened them. War has given history momentum and it is now flying with locomotive speed."

If the arguments of the Khrushchev revisionists are to be believed, would not that make Lenin the worst of all "bellicose elements?"

In diametrical opposition to the Khrushchev revisionists, the Marxist-Leninists and revolutionary peoples never take a gloomy view of war. Our attitude toward imperialist wars of aggression has always been clear-cut. First, we are against them, and secondly, we are not afraid of them. We will destroy whoever attacks us. As for revolutionary wars waged by the oppressed nations and peoples, so for from opposing them, we invariably give them firm support and active aid. It has been so in the past, it remains so in the present and, when we grow in strength as time goes on, we will give them still more support and aid in the future. It is sheer daydreaming for anyone to think that, since our revolution has been victorious, our national construction is forging ahead, our national health is increasing and our living conditions are improving, we, too, will lose our revolution and discard Marxism-Leninism and proletarian internationalism. Of course, every revolution in a country stems from the demands of its own people. Only when the people in a country are awakened, mobilized, organized, and armed can they overthrow the reactionary rule of imperialism and its lackeys through struggle; their role cannot be replaced or taken over by any people from outside. In this sense, revolution cannot be imported, but this does not exclude mutual sympathy and support on the part of revolutionary peoples in their struggles against the imperialists and their lackeys. Our support and aid to other revolutionary peoples serves precisely to help their self-reliant struggle.

The propaganda of the Khrushchev revisionists against people's war and the publicity they give to defeatism and capitulationism tend to demoralize and spiritually disarm revolutionary people everywhere. These revisionists are doing what the U.S. imperialists are unable to do themselves and are rendering them great service. They have greatly encouraged U.S. imperialism in its war adventures. They have completely betrayed the Marxist-Leninist revolutionary theory of war and have become betrayers of people's war.

To win the struggle against U.S. imperialism and carry people's wars to victory, the Marxist-Leninists and revolutionary people throughout the world must resolutely oppose Khrushchev revisionism.

Today, Khrushchev revisionism has a small audience among the revolutionary people of the world. Wherever there is armed aggression and suppression by imperialism and its lackeys, there are bound to be people's wars against aggression and oppression. It is certain that such wars will develop vigorously. This is an objective law independent of the will of either the U.S. imperialists or the Khrushchev revisionists. The revolutionary people of the world will sweep away everything that stands in the way of their advance. Khrushchev is finished. And the successors to Khrushchev revisionism will fare no better than the imperialists, the reactionaries and the Khrushchev revisionists, who have all set themselves against people's war, and who will be swept like dust from the stage of history by the mighty broom of the revolutionary people.[36]

This passage illuminates both the Soviet and the Chinese Communist strategic concepts, and the divergence between them—even allowing for intentional polemical distortions by both sides. It is also an interesting commentary read in conjunction with the evaluation of *Military Thought* two years earlier, representing, in a sense, Peking's view of "the Moscow version of total strategy."

10. The Soviet Generals' View of China in the 1960's

By J. MALCOLM MACKINTOSH

The Sino-Soviet dispute, initially thinly disguised as an ideological quarrel between two Communist parties, is clearly a full-scale disagreement on a state-to-state level. As such, it raises, at once, the problem of future military relations between the Soviet Union and China. Is this situation likely to alter Soviet military planning, intentions, or deployments to meet a nationalistic and hostile China on the U.S.S.R.'s eastern frontier, and if so, where are these changes occurring or most likely to occur?

Since the establishment of the Communist government in China in 1949, Soviet military deployment along the Chinese frontier has been negligible, with the exception of troops in the Maritime Province running down the Pacific coastline from the Amur River to the port of Vladivostok. This province has been the center of the Soviet Army's defense deployment against U.S. power in the Pacific, and has contained a concentration of a dozen well-equipped divisions, supported by an Air Army, and the Pacific Fleet based on Vladivostok. Its command was vested in the headquarters of the Far Eastern Military District at Khabarovsk, which, from 1945 to 1955, was commanded by the present Minister of Defense, Marshal Rodion Malinovsky. Small detachments of ground and air forces (and, in some areas, frontier guards of the Committee of State Security) are maintained on Sakhalin and in the Kuril Islands, in the Kamchatka peninsula, along the Amur River above Khabarovsk, and, also, in the Trans-Baikal Military District, with headquarters at Chita.

Apart from these forces, the vast area between Lake Baikal and the Ural Mountains (the Siberian and Ural Military Districts, through which the Trans-Siberian Railroad passes) contain only small numbers of low-strength formations used mainly for basic training. Along the Sino-Soviet frontier in Central Asia (including the Soviet-Mongolian frontier) the border was virtually unmanned except for State Security frontier guards. The main forces of the Turkestan Military District (with headquarters at Tashkent) have been directed at Iran, with smaller concentrations along the Afghan frontier. In all, from 1949 to the present day, the whole area north of the 4,000-mile-long Sino-Soviet frontier have held not more than twenty Soviet divisions, of which less than half could readily have undertaken defensive or offensive operations against Chinese military power in Manchuria or Sinkiang.

Is tension between the Soviet Union and China likely to result in any significant redeployment of Soviet forces in the Far East? It is extremely probable that the Soviet General Staff, on the instructions of the Government, has been studying both the short-and long-term military effects of the split; and, since the military leadership is, on the whole, conservative in outlook and inclined to lay emphasis upon the worst situations that could arise, their presentation and recommendations to the Party and Government are likely to be on the pessimistic side. In particular, the Soviet military leaders are likely to call, if they have not already done so, for an early increase in ground and air forces in the Far Eastern and Trans-Baikal Military Districts, added to the strengthening of the frontier guards along the whole Chinese border.

In view of the Soviet Army's heavy commitments in western Russia and eastern Europe, where the strength of Soviet ground and air forces is regarded by the High Command as the minimum required to keep the Warsaw Pact functioning effectively, it is unlikely that the marshals would agree to any sizeable transfer of units from the West to the Chinese border. They are more likely, in general, to suggest bringing a number of training and low-strength divisions already in the area up to higher manpower-and-equipment strength. They would probably also recommend the redeployment of some tactical bombers, fighter-bombers, and fighters to Far Eastern airfields, and, perhaps, even increase the size of the Far East-based long-range bomber force, which has a nuclear capability.

In the field of air defense, the High Command will undoubtedly want to improve the ability of the Air Defense Command (which combines interceptor fighters, surface-to-air missiles, and the early-warning network) to deal with any Chinese air reconnaissance or probing activity that might take place along the border—or, perhaps, over Outer Mongolia—with special reference to the air defense of the vital Trans-Siberian Railroad. Finally, the High Command would press for completing modernization plans for the Pacific Fleet, which acquired a new and much younger commander in 1962, and its naval air force, which also has a nuclear capability. Road and rail communications may well require a special short-term overhaul, and the High Command's recommendations probably end with a general appeal for increased stockpiles of weapons and equipment, and for improved facilities in the Far East to handle transport aircraft carrying military cargoes.

In addition to these projected short-term recommendations, it is very likely that the Soviet General Staff is preparing a much longer-range study of the effect of the dispute in the defense field, dealing, perhaps, with the period twenty to thirty years ahead, when China may be a much more formidable military power than she is today. Such a study might take into consideration an aggressively chauvinistic Chinese Communist Government with a land-army war potential of 300–400 divisions, armed with nuclear weapons and tactical missiles. (In case this figure should sound fantastic, it is worth recalling that, in 1943–45, the Soviet Army had nearly 500 divisions in the field after two years of mobilizing a population of some 200 million, at a time when many of the country's industrial centers were in German hands; China's population is already more than three times larger than that of the Soviet Union, and in twenty years may be over 850 million.) Even taking into consideration the inferior Chinese industrial base, slow economic progress to date, and difficulty in acquiring new weapons, it is still not impossible that, in Soviet calculations, an actively hostile, militaristic China could put at least twice the 115 line divisions the country now maintains, as a peacetime army, into the field against the Soviet Union in the 1980's.

On such data and calculations as these, the present Soviet military leadership would be likely to form its conclusions—although a caveat should be entered here that the next generation of Soviet military men may adopt different criteria in assessing the Chinese threat. The central question for the military to answer would be, ironically enough, the question that NATO leaders have had to answer vis-à-vis Soviet manpower strength: Can we match our adversaries' strength by men on the ground, or do we have to rely on weapons of mass destruction to redress the balance?

The main conclusion of this hypothetical long-term staff study doubtless would be that, in view of the distances east of the Ural

Mountains and the capacities of the Trans-Siberian Railroad and of airfields in Asiatic Russia, any attempt to match the numbers that the Chinese could put into the field would be hopeless. It is interesting to recall that, in 1945, it took the Soviet High Command from three and a half to four months to move 27 infantry divisions and 3 division-sized armored corps to the Manchurian frontier in time to take part in the occupation of Manchuria against the Japanese.* The Soviet High Command would, therefore, recommend the use of nuclear weapons and other means of mass destruction in defense of the Soviet Far East. If the Soviet military have the last word, the Sino-Soviet dispute may indeed give a new lease on life to nuclear and chemical weapons.

The foregoing suggestions and hypotheses may be among those that could appear on the desks of the Soviet political leaders when they call for a military appreciation of the situation. In practice, the political leaders are likely to pigeon-hole the long-term analysis, while not necessarily disagreeing with its conclusions. To the report on short-term measures, they are likely to react by accepting the need for some build-up, but turning down the more extensive military measures proposed by the High Command—such as increasing the call-up, immediately activating training formations, and extensively stockpiling weapons and equipment in the Far East.

The Soviet leaders have been at pains to emphasize that China's military power is still at a relatively low level. They will not, therefore, spend money and resources on military preparations to meet threats that they obviously regard as remote. Nevertheless, the Soviet leaders have, evidently, agreed to precautionary strengthening of the frontier guards in Central Asia and the Far East, to improving air defense measures, and to increasing ground and air patrolling and reconnaissance of the frontier areas, particularly along sectors shown as "undemarcated" on Chinese maps and where some frontier incidents have already been provoked.

In addition, it seems probable that the political leaders will find ways of demonstrating to the Chinese the extent of Soviet military power and their determination to use it on the frontier if provoked. Such an effort may have been intensified since 1963. The exceptionally imposing naval parade of the Pacific Fleet in Vladivostok harbor on July 28, 1963 which was attended by the Commander in Chief of the Soviet Navy, Admiral S. G. Gorshkov, and the senior naval political officer, Vice Admiral V. M. Grishanov, was un-

* See Chapter 4.

doubtedly intended to impress the Chinese, as was the wide publicity given to the display in the press. Again, the lengthy and imposing visit of the Commander in Chief of the Mongolian Army to the Soviet Union, in April and May of that same year, probably served the same ends. And, perhaps, the appointment of a very senior officer, who was Chief of Staff of the Soviet forces occupying Manchuria in 1945, as Chief of Staff of the Siberian Military District in 1963 may be significant. This officer, General S. P. Ivanov, has since been promoted to command the Siberian Military District.

In short, what the Soviet Government is likely to continue to do in the late 1960's is to secure its physical control over a long frontier, which for many years has been only lightly guarded, and to take precautionary military measures relevant to dealing with frontier incidents and impressing the Chinese with Soviet military power in the area. It is difficult to learn exactly what these measures are, but it is not impossible that the commands of the Asian military districts in the Sovet Union have been given new responsibilities in the border areas, and in the field of study and planning dealing with situations of tension along the Sino-Soviet frontier. Indeed, it has been reported that, in 1964, Soviet ground forces in the area of Vladivostok conducted maneuvers that assumed a nonnuclear Chinese invasion of the Maritime Province.

If the foregoing estimate of the Soviet political leaders' reaction to the demands of the Ministry of Defense is approximately correct, it is interesting to look, in a little more detail, at the likely relation of forces in the Far East during the 1960's, as seen through the eyes of the Soviet marshals. On the Soviet side, there are three main elements of military power: strategic striking forces, naval forces, and ground forces, all of which have a nuclear, as well as a conventional, capability. One of the three Soviet Long-Range Air Armies is permanently stationed in the Far East, and probably has about 200 medium and heavy bombers and tanker aircraft (for in-flight refueling), which would enable the Russians to strike at any target in China with nuclear or conventional weapons. Little is known of Soviet land-based strategic-missile strength in the Far East, but it is to be asumed that missiles of intermediate and medium range deployed there could be used against Chinese targets, if required. The Soviet Pacific Fleet is estimated to have 120 submarines, 6 cruisers, 30 destroyers, and 500 other vessels, backed up by about 200 naval shore-based aircraft, some of them armed with air-to-surface missiles. On the ground, the Soviet marshals have a force of 12 to 15 divisions in the area between Vladivostok and Lake Baikal, with another 7 or 8 in Central Asia. Of these divisions, which could be brought in to operate on the Chinese border, perhaps two are airborne divisions, and the remainder tank or motorized-rifle divisions, supported by limited numbers of tactical surface-to-surface missiles with conventional, nuclear, or chemical warheads. In all, the ground Forces in the area between the Caspian Sea and the Pacific probably number 250,000 men, and are, undoubtedly, a very hard-hitting and well-trained force, even if employed only on a conventional basis.

Given these force levels, the problem for the Soviet marshals would be to plan for their most effective use against Chinese military power, should this action become necessary. The two main factors that would figure in Soviet staff studies would be Chinese manpower superiority in the event of China's full or even partial mobilization, and the relatively small number of military and military-industrial targets vital to Chinese effectiveness in war. On the first score, the Soviet military planners would assume that their 12 to 15 divisions in the Far East could be opposed by a Chinese concentration of three or four times that number in Manchuria. This Chinese force, in the last resort, might have to be stopped by the use of nuclear or chemical weapons. If, however, Chinese military action were mounted at a lower level, the Soviet defense planners would probably estimate that they could defeat up to twice their own number of Chinese—using conventional weapons only. An important factor here would be the small number of armored formations, compared with the Soviet Far Eastern Forces, which the Chinese could put into the field. Only four of the 115 divisions in the Chinese Army are believed to be armored—less armored forces than the Russians already maintain in Central Asia and the Far East in peacetime. At sea, the Chinese Navy, under its land-trained commanders, would be no match at all for the Soviet Far Eastern Fleet, which has 120 submarines, compared with the Chinese total of 30.

But, it would probably be the second factor in the correlation of forces that would interest the Soviet defense planners most closely. This factor is the relatively small number of targets vulnerable to Soviet air attack that would be vital to any Chinese war effort. First among these targets would be the few facilities connected with the Chinese nuclear-weapons program. There can surely be no doubt that the Russians know exactly where these targets are, including the site of the Chinese nuclear tests, and the Soviet Long

Range Air Force in the Far East would be quite capable of carrying out such a strike, probably even using conventional weapons only. Then, too, the Soviet authorities certainly know exactly where all the Chinese arms production centers are, and all the most important army supply bases, as well as deployment areas of the few armored and artillery divisions on which the Chinese Army depends for its mobility and heavy fire-power. Chinese airfields, too, would be vulnerable to Soviet air strikes. All in all, therefore, the weight of attack that the Soviet armed forces could bring to bear on vital elements of Chinese military power must make the Soviet defense planners reasonably confident of defeating the Chinese with conventional weapons in all but an overwhelming attack by a fully mobilized China putting millions of men into the field.

The appearance of Chinese nuclear weapons is not, in all probability, going to alter the Soviet defense planners' estimate of the relation of forces in the Far East in the foreseeable future. Should the Chinese be the first to use nuclear weapons in the future war against Russia they could, of course, attempt to inflict an immense amount of damage on a few large cities—for instance, Vladivostok or Chita—or, possibly, on sensitive areas in Soviet Central Asia. But, unless the Chinese can radically improve their own means of delivery, there is little likelihood that their present air force could penetrate Soviet air defenses, and, in any case, a Chinese attempt to initiate the use of nuclear weapons would remove all Soviet inhibitions against their use, with catastrophic results for the Chinese. It seems probable that this line of argument would appear in Soviet staff studies of the military implications of the acquisition of nuclear weapons by China, as long as Chinese nuclear stockpiles and delivery capabilities remain within the range predictable for the next five to ten years.

Although the present Soviet leaders, Leonid I. Brezhnev and Aleksei N. Kosygin, appear to have diverted the Soviet Union from the collision course with China on which Khrushchev seemed determined to embark, all the political evidence suggests that this change in course has not altered the fundamental nature of the dispute between the two countries. Indeed, if anything, China's disappointment over the failure of Brezhnev and Kosygin to abandon Khrushchev's policies toward the United States, the nuclear-test-ban treaty, and the world Communist movement has led the Chinese to new heights of bitterness and resentment against the Soviet Union. The military estimates probably first drawn up under Khrushchev's rule are not likely to have been much changed—with one possible exception. The reappointment of Marshal Matvei V. Zakharov as Chief of the Soviet General Staff brought to this key post a man who seems to have disagreed with Khrushchev on defense policy, and who had been dismissed in March, 1963. Zakharov's return may have led to a reassessment of the general requirements of the Soviet ground forces, including those in the Far East. And, since one trend in Soviet military thinking today seems to involve consideration of the employment of nonnuclear forces, with stress on amphibious and airborne operations, it is possible that these types of operation will be given greater attention in Soviet military planning on China in the future than had been the case in the late Khrushchev years.

So much for the details of Soviet military planning. But what are, in fact, the possible trouble spots in the next few years? First of all, there is the problem of those areas in which the Chinese regard the frontier as undemarcated, particularly in Central Asia, where the border cuts through lands occupied by Muslim peoples, such as the Kazakhs, leaving elements on both sides of the frontier. The most sensitive spot here is the Ili Valley, which was filched from the Chinese by the Imperial Russian Government during the latter half of the nineteenth century. But the whole province of Sinkiang was the scene of sporadic Soviet intervention during the 1930's and 1940's; and active Soviet intrigues with nationalist anti-Chinese movements in Sinkiang were suspended only after the Communists came to power in 1949.*

Since 1950, there has been considerable movement of population from Sinkiang into Soviet Central Asia, which, the Chinese say, has taken place with Soviet connivance and encouragement. This area is especially dangerous in the military sense because Soviet Central Asia is believed to be a particularly sensitive area in the field of new weapons. If a prediction is in order, it is possible that we may see frontier incidents provoked by the Chinese in this area; the Chinese have been pushing road and rail development westward through Sinkiang, and in 1962, they successfully moved troops from northern and central Sinkiang southward to their Ladakh battlefield with the Indian army. Another reason for potential trouble in this remote corner of the world may be underlined: Soviet Central Asia's proximity to Kashmir. In view of recent Chinese agreement with Pakistan, the Soviet Union is likely to fear forward Chinese moves in southwest Sinkiang, since such

* See Chapter 2.

moves may be designed to intimidate India and encourage extremists in Pakistan.

The second problem concerns Mongolia. Although the Sino-Mongolian frontier has recently been demarcated, the Mongolian Government has strongly supported the Soviet line in the dispute, and has, undoubtedly, incurred Chinese hositility. But any Chinese-provoked frontier incidents here, if persisted in, would bring Soviet troops into Mongolia under the Soviet-Mongolian defense treaty renewed in early 1966; therefore, border trouble on this frontier is less likely.

The extensive territorial claims in the Pacific area, already mentioned by China in the debate with the Soviet Union, constitute the third problem. These claims include the Maritime Province and a large part of Amur Province, which were ceded by China to Russia by the "unequal" treaties of Aigun and Peking in the nineteenth century. These territories are so extensive, so well-garrisoned, and so vital to the whole Soviet position in the Far East, and have been so completely Russified, that actual Chinese claims for their return are remote and unrealistic. There are, however, minor points in dispute along this border—the ownership of certain uninhabited islands in the Amur River, for example, could be exploited if either side wanted to cause trouble—and, to this extent, frontier incidents here, though less likely, cannot be ruled out entirely. Moreover, Chinese military strength in Manchuria has been maintained at a high level since the Korean War.

To sum up, the "state-to-state" nature of the Sino-Soviet dispute since the early 1960's focuses attention in Moscow and Peking on their common border, and, with the Chinese in their present aggressive mood, frontier incidents (particularly in Central Asia) may well occur. Very little is known of the outlook of the Chinese military, but the Soviet High Command is likely to press for the military strengthening of the border, while the Soviet political leaders, less alarmist than their military advisers, will probably tone down the recommendations. In the long term, the Russians are likely to hold the view that an ultimate Chinese military threat could be countered only by the use of weapons of mass destruction; but the Soviet Government does not appear to expect that China will acquire a serious nuclear-weapons capability in the near future.

In the very long run, however, probably the most nagging Russian fear is Chinese domination of the Indian subcontinent, either through military erosion or political subversion, for this dominance would outflank the Soviet Union, and place the whole of Soviet Asia under a greater threat than ever before. If the Chinese continue to develop their hostility to the Soviet Union along extreme nationalistic lines, one result may be a closer Soviet interest in Indian defense, combined with attempts to wean Pakistan away from her new contacts with China. And, here, as the Tashkent accord of 1965 already foreshadows, Russia and the West might find some unexpected common ground.

11. Sino-Soviet War in 19xx?

By O. FERDINAND MIKSCHE

Although it is not possible to foresee whether and when Sino-Soviet disagreements may intensify, even a war between the two giant Communist states cannot be excluded from the range of possible future developments. Accordingly, this chapter sketches some of the fundamental underlying geopolitical and strategic factors that would set the conditions of such a conflict.

If a military conflict should break out between the Soviet Union and China, it would be set off by a variety of causes, many of which may not yet even be discernible. From its inception, Chinese Communism has differed from Soviet Marxism in many respects. Indeed, it came into its own even against the will of Moscow (which, for twenty years, gave its support to Chiang Kai-shek). Despite all protestations of international solidarity, the Russians have, subconsciously, long been afraid of the Communist Middle Kingdom (as the Chinese call their country), not only because they regard the Chinese as dangerous ideological deviationists, but also, and more particularly, because they view them as serious obstacles to their own world political aspirations. Other motives than the purely ideological apparently also play an important part in the Russian reaction; it was the Russians who most shamelessly exploited China's weakness during the nineteenth century and the early part of the twentieth. No wonder, then, that the Chinese, despite being Communists, look upon the Russians (and other white-skinned peoples) as "foreign devils."

The decisive factor, however, is the impossibility of feeding the Chinese people at the present rate of increase (15 million a year), which compels Peking to pursue an aggressive policy. The over-populated Middle Kingdom is seeking *Lebensraum*, particularly in Southeast Asia. Although she must export food in order to be able

193

to import many important raw materials, China is not poor in mineral resources. Exploitation of these resources, however, requires enormous investments, which China alone cannot finance. Since the Russians refuse to come to her aid, China is trying to gain possession, through subversion, of the tin and copper mines, rubber plantations, and oil fields provided with modern equipment by the "Western imperialists," and of the rich rice granary of Southeast Asia. By conquering one of the most important raw-materials areas of the world, would it not be possible for China to acquire the means it needs for its struggle against the wealthy white Communists in Moscow? Is this perhaps the reason why the Russians as well as the Americans, but for other reasons, have begun to develop their activity in Southeast Asia in these last few years? Moscow is generously supplying Indonesia with modern weapons, naval vessels, and aircraft, which at least originally were aimed against the Western powers, but perhaps also are supplied with the ulterior motive of equipping Indonesia as a potential ally against the Middle Kingdom.

Peking's sphere of power today extends as far as the Gulf of Tonkin. There is danger of Communist influence eventually expanding through Burma and Thailand to the shores of the Indian Ocean, and working its way through Viet-Nam and Malaysia to Singapore, a world traffic center of the highest importance to the entire West. If it should come to this point, it is still possible that, despite recent setbacks for the Chinese Communists, Indonesia might some day serve the Chinese as the bridge for an advance to the gates of Australia—not by the use of nuclear weapons, but by relentless revolutionary underground work by the "yellow ant men," against which nuclear weapons are quite ineffective.

Such a development would be equivalent to breaking through and turning the flank of the U.S. position in the Pacific. China's push through Southeast Asia to the shores of the Indian Ocean passes through areas that, in past centuries, generally owed feudal allegiance to Peking. As a matter of fact, all of Southeast Asia is today exposed to the pressure of the steadily increasing mass of Chinese, whose push for *Lebensraum* cannot be stemmed in the long run. It would be wise to concentrate on the defense of the island chain, especially since that would afford the only chance of blocking Chinese infiltration into the Pacific area.

India's future could be another factor determining the evolution of relations between the Russians and the Chinese. India is afflicted with many weaknesses, and possesses a population of more than 450 million today, with an increase of 4.5 million annually. Whose sphere of influence will this gigantic country eventually become? What will happen if, within the next few years, the Congress Party should become exhausted and thus less a match for Chinese dynamism than it is today? Communists hold that India's problem can be solved only by a socialist regime. But now, two antagonistic Communist movements, the Chinese and the Russian, are contending for hegemony in Asia.

Given the passivity of its people, will India hold her ground in the gigantic struggle for a new division of Asia, or will she become the prey of a new colonialism? The latter development is entirely conceivable, especially in the event that, sooner or later, the Japanese should promote the industrialization of China. It is worth noting that China's aggression against India ran in the direction of the strategically important river valleys of the Brahmaputra and the Indus, both of which empty into the Indian Ocean. Should Peking's plans call for more than a mere border rectification, neither the West nor the Soviet Union should allow China to use India as a springboard in the direction of East Africa and the Arab world. But even if rivalry arising over India should be the eventual cause of war between the Russians and the Chinese, the principal theater of the struggle would presumably include the areas along the border between the two gigantic Communist powers, where, from the Pamir Plateau to Vladivostok, Sino-Soviet interests are in direct conflict.

Not only Tibet, and other countries of the Himalayan region now under Indian rule, but also present-day Soviet Central Asia, were, up to the eighteenth century, included in the Middle Kingdom's sphere of influence. Eastern Siberia's principal cities— Blagoveshchensk, Khabarovsk, Nikolaevsk, Komsomolsk, and Vladivostok—are situated on formerly Chinese territory acquired by the Czars. The Soviet Russians, later on, showed themselves no less imperialistic. In 1921, Moscow took from China by force the province of Tannu Tuva; in 1924, Outer Mongolia came under Soviet hegemony. Manchuria, "liberated" from the Japanese at the end of World War II, was returned to China, totally stripped, by the Russians, in 1946. Much of Sinkiang, rich in uranium and gold deposits, was under Soviet "administration" from 1934 to 1949. Will the 750 million Chinese forever passively watch the exploitation by the Soviet "master race" of Asiatic territories that once belonged to the Middle Kingdom, or will they not rather press for "independence" also for Turkestan, Tannu Tuva, and Mongolia, to make it easier for China to get possession of these countries?

The Russians appear to be conscious of the dangers threatening them in the Far East. They sense that, on the other side of the border, there is a China, three to four times more populous than their own country, thirsty for power and becoming increasingly self-assertive, a country whose people are industrious—a big country that has, at all times, thought of itself as the dominant power of Asia, and that is daily becoming more disquieting to Moscow. Moscow is displaying conspicuous haste in colonizing Siberia. But might it not be precisely this policy that makes Siberia's wealth even more attractive to the Chinese, who (as in the case of Southeast Asia) perhaps wish to take possession of raw-materials resources already developed and the modern industries necessary for their conversion?

From a military point of view, much would depend on the circumstances attending the outbreak of a Sino-Soviet war. Predicting the circumstances now would be as impossible as it would have been, in 1914, to foresee that World War I would be triggered by two revolver shots. It might be of some interest, however, to try to puzzle out, at least in broad outline, some of the military aspects of such a potential struggle. A primary determinant would be the character of the initial combat operations, from which the others would evolve, as by a chain reaction. Possibly there will be no direct hostilities at all for a long time. The existing rivalry between these two adversaries, which are antagonistic to each other on both power-political and ideological grounds, has led initially to a cold war, with the Russians and Chinese waging subversive warfare against each other—a method of war undoubtedly congenial to these two Communist systems.

It would, thus, be entirely conceivable that a tension generated in the Far East, India, or Southeast Asia might shift gradually to areas along the 4,300-mile boundary between the Soviet Union and China, where each would try—probably by revolutionary action at first—to penetrate as far as possible into the adversary's hinterland. Probably it would be easier for the Chinese to incite some of the peoples of Siberia or Turkestan, already somewhat hostile to the Russians, than it would be for the Russians to recruit partisans in China's interior. Revolts organized in not easily accessible areas of Central and East Asia could degenerate into guerrilla warfare lasting for years. Leaders dropped from the air, gathering around themselves thousands of "volunteers," operating in large bands, and equipped with huge supplies of small arms, could paralyze large areas. Since modern armaments would be of only minor importance in such a struggle, the Chinese could hope to enjoy superiority over the Russians. The Russians would be compelled to deploy an increasing number of troops to police the vast areas of Siberia and, at the same time, the immensely long border with China, and still would be unable to bring about an end of the conflict on their own terms. Sooner or later, a mounting tension would explode into open hostilities.

But, quite aside from the question of whether a war would come about in this or that manner, it is more important to note the fact that, for the first time in her history, Russia would be faced with an enemy to whom she would be far superior technologically but, in a similar degree, inferior in manpower by a ratio of between 1:3 and 1:4—the situation in which Russia's adversaries found themselves in the last two wars. This time, the Russians would have to battle with troops even more frugal than their own. In addition, the Russians would, in China, have to contend with geographical problems such as confronted Napoleon in 1812, the former Central Powers in 1914–17, and the German *Wehrmacht* in 1941–45. It would suffice for China to equip, even if only with small arms, one-third of her 125 million able-bodied men, to be unconquerable in the conventional military sense.

In case of a general mobilization, Soviet ground strength could be as much as 200 divisions, equipped with the latest weapons. The Soviet air force has over 10,000 aircraft. The Soviet Pacific Fleet alone would be far superior to the Chinese. China's military strength, at the present time, consists chiefly of 2.5 million men, comprising about 115 infantry divisions, but apparently only about 4 tank divisions and 1 airborne division. The ground forces are organized into about 35 armies, each of 3 divisions (or 50,000 to 60,000 men). The air force comprises nearly 2,500 aircraft, and the navy consists of only 4 destroyers, 4 destroyer escorts, 30 submarines, and smaller vessels.

Advanced technical armaments were formerly supplied to the Chinese by the Russians, but deliveries were virtually stopped in 1960, thus imposing a disastrous spare-parts shortage on the Chinese air force and navy. China's aviation and shipbuilding industries, still in their infancy, found themselves in a critical situation after the stoppage of Soviet assistance. But this state of affairs could change considerably within a few years, especially since morale remains a decisive element determining the value of any military force—and China's army is rooted in the people.

From the time of the first Chinese nuclear test explosion in the Central Asian desert in October, 1964, at least five years will be required for Peking to build up a *force de frappe* sufficiently strong to threaten Siberia's industrial centers; this threat may be presumed to have a significant effect on Moscow's policy for Asia. A situation could, in time, arise in which the Russians could employ their atomic weapons only if they accept the risk of enormous destruction in their own country. Moreover, psychologically as well as physically, the Russians would be far more vulnerable than the numerically immensely stronger Chinese.

Time seems to work for Peking, and not for Moscow. It is, therefore, not at all pointless to ask whether the Russians will simply try to live with this continuously growing threat to their interests, or whether they will, instead, choose to take preventive action before the Chinese have acquired the capacity to provide atomic support for their world political aspirations. In any case, on the military plane, the Russians could rely exclusively on atomic weapons (i.e., without employing conventional forces). Even if, as a matter of precaution, the Russians used only conventional forces, desperate situations might easily provoke the Chinese, less vulnerable to atomic attack, to resort to tactical or strategic employment of nuclear weapons as the *ultima ratio,* which would inevitably unleash a nuclear duel. And yet, the question remains whether it would be possible, even by nuclear means, to crush the resistance of 750 million people, and to wipe out their will to carry on protracted guerilla warfare. Prevention of such warfare would, naturally, have to be the primary goal of Moscow's strategy. Even so, it is difficult to see how the Russians could avoid the employment of mass armies. Even in the event that the Russians waged the war only strategically and with atomic weapons, they would have to deploy a large number of divisions for securing the long border against Chinese infiltration. Whether or not atomic weapons are employed, a Russo-Chinese war doubtless would be an extremely risky affair—very costly in matériel and casualties—for the Soviet Union. But, in such a struggle, the Chinese, too, would have little prospect of winning.

All these foregoing speculations may not be entirely idle, since the evolution of relations between China and Russia could easily become the most crucial question of our century. In this matter, might not the interests of Russia and the United States coincide—a development that, all antagonisms notwithstanding, is already beginning to take shape?

While 165 million people live in European Russia, only 60 million inhabit the area between the Caspian Sea and the Pacific coast. The areas forming Russian Asia, eight times the size of Europe from the Elbe to Gibraltar including Italy and Great Britain, are underpopulated. The northern two-thirds of Siberia is uninhabitable for climatic reasons. In the south, the population is settled mainly along the Trans-Siberian Railroad and in the industrial centers.

Of the 60 million Soviet citizens living east of the Ural Mountains, about one-half are of Asiatic origin. The majority of the population of Turkestan, as well as many Mongols and Chinese who live in the East and in the Pacific Maritime Province, may not be entirely reliable to Moscow. With great difficulties, the Soviet Government is exerting great efforts to bring people to Siberia, and it seems unlikely that it will establish an effective counterweight in the foreseeable future against the Chinese.

China, like Siberia, is also settled very unevenly. Although the heaviest population concentrations in the world have arisen along the Pacific coast, in the valleys of the Hwang Ho and Yangtze rivers, and around Canton, Peking, and Shanghai, large areas of central and western China remain practically uninhabited. These areas offer very poor conditions for settlement, unless development projects are carried out in them. Such projects not only call for immense investments, but also could not do more than keep up with the rapid rate of population growth. Hence, China's push for *Lebensraum*, for the time being directed southward toward the Indian Ocean, will eventually turn northward toward Siberia.

In the event of a military conflict between Russia and China, the initial front would extend over 4,300 miles. This immense theater of war falls into three sectors that are nearly equal in size but that differ radically from a geostrategic viewpoint, each measuring close to 1,400 miles (compared to the length of the eastern front between Leningrad and Sevastopol, which was about 1,000 miles).

The eastern sector, where Siberia's Maritime Province and Manchuria are partly level and partly hilly (traversed here and there by secondary mountain ranges), offers a terrain that, owing to the density of the existing communications network, is suited for operations by mechanized forces.

The central sector encompasses the nearly unpopulated area of

Mongolia—the Gobi Desert—where modern desert warfare, similar to World War II operations in North Africa could probably be waged. It would be difficult to operate with large masses of troops in this area.

The western sector is formed by distinct alpine ranges, with peaks rising to over 25,000 feet, where infiltration tactics and guerrilla warfare would be possible but operations with mechanized troops would be difficult to imagine. Deep thrusts would bog down in the endless wastes of Central Asia, and would, in any case, merely be punches in a void. These geostrategic factors would have a decisive effect on the conduct and the forms of land military operations.

Russia lost the war with Japan (1904–5) mainly because of adverse logistic conditions. The carrying capacity of the single-track Trans-Siberian Railroad was inadequate to meet the requirements of Russia's strategic concentration and assure supply in Manchuria. Profiting from this experience, the Soviet Government has followed a policy that attempts to make the eastern Siberian provinces self-sufficient militarily, in order, as far as possible, to assure the defense of this area without help from European Russia.

The Trans-Siberian Railroad was turned into a two-track system, and supplemented by a motor highway. The plan to build a second railroad line farther north has not yet been carried out. A disadvantage for the Russians is the fact that the Trans-Siberian Railroad, in following the Amur River, runs for a long distance in the immediate vicinity of the Chinese border.

The development of the defense system of eastern Siberia, which was originally directed against the Japanese and designed to be as nearly self-sufficient as possible, required the construction of many new industries. Giant integrated industrial complexes presumably would be able to supply about one-third of the matériel requirements of the front, but two-thirds of the supplies would still have to be brought from European Russia. The oil wells and refineries of Sakhalin Island are theoretically sufficient to supply the entire motor fuel needs of the eastern sector by means of existing pipelines.

It is even conceivable that the Soviet Union and the United States might sign a "lend-lease pact" similar to that of World War II. Ships of the Western powers could carry war matériel, and other strategic commodities, to Russia's European ports, as well as to Vladivostok.

Suspicious as the Russians would still be of the West, they have the shield afforded by the Warsaw Pact countries.

Even if, owing to outside assistance, China's industrialization should make rapid progress, China would certainly remain technologically inferior to the Soviet Union for several decades. China's major industrial concentrations are situated mainly in the North —in Manchuria, and in the Peking and Shanghai areas—and they would be difficult to defend against air attacks.

In order to interdict the arms smuggling traffic to China along the Pacific coast, the Russians would have to establish a naval blockade. It is doubtful, however, whether effective policing of the 4,800-mile stretch between Vladivostok and Saigon could be accomplished by this means. Among possible centers of arms smuggling traffic would be Japan, Korea, the Philippines, Viet-Nam, Malaysia, and Burma.

Manning the 4,300-mile land front between Turkestan and Vladivostok could require up to 250 to 300 divisions—that is, including air forces, some 10 to 15 million men. The Russians could, perhaps, raise that number on the basis of their present military system. The relatively large number of units would be necessary not only for offensive operations, but for defense, and even to secure large areas of Russian Central Asia against infiltration attempts and guerrilla operations.

There is no doubt that the principal theater of a Sino-Soviet war would again be Manchuria, where a relatively highly developed communications network would afford the easiest access to the most vital centers of the Middle Kingdom. The Russians would probably attempt to seize Manchuria as they did in 1945, by a maneuver of three converging thrusts—from the west, north, and east. Their next objective would probably be Peking, which, in a second phase, could be captured by a pincers movement carried out from the north (through Manchuria) and the west (through Mongolia). This would mean a 1,200-mile-deep penetration into China.

But would these operations suffice to achieve victory in the war? South and Central China would be able, despite the loss of the North, to continue fighting for years after that.

The deeper the spearheads of the Soviet attack penetrated into China, the weaker their thrust would become. The security requirements of the overextended supply lines, and the policing of vast areas against partisans, would present unconquerable problems even to a country as rich in manpower as Russia. A guerrilla war of unprecedented dimensions could easily explode in the rear of the Soviet army.

All victories of the Russian regular forces notwithstanding, a struggle lasting years, and virtually impossible to win, would be difficult to avoid. Faced with such a situation, might not the Russians rather choose a single all-destroying atomic blow?

Critically important would be the question whether China already had a stock of atomic weapons at the time of the outbreak of war. Because the Russians have available only the two-track Trans-Siberian Railroad and a motor highway, their supply system is extremely vulnerable. Should the Chinese have achieved an atomic delivery capacity up to a range of 1,000 miles, they could threaten not only these communication lines but also the industrial centers of Russian Asia farther west. To threaten European Russia, the Chinese would need missiles or aircraft with a range of up to 3,000 miles.

In the field of conventional warfare, the Chinese would seek mainly to operate through their overwhelming manpower superiority; they would probably develop a large-scale infiltration strategy with the objective of establishing tenacious footholds in Russian territory. The political situation in Muslim Turkestan is uncertain, and Peking might seek to incite revolts.

Chinese operations with regular military forces on any large scale could, at most, be expected in the eastern sector, where the Chinese might employ their forces—which, though technically inferior, would be vastly superior in strength to the Russians—in an attempt to capture, by surprise, the East Siberian Maritime Province with the cities of Vladivostok, Komsomolsk, and Khabarovsk.

In order to mount such an offensive (while at the same time securing their border and protecting the Peking area), the Chinese would need at least 50 divisions with modern equipment, supported by 5,000 aircraft. They are not likely to have these forces before 1975.

Appendix A

In this annex, the full text of the Sino-Soviet Treaty of August 14, 1945, is reproduced, along with several other agreements, reached at the same time, pertinent to the subject matter of the present book.

Treaty of Friendship and Alliance Between the Republic of China and the U.S.S.R. (August 14, 1945)

The President of the National Government of the Republic of China, and the Presidium of the Supreme Soviet of the U.S.S.R.,

Desirous of strengthening the friendly relations that have always existed between China and the U.S.S.R., through an alliance and good neighborly postwar collaboration,

Determined to assist each other in the struggle against aggression on the part of enemies of the United Nations in this world war, and to collaborate in the common war against Japan until her unconditional surrender,

Expressing their unswerving aspiration to cooperate in the cause of maintaining peace and security for the benefit of the peoples of both countries and of all the peace-loving nations,

Acting upon the principles enunciated in the joint declaration of the United Nations of January 1, 1942, in the four power Declaration signed in Moscow on October 30, 1943, and in the Charter of the International Organization of the United Nations,

Have decided to conclude the present Treaty to this effect and appointed as their plenipotentiaries:

The President of the National Government of the Republic of China;
His Excellency Dr. Wang Shih-chieh, Minister for Foreign Affairs of the
    Republic of China,
The Presidium of the Supreme Soviet of the U.S.S.R.;
His Excellency Mr. V. M. Molotov, the People's Commissar of Foreign
    Affairs of the U.S.S.R.,
Who, after exchanging their Full Powers, found in good and due form, have agreed as follows:

ARTICLE I: The High Contracting Parties undertake in association with the other United Nations to wage war against Japan until final victory is won. The High Contracting Parties undertake mutually to render to one another all necessary military and other assistance and support in this war.

ARTICLE II: The High Contracting Parties undertake not to enter into separate negotiations with Japan and not to conclude, without mutual consent, any armistice or peace treaty either with the present Japanese Government or with any other government or authority set up in Japan which do not renounce all aggressive intentions.

ARTICLE III: The High Contracting Parties undertake after the termination of the war against Japan to take jointly all measures in their power to render impossible a repetition of aggression and violation of the peace by Japan.

In the event of one of the High Contracting Parties becoming involved in hostilities with Japan in consequence of an attack by the latter against the said High Contracting Party, the other High Contracting Party shall at once give to the High Contracting Party so involved in hostilities all the military and other support and assistance with the means in its power.

This article shall remain in force until such time as the organization "The United Nations" may on request of the two High Contracting Parties be charged with the responsibility for preventing further aggression by Japan.

ARTICLE IV: Each High Contracting Party undertakes not to conclude any alliance and not to take any part in any coalition directed against the other High Contracting Party.

ARTICLE V: The High Contracting Parties, having regard to the interests of the security and economic development of each of them, agree to work together in close and friendly collaboration after the coming of peace and to act according to the principles of mutual respect for their sovereignty and territorial integrity and of noninterference in the internal affairs of the other contracting party.

ARTICLE VI: The High Contracting Parties agree to render each other every possible economic assistance in the postwar period with a view to facilitating and accelerating reconstruction in both countries and to contributing to the cause of world prosperity.

ARTICLE VII: Nothing in this treaty shall be so construed as may affect the rights or obligations of the High Contracting Parties as members of the organization "The United Nations."

ARTICLE VIII: The present Treaty shall be ratified in the shortest possible time. The exchange of the instruments of ratification shall take place as soon as possible in Chungking.

The Treaty comes into force immediately upon its ratification and shall remain in force for a term of thirty years.

If neither of the High Contracting Parties has given notice, a year before the expiration of the term, of its desire to terminate the Treaty, it shall remain valid for an unlimited time, each of the High Contracting Parties being able to terminate its operation by giving notice to that effect one year in advance.

In faith whereof the Plenipotentiaries have signed the present Treaty and affixed their seals to it.

Done in Moscow, the Fourteenth August, 1945, corresponding to the Fourteenth day of the Eighth month of the Thirty-fourth year of the Chinese Republic, in two copies, each one in the Russian and Chinese languages, both texts being equally authoritative.

The Plenipotentiary of the Supreme Soviet of the U.S.S.R.

The Plenipotentiary of the President of the National Government of the Republic of China.

The People's Commissar for Foreign Affairs (Molotov) to the Chinese Minister for Foreign Affairs (Wang)

August 14, 1945

Your Excellency, With reference to the Treaty of Friendship and Alliance signed today between the Republic of China and the U.S.S.R., I have the honor to put on record the understanding between the High Contracting Parties as follows:

1. In accordance with the spirit of the aforementioned Treaty, and in order to put into effect its aims and purposes, the Government of the U.S.S.R. agrees to render to China moral support and aid in military supplies and other material resources, such support and aid to be entirely given to the National Government as the central government of China.

2. In the course of conversations regarding Dairen and Port Arthur and regarding the joint operation of the Chinese Changchun Railway, the Government of the U.S.S.R. regarded the Three Eastern Provinces [Manchuria] as part of China and reaffirmed its respect for China's full sovereignty over the Three Eastern Provinces and recognized their territorial and administrative integrity.

3. As for the recent developments in Sinkiang the Soviet Government confirms that, as stated in Article V of the Treaty of Friendship and Alliance, it has no intention of interfering in the internal affairs of China.

If Your Excellency will be so good as to confirm that the understanding is correct as set forth in the preceding paragraphs, the present note and Your Excellency's reply thereto will constitute a part of the aforementioned Treaty of Friendship and Alliance.

I take [etc.]

V. M. Molotov

*The Chinese Minister for Foreign Affairs (Wang) to the People's
Commissar for Foreign Affairs (Molotov)*

August 14, 1945

Your Excellency: I have the honor to acknowledge receipt of Your Excellency's Note of today's date reading as follows:

"With reference to the Treaty of Friendship and Alliance signed today between the Republic of China and the U.S.S.R., I have the honor to put on record the understanding between the High Contracting Parties as follows:

"1. In accordance with the spirit of the aforementioned Treaty, and in order to put into effect its aims and purposes, the Government of the U.S.S.R. agrees to render to China moral support and aid in military supplies and other material resources, such support and aid to be entirely given to the National Government as the central Government of China.

"2. In the course of conversations regarding Dairen and Port Arthur and regarding the joint operation of the Chinese Changchun Railway, the Government of the U.S.S.R. regarded the Three Eastern Provinces as part of China and reaffirmed its respect for China's full sovereignty over the Three Eastern Provinces and recognized their territorial and administrative integrity.

"3. As for the recent developments in Sinkiang the Soviet Government confirms that, as stated in Article V of the Treaty of Friendship and Alliance, it has no intention of interfering in the internal affairs of China.

"If Your Excellency will be so good as to confirm that the understanding is correct as set fourth in the preceding paragraphs, the present note, and Your Excellency's reply thereto will constitute a part of the aforementioned Treaty of Friendship and Alliance."

I have the honor to confirm that the understanding is correct as set forth above.

I avail [etc.]

Wang Shih-Chieh

Agreement on Port Arthur

In conformity with and for the implementation of the Treaty of Friendship and Alliance between the Republic of China and the U.S.S.R., the High Contracting Parties have agreed as follows:

ARTICLE I: With a view to strengthening the security of China and the U.S.S.R. against further aggression by Japan, the Government of the Republic of China agrees to the joint use of the two countries of Port Arthur as a naval base.

ARTICLE II: The precise boundary of the area provided in Article I is described in the Annex and shown in the map (Annex 1). [Map not reproduced —R.L.G.]

ARTICLE III: The High Contracting Parties agree that Port Arthur, as an exclusive naval base, will be used only by Chinese and Soviet military and commercial vessels.

There shall be established a Sino-Soviet Military Commission to handle the matters of joint use of the above-mentioned naval base. The Commission shall consist of two Chinese and three Soviet representatives. The chairman of the Commission shall be appointed by the Soviet side and the Vice Chairman shall be appointed by the Chinese side.

ARTICLE IV: The Chinese Government entrusts to the Soviet Government the defense of the naval base. The Soviet Government may erect at its own expense such installations as are necessary for the defense of the naval base.

ARTICLE V: The Civil Administration of the whole area will be Chinese. The leading posts of the Civil Administration will be appointed by the Chinese Government taking into account Soviet interests in the area.

The leading posts of the civil administration in the city of Port Arthur are appointed and dismissed by the Chinese Government in agreement with the Soviet military command.

The proposals which the Soviet military commander in that area may address to the Chinese civil administration in order to safeguard security and defense will be fulfilled by the said administration. In cases of disagreement, such cases shall be submitted to the Sino-Soviet Military Commission for consideration and decision.

ARTICLE VI: The Government of the U.S.S.R. has the right to maintain in the region mentioned in Article II, their army, navy and air force and to determine their location.

ARTICLE VII: The Government of the U.S.S.R. also undertakes to establish and keep up lighthouses and other installations and signs necessary for the security of navigation of the area.

ARTICLE VIII: After the termination of this agreement all the installations and public property installed or constructed by the U.S.S.R. in the area shall revert without compensation to the Chinese Government.

ARTICLE IX: The present agreement is concluded for thirty years. It comes into force on the day of its ratification.

In faith whereof the plenipotentiaries of the High Contracting Parties have signed the present agreement and affixed thereto their seals. The present agreement is made in two copies, each in the Russian and Chinese language, both texts being authoritative.

Done in Moscow, August 14, 1945, corresponding to the 14th day of the 8th month of the 34th year of the Chinese Republic.

The Plenipotentiary of the Presidium of the Supreme Soviet of the U.S.S.R.	The Plenipotentiary of the President of the National Government of the Republic of China.

Appendix to "Agreement on Port Arthur" Signed in Moscow
(August 14, 1945)

The territory of the area of the naval base provided for by paragraph II of the Agreement on Port Arthur is situated south of the line which begins on the west coast of Liaotung Peninsula—south of Housantaowan—and follows a general easterly direction across Shihe Station and the point of Tsoukiachutse to the east coast of the same peninsula, excluding the town of Dalny (Dairen).

All the islands situated in the waters adjoining the west side of the area on Liaotung Peninsula established by the Agreement, and south of the line passing through the points 39°00' North latitude, 120°49' East longitude; 39°20' North latitude, 121°31' East longitude, and beyond in a general northeasterly direction along the axis of the fairway leading to port Pulantien to the initial point on land, are included in the area of the naval base.

All the islands situated within the waters adjoining the eastern part of the area of Liaotung Peninsula and south of the line passing from the terminal point on land in an easterly direction toward the point 39°20' North latitude, 123°08' East longitude, and farther southeast through the point 39°00' North latitude, 123°16' East longitude, are included in the area. (See attached map, scale 1:500,000.) [Map not attached—RLG]

The boundary line of the district will be demarcated on the spot by a mixed Soviet-Chinese Commission. The Commission shall establish the boundary posts and, when need arises, buoys on the water, compile a detailed description of this line, enter it on a topographical map drawn to the scale of 1:25,000, and the water boundary on a naval map drawn to the scale of 1:300,000.

The time when the Commission shall start its work is subject to special agreement between the parties.

Descriptions of the boundary line of the area and the maps of this line compiled by the above Commission are subject to approval by both Governments.

W. S.   V. M.

*Agreement Regarding Relations between the Chinese Administration
and the Commander in Chief of the Soviet Forces After the Entry
of Soviet Troops Into the "Three Eastern Provinces" * of China
During the Present Joint Military Operations Against Japan*

The President of the National Government of China and the Presidium of
the Supreme Council of the Union of Soviet Socialist Republics, desirous
that relations between the Chinese Administration and the Commander in
Chief of the Soviet forces after the entry of Soviet troops into the "Three
Eastern Provinces" of China during the present joint military operations
against Japan should be governed by the spirit of friendship and alliance
existing between the two countries, have agreed on the following:

1. After the Soviet troops enter the "Three Eastern Provinces" of China
as a result of military operations, the supreme authority and responsibility
in all matters relating to the prosecution of the war will be vested, in the zone
of operations for the time required for the operations, in the Commander in
Chief of the Soviet forces.

2. A Chinese National Government representative and staff will be appointed for the recovered territory, whose duties will be:

(a) To establish and direct, in accordance with the laws of China, an
administration for the territory cleared of the enemy.

(b) To establish the cooperation between the Chinese armed forces, both
regular and irregular, and the Soviet forces in recovered territory.

(c) To ensure the active cooperation of the Chinese administration with
the Commander in Chief of the Soviet forces and, specifically, to give the
local authorities directions to this effect, being guided by the requirements and
wishes of the Commander in Chief of the Soviet forces.

3. To ensure contact between the Commander in Chief of the Soviet
forces and the Chinese National Government representative a Chinese
military mission will be appointed to the Commander in Chief of the Soviet
forces.

4. In the zones under the supreme authority of the Commander in Chief of
the Soviet forces, the Chinese National Government administration for the
recovered territory will maintain contact with the Commander in Chief of
the Soviet forces through the Chinese National Government representative.

5. As soon as any part of the liberated territory ceases to be a zone of
immediate military operations, the Chinese National Government will assume
full authority in the direction of public affairs and will render the Commander in Chief of the Soviet forces every assistance and support through its
civil and military bodies.

6. All persons belonging to the Soviet forces on Chinese territory will be
under the jurisdiction of the Commander in Chief of the Soviet forces. All
Chinese, whether civilian or military, will be under Chinese jurisdiction.

* Manchuria.

This jurisdiction will also extend to the civilian population on Chinese territory even in the case of offenses against the Soviet armed forces, with the exception of offenses committed in the zone of military operations under the jurisdiction of the Commander in Chief of the Soviet forces. In disputable cases the question will be settled by mutual agreement between the Chinese National Government representative and the Commander in Chief of the Soviet forces.

7. With regard to currency matters after the entry of Soviet troops into the "Three Eastern Provinces" of China, a separate agreement shall be reached.

8. The present Agreement comes into force immediately upon the ratification of the Treaty of Friendship and Alliance between China and the U.S.S.R. signed this day. The Agreement has been done in two copies, each in the Chinese and Russian languages. Both texts are equally valid.

On the Authorization of the National Government of the Republic of China.

On the Authorization of the Government of the Union of Soviet Socialist Republics.

Agreement Between the Republic of China and the U.S.S.R. Concerning the Chinese Changchun Railway

The President of the Republic of China and the Presidium of the Supreme Council of the U.S.S.R., desiring to strengthen the friendly relations and economic bonds between the two countries on the basis of the full observation of the rights and interests of each other, have agreed as follows:

ARTICLE I: After the Japanese armed forces are driven out of the Three Eastern Provinces of China, the trunk line of the Chinese Eastern Railway and the South Manchurian Railway from Manchuli to Suifenho and from Harbin to Dairen and Port Arthur united into one railway under the name "Chinese Changchun Railway" shall be in joint ownership of the U.S.S.R. and the Republic of China and shall be operated by them jointly.

There shall be joint ownership and operation only of those lands acquired and railway auxiliary lines built by the Chinese Eastern Railway during the time of Russian and joint Sino-Soviet administration and by the South Manchurian Railway during the time of Russian administration and which are designed for direct needs of these railways as well as the subsidiary enterprises built during the said periods and directly serving these railways. All the other railway branches, subsidiary enterprises and lands shall be in the complete ownership of the Chinese Government.

The joint operation of the aforementioned railway shall be undertaken by a single management under Chinese sovereignty and as a purely commercial transportation enterprise.

ARTICLE II: The High Contracting parties agree that their joint ownership of the railway shall be in equal shares and shall not be alienable in whole or in part.

ARTICLE III: The High Contracting parties agree that for the joint operation of the said railway the Sino-Soviet Company of the Chinese Changchun Railway shall be formed. The Company shall have a Board of Directors to be composed of ten members of whom five shall be appointed by the Chinese Government and five by the Soviet Government. The Board of Directors shall be in Changchun.

ARTICLE IV: The Chinese Government shall appoint one of the Chinese Directors as President of the Board of Directors and one as the Assistant President. The Soviet Government shall appoint one of the Soviet Directors as Vice-President of the Board of Directors, and one as the Assistant Vice-President. Seven persons shall constitute a quorum. When questions are decided by the Board, the vote of the President of the Board of Directors shall be counted as two votes.

Questions on which the Board of Directors cannot reach an agreement shall be submitted to the Governments of the Contracting Parties for consideration and settlement in an equitable and friendly spirit.

ARTICLE V: The Company shall establish a Board of Auditors which shall be composed of six members of whom three are appointed by the Chinese Government and three appointed by the Soviet Government. The Chairman of the Board of Auditors shall be elected from among the Soviet Auditors, and Vice-Chairman from among the Chinese auditors. When questions are decided by the Board the vote of the Chairman shall be counted as two votes. Five persons shall constitute a quorum.

ARTICLE VI: For the administration of current affairs the Board of Directors shall appoint a manager of the Chinese Changchun Railway from among Soviet citizens and one assistant manager from among Chinese citizens.

ARTICLE VII: The Board of Auditors shall appoint a General Comptroller from among Chinese citizens, and an Assistant General Comptroller from among Soviet citizens.

ARTICLE VIII: The Chiefs and Assistant Chiefs of the various departments, Chiefs of sections, station masters at important stations of the railway shall be appointed by the Board of Directors. The Manager of the Railway has right to recommend candidates for the above-mentioned posts. Individual members of the Board of Directors may also recommend such candidates in agreement with the Manager. If the Chief of a department is a national of China, the Assistant Chief shall be a national of the Soviet Union, and vice versa. The appointment of the Chiefs and Assistant Chiefs of departments and Chiefs of sections and station masters shall be made in accordance with the principle of equal representation between the nationals of China and nationals of the Soviet Union.

ARTICLE IX: The Chinese Government will bear the responsibility for the protection of the said Railway.

The Chinese Government will also organize and supervise the railway guards who shall protect the railway buildings, installations and other properties and freight from destruction, loss and robbery, and shall maintain the normal order on the railway. As regards the duties of the police in execution of this Article, they will be determined by the Chinese Government in consultation with the Soviet Government.

ARTICLE X: Only during the time of war against Japan the railway may be used for the transportation of Soviet troops. The Soviet Government has the right to transport by the above-mentioned railway for transit purpose military goods in sealed cars without customs inspection. The guarding of such military goods shall be undertaken by the railroad police and the Soviet Union shall not send any armed escort.

ARTICLE XI: Goods for through transit and transported by the Chinese Changchun Railway from Manchuli to Suifenho or vice versa and also from Soviet territory to the ports of Dairen and Port Arthur or vice versa shall be free from Chinese Customs duties or any other taxes and dues, but on entering Chinese territory such goods shall be subject to Chinese Customs inspection and verification.

ARTICLE XII: The Chinese Government shall ensure, on the basis of a separate agreement, that the supply of coal for the operation of the railway will be fully secured.

ARTICLE XIII: The railway shall pay taxes to the Government of the Republic of China the same as are paid by the Chinese state railways.

ARTICLE XIV: Both Contracting Parties agree to provide the Board of Directors of the Chinese Changchun Railway with working capital the amount of which will be determined by the Statute of the Railway.

Profits and losses and exploitation of the railway shall be equally divided between the Parties.

ARTICLE XV: For the working out in Chungking of the Statutes of joint operation of the railway the High Contracting Parties undertake within one month of the signing of the present Agreement, to appoint their representatives—three representatives from each Party. The Statute shall be worked out within two months and reported to the two Governments for their approval.

ARTICLE XVI: The determination, in accordance with the provisions in Article I, of the properties to be included in the joint ownership and operations of the railway by China and the U.S.S.R. shall be made by a Commission to be composed of three representatives each of the two Governments. The Commission shall be constituted in Chungking within one month after the signing of the present Agreement and shall terminate its work within three months after the joint operation of the railway shall have begun.

The decision of the Commission shall be reported to the two Governments for their approval.

ARTICLE XVII: The term of this present Agreement shall be thirty years. After the expiration of the term of the present Agreement, the Chinese Changchun Railway with all its properties shall be transferred without compensation to the ownership of the Republic of China.

ARTICLE XVIII: The present Agreement shall come into force from the date of its ratification.

Done in Moscow, August 14, 1945, corresponding to the 14th day of the 8th month of the 34th year of the Chinese Republic, in two copies each in the Russian and Chinese languages, both texts being equally authoritative.

The Plenipotentiary of the President of the National Government of the Republic of China.

The Plenipotentiary of the Presidium of the Supreme Soviet of the U.S.S.R.

Appendix B

The full texts of the Sino-Soviet Treaty of 1950, and the most relevant accompanying documents, are given in this annex. The subsequent agreements of 1952 and 1954 first extending, and then terminating, the Soviet military base rights at Port Arthur are also given. All are unofficial translations of official texts in Chinese and Russian.

*Treaty of Friendship, Alliance, and Mutual Assistance Between
The People's Republic of China and the U.S.S.R.*
(February 14, 1950)

The Central People's Government of the People's Republic of China and the Presidium of the Supreme Soviet of the Union of Soviet Socialist Republics;

Fully determined jointly to prevent, by strengthening friendship and cooperation between the People's Republic of China and the Union of Soviet Socialist Republics, the revival of Japanese imperialism and the resumption of aggression on the part of Japan or any other state that may collaborate in any way with Japan in acts of aggression;

Imbued with the desire to consolidate lasting peace and universal security in the Far East and throughout the world in conformity with the aims and principles of the United Nations;

Profoundly convinced that the consolidation of good neighborly relations and friendship between the People's Republic of China and the Union of Soviet Socialist Republics meets the vital interests of the peoples of China and the Soviet Union;

Resolved toward this end to conclude the present Treaty and have appointed as their plenipotentiary representatives:

Chou En-lai, Premier of the Government Administration Council and Minister of Foreign Affairs, acting for the Central People's Government of the People's Republic of China; and Andrei Yanuaryevich Vyshinsky, Minister of Foreign Affairs of the U.S.S.R., acting for the Presidium of the Supreme Soviet of the Union of Soviet Socialist Republics.

Both plenipotentiary representatives having communicated their full powers, and found them in good and due form, have agreed upon the following:

ARTICLE I: Both High Contracting Parties undertake jointly to adopt all necessary measures at their disposal for the purpose of preventing the resump-

214

tion of aggression and violation of peace on the part of Japan or any other state that may collaborate with Japan directly or indirectly in acts of aggression. In the event of one of the High Contracting Parties being attacked by Japan or any state allied with her, and thus being involved in a state of war, the other High Contracting Party shall immediately render military and other assistance by all means at its disposal.

The High Contracting Parties also declare their readiness to participate in a spirit of sincere cooperation in all international actions aimed at ensuring peace and security throughout the world, and to contribute their full share to the earliest implementation of these tasks.

ARTICLE II: Both High Contracting Parties undertake in a spirit of mutual agreement to bring about the earliest conclusion of a peace treaty with Japan, jointly with the other powers which were allies in the Second World War.

ARTICLE III: Both High Contracting Parties undertake not to conclude any alliance directed against the other High Contracting Party, and not to take part in any coalition or in any actions or measures directed against the other High Contracting Party.

ARTICLE IV: Both High Contracting Parties will consult with each other in regard to all important international problems affecting the common interests of China and the Soviet Union, being guided by the interests of consolidating peace and universal security.

ARTICLE V: Both High Contracting Parties undertake, in a spirit of friendship and cooperation and in conformity with the principles of equality, mutual benefit, mutual respect for national sovereignty and territorial integrity, and noninterference in the internal affairs of the other High Contracting Party, to develop and consolidate economic and cultural ties between China and the Soviet Union, to render the other all possible economic assistance, and to carry out necessary economic cooperation.

ARTICLE VI: The present Treaty shall come into force immediately after its ratification; the exchange of instruments of ratification shall take place in Peking.*

The present Treaty shall be valid for thirty years. If neither of the High Contracting Parties gives notice a year before the expiration of this term of its intention to denounce the Treaty, it shall remain in force for another five years and shall be further extended in compliance with this provision.

Done in Moscow on February 14, 1950, in two copies, each in the Chinese and Russian languages, both texts being equally valid.

* The treaty was separately but simultaneously ratified by both Governments on April 11, 1950; the instruments of ratification were exchanged in Peking on September 30, 1950.

On the authorization of the
Central People's Government of
the People's Republic of China

Chou En-lai

On the authorization of the Presidium of the Supreme Soviet of
the Union of Soviet Socialist Republics

A. Ya. Vyshinsky

Agreement Between the People's Republic of China and the U.S.S.R.
Concerning the Chinese Changchun Railway, Port Arthur
and Dairen
(February 14, 1950)

The Central People's Government of the People's Republic of China and
the Presidium of the Supreme Soviet of the Union of Soviet Socialist Republics record that since 1945 fundamental changes have occurred in the
situation in the Far East, namely: Imperialist Japan has suffered defeat;
the reactionary Kuomintang Government has been overthrown; China has
become a People's Democratic Republic; a new People's Government has
been established in China which has unified the whole of China, has carried
out a policy of friendship and cooperation with the Soviet Union, and has
proved its ability to defend the national independence and territorial integrity
of China and the national honor and dignity of the Chinese people.

The Central People's Government of the People's Republic of China and
the Presidium of the Supreme Soviet of the Union of Soviet Socialist Republics consider that this new situation permits a new approach to the question of the Chinese Changchun Railway, Port Arthur, and Dairen.

In conformity with these new circumstances, the Central People's Government of the People's Republic of China and the Presidium of the Supreme
Soviet of the Union of Soviet Socialist Republics have decided to conclude
the present Agreement on the Chinese Changchun Railway, Port Arthur, and
Dairen:

ARTICLE I: Both High Contracting Parties agree that the Soviet Government transfer without compensation to the Government of the People's
Republic of China all its rights in the joint administration of the Chinese
Changchun Railway, together with all the property belonging to the Railway. The transfer shall be effected immediately upon the conclusion of a
peace treaty with Japan, but not later than the end of 1952.

Pending the transfer, the existing Sino-Soviet joint administration of the Chinese Changchun Railway shall remain unchanged. After this Agreement becomes effective, posts (such as Manager of the Railway, Chairman of the Board of Directors, and others) will be periodically alternated between representatives of China and the U.S.S.R.

As regards concrete methods of effecting the transfer, they shall be agreed upon and determined by the Governments of both High Contracting Parties.

ARTICLE II: Both High Contracting Parties agree that Soviet troops shall be withdrawn from the jointly utilized naval base of Port Arthur, and that the installations in this area be handed over to the Government of the People's Republic of China, immediately upon the conclusion of a peace treaty with Japan, but not later than the end of 1952. The Government of the People's Republic of China will compensate the Soviet Union for expenses which it has incurred in restoring and constructing installations since 1945.

For the period pending the withdrawal of Soviet troops and the transfer of the above-mentioned installations, the Governments of China and the Soviet Union will each appoint an equal number of military representatives to form a joint Chinese-Soviet Military Commission which will be alternately presided over by each side and which will be in charge of military affairs in the area of Port Arthur; concrete measures in this sphere will be drawn up by the joint Chinese-Soviet Military Commission within three months after the present Agreement comes into force, and shall be implemented upon approval of these measures by the Governments of both countries.

The civil administration in the aforementioned area shall be under the direct authority of the Government of the People's Republic of China. Pending the withdrawal of Soviet troops, the zone for billeting Soviet troops in the area of Port Arthur will remain unaltered in conformity with existing borders.

In the event that either of the High Contracting Parties becomes the victim of aggression on the part of Japan or any state that may collaborate with Japan, and as a result thereof becomes involved in hostilities, China, and the Soviet Union may, on the proposal of the Government of the People's Republic of China and with the agreement of the Government of the U.S.S.R., jointly use the naval base of Port Arthur for the purpose of conducting joint military operations against the aggressor.

ARTICLE III: Both High Contracting Parties agree that the question of Dairen Port be further considered on the conclusion of a peace treaty with Japan. As regards the administration of Dairen, it is in the hands of the Government of the People's Republic of China.

All the property in Dairen now temporarily administered by or leased to the Soviet Union, shall be taken over by the Government of the People's Republic of China. To carry out the transfer of the aforementioned property, the Governments of China and the Soviet Union shall appoint three representatives each to form a Joint Commission which, within three months after the present Agreement comes into effect, shall draw up concrete measures for the transfer of the property; these measures proposed by the Joint Commission shall be fully carried out in the course of 1950 after their approval by the Governments of both countries.

ARTICLE IV: The present Agreement shall come into force on the day of its ratification. The exchange of instruments of ratification shall take place in Peking.

Done in Moscow on February 14, 1950, in two copies, each in the Chinese and Russian languages, both texts being equally valid.

> On the authorization of the Central People's Government of the People's Republic of China
>
> Chou En-lai
>
> On the authorization of the Presidium of the Supreme Soviet of the Union of Soviet Socialist Republics
>
> A. Ya. Vyshinsky

Exchange of Notes Between the People's Republic of China and the U.S.S.R. Extending Soviet Participation in the Joint Use of the Chinese Naval Base at Port Arthur
(September 15, 1952)

Dear Comrade Minister:

Inasmuch as Japan has refused to conclude an over-all peace treaty and concluded a separate treaty with the United States and certain other countries, as a result of which Japan has not and apparently does not want to have any peace treaty with the People's Republic of China and the Soviet Union, conditions dangerous to the cause of peace and favorable for recurrence of Japanese aggression have arisen.

In view of this and for the purpose of ensuring peace, and also on the basis of the Treaty of Friendship, Alliance, and Mutual Assistance between the People's Republic of China and the Union of Soviet Socialist Republics, the Government of the People's Republic of China suggests and asks the Soviet Government to agree to postpone the withdrawal of the Soviet troops from the jointly used Chinese naval base of Port Arthur, provided for in

Article Two of the Sino-Soviet Agreement on Port Arthur, until the time when a peace treaty between the People's Republic of China and Japan and a peace treaty between the Soviet Union and Japan are concluded.

If the Soviet Government agrees to the aforestated proposal of the Government of the People's Republic of China, the present note and your note of reply will be regarded as a competent part of the agreement of February 14, 1950, between the People's Republic of China and the U.S.S.R. concerning the naval base of Port Arthur, and will go into force on the day of the exchange of notes.

I beg you, Comrade Minister, to accept assurances of my profound respect for you.

September 15, 1952

Chou En-lai

A. Ya. Vyshinsky,
Minister of Foreign Affairs
Union of Soviet Socialist Republics

Dear Comrade Premier and Minister:

I acknowledge the receipt of your note of September 15th of the current year which says:

Inasmuch as Japan has refused to conclude an over-all peace treaty and concluded a separate treaty with the United States and certain other countries, as a result of which Japan has not and apparently does not want to have any peace treaty with the People's Republic of China and the Soviet Union, conditions dangerous to the cause of peace and favorable for recurrence of Japanese aggression have arisen.

In view of this and for the purpose of ensuring peace, and also on the basis of the Treaty of Friendship, Alliance, and Mutual Assistance between the People's Republic of China and the Union of Soviet Socialist Republics, the Government of the People's Republic of China suggests and asks the Soviet Government to agree to postpone the withdrawal of the Soviet troops from the jointly used Chinese naval base of Port Arthur, provided for in Article Two of the Sino-Soviet Agreement on Port Arthur, until a time when a peace treaty between the People's Republic of China and Japan and a peace treaty between the Soviet Union and Japan are concluded.

The Soviet Government agrees to the aforementioned proposal of the Government of the People's Republic of China and also to the proposal that your note and this reply to it become a component part of the aforementioned agreement of February 14th, 1950, concerning the naval base of Port Arthur from the day of exchange of these notes.

I beg you, Comrade Premier and Minister, to accept assurances of my profound respect for you.

September 15, 1952

A. Ya. Vyshinsky

Chou En-lai,
Premier, State Administrative Council, and
Minister of Foreign Affairs,
Central People's Government,
Chinese People's Republic

Joint Communiqué on the Transfer of Soviet Rights in the Management of the Chinese Changchun Railway to the People's Republic of China
(September 15, 1952)

In accordance with the established relations of friendship and cooperation between the People's Republic of China and the U.S.S.R., an Agreement on the Chinese-Changchun Railway was signed in Moscow on February 14, 1950, under which the Soviet Government transfers without compensation to the Government of the People's Republic of China all its rights to point administration of the Chinese-Changchun Railway together with all property belonging to the railway. Under this agreement the transfer of the aforementioned Chinese-Changchun Railway shall be effected not later than by the end of 1952.

At present the Government of the People's Republic of China and the Soviet Government have begun carrying out measures for implementing this agreement and with this end in view have agreed to form a joint Sino-Soviet Commission.

The joint Sino-Soviet Commission shall complete the transfer of the Chinese-Changchun Railway to the People's Republic of China not later than by December 31, 1952.

Joint Communiqué of the People's Republic of China and the U.S.S.R. on the Withdrawal of Soviet Armed Forces from the Port Arthur Naval Base Area
(October 12, 1954)

The Government of the People's Republic of China and the Government of the Soviet Union, in view of the changes in the international situation in the Far East following the termination of the war in Korea and the strengthened national defenses of the People's Republic of China, and in the light of the relations of friendship and cooperation between the two countries which are being daily strengthened, have agreed that Soviet armed forces will withdraw from the jointly used naval base of Port Arthur and that the installations in this area be transferred without compensation to the Government of the People's Republic of China.

Both sides agree that the joint Sino-Soviet Commission at Port Arthur set up in accordance with the agreement of February 14, 1950, be responsible for carrying out measures connected with the withdrawal of Soviet armed forces and the transfer of the installations in the area of the Port Arthur naval base to the Government of the People's Republic of China.

The withdrawal of the Soviet armed forces and the transfer of the installations in the area of the Port Arthur naval base to the Government of the People's Republic of China shall be completed by May 31, 1955.

Appendix C

While many of the statements made by both the Soviet and Chinese governments, Communist parties, and writers in the polemics of the past several years bear on Sino-Soviet military relations, and are used in the analyses presented in this volume, one in particular is a source worth citing in full: the following Chinese Government Statement of September 1, 1963.

Statement by the Spokesman of the Chinese Government
(Peking, September 1, 1963)

On August 21, the Soviet Government issued a statement in reply to the statement made by the spokesman of the Chinese Government on August 15. This Soviet statement is even less presentable than its forerunners. It is unable to advance a single logical argument in defense of the Soviet leaders' act of betrayal; it cannot answer any of the questions of substance we raised in our last statement. The only new element in it is its assertion that China wants to gain victory through the launching of thermonuclear war and to bring about the death of half of mankind. With this assertion, the latest slander campaign of the Soviet leaders against China plumbs new depths. Apparently the Soviet leaders have already become so degenerate that they now depend on telling lies for a living.

More and more facts bear witness that on the question of war and peace the Soviet leaders' theory is one of forbidding revolution and their practice is one of moving from adventurism to capitulationism, and the conclusion of the tripartite [nuclear test ban] treaty marks the further development of their capitulationism. And to cover all this up they are desperately distorting the Marxist-Leninist line of the Chinese Communist Party and the Chinese Government on the question of war and peace, asserting that China wants to impose its "adventurist program" on other countries.

The Soviet Government in its statement is insolent enough to say that we are able to criticize them only because China enjoys the protection of Soviet nuclear weapons. Well, then, leaders of the Soviet Union, please continue to protect us awhile with your nuclear weapons. We shall continue to criticize you, and we hope you will have the courage to argue the matter out with us.

In our statements of July 31 and August 15, we demonstrated irrefutably that in signing the tripartite treaty the Soviet leaders betrayed their original stand, betrayed the interests of the Soviet people, betrayed the interests of the peoples in the socialist camp, and betrayed the interests of the peoples

222

throughout the world. In its statement on August 3, the Soviet Government erected the shield of state sovereignty against this criticism of ours. Now they are erecting a shield out of national defense secrets. They say that what has changed are objective circumstances and not the Soviet leaders. And what were the changed circumstances? Ah! That cannot be divulged because it is a national defense secret.

This is sheer hypocrisy. National defense secret indeed! The simple fact is that after its tests in 1961 and 1962 the Soviet Union came into possession of the technical data which it needed. Who does not know this so-called national defense secret? That took place back in 1962, but as late as June 15, 1963, the Soviet leaders were still saying that the position of the West was unacceptable. How can the 180-degree turn made by the Soviet leaders after June 15, 1963, in betrayal of their original position be explained away by the change which took place in 1962?

With the conclusion of the tripartite [nuclear test ban] treaty, the Soviet statement asserts, at the worst the situation is the same as without the treaty. How can anyone say the treaty has increased the danger of war? The United States may conduct underground nuclear tests, but cannot the Soviet Union do the same?

This assertion can only delude people who do not look beyond the surface or are most naive. The essence of the matter is that the United States is in the lead in the field of underground nuclear testing. Without the tripartite treaty, the United States would have been condemned when it engaged in underground nuclear testing. The tripartite treaty legalizes underground nuclear testing, which precisely helps the United States maintain and improve on its lead.

In the short period since the conclusion of the tripartite treaty the United States has already conducted three underground nuclear tests. On August 24, the U.S. Defense Department submitted a program to the Senate, proposing a great increase in underground nuclear tests. Deputy Defense Secretary Gilpatric said:

> The underground testing program (of the United States) will be comprehensive. Therefore, it will be revised to include as many as feasible of the objectives of the tests which we would otherwise do under conditions of unrestricted testing, so as to ensure the highest practicable rate of progress in nuclear technology.

All this is shocking to people who are truly concerned about peace. How can the Soviet leaders pretend blindness?

The whole world knows that the tripartite treaty is designed to manacle all the socialist countries other than the Soviet Union and all the peace-loving countries, and that it has no restraining effect whatsoever on U.S. imperialism. It does not hinder the United States from using nuclear weapons in time of war, manufacturing and stockpiling nuclear weapons, and proliferating nuclear weapons among its allies. After the conclusion of the tripartite treaty, U.S. imperialism has continuously declared that it is not bound in any way, and the Soviet leaders have not uttered a sound of protest. The Soviet statement pretends ignorance of all this and maintains that the Soviet leaders' position on the question of preventing the proliferation of nuclear weapons is perfectly reasonable.

The Soviet statement says it would not mean much if one or two more socialist countries came into possession of nuclear weapons, but it would be terrible if one or two more capitalist countries did so; that the Soviet Union cannot on the one hand give nuclear weapons to China and on the other oppose the United States giving nuclear weapons to West Germany; and that if the Soviet Union did so, the United States would surely arm West Germany with nuclear weapons. The Soviet statement boastfully proclaims this to be the Soviet leaders' "principled stand" on the question of preventing nuclear proliferation.

My! What a "principled stand!" But let us see what this "principled stand" amounts to. Anyone with some knowledge of Marxism-Leninism who but slightly uses his head will see

—that it is a cowardly stand, which utterly despises the strength of one's own class brothers and holds in awe and veneration the strength of the imperialists;

—that it is an absurd stand, which puts the socialist camp and the imperialist camp on a par and makes no distinction between the enemy and ourselves; and

—that it is a reactionary stand, which implies that nuclear proliferation by U.S. imperialism is not for aggression but for defense and that the aggressive nature of imperialism has already changed.

Even a bourgeois statesman with some common sense understands that a commitment undertaken must be premised on a commitment accepted by the other party. The Soviet Union is not giving nuclear weapons to China, but has the United States undertaken an obligation not to arm West Germany with nuclear weapons?

In our view, the dogged adherence by the Soviet leaders to their "principled stand" is a matter of unrequited love. Look how pitiless the U.S. imperialists are. After signing the tripartite treaty, they noisily proceed with building up the NATO "multilateral nuclear force" and continue to ship nuclear weapons to West Germany. Where is there any sign of a commitment?

The tripartite treaty marks the surrender of the Soviet leaders to U.S. imperialism. It is rotten to the core. China of course cannot be a party to it.

The Soviet statement asserts that in refusing to sign this treaty, China is assuming the role of those in the right wing of the ranks of the U.S. "madmen," the West German revanchists, and the French extremists. If that is the case, do not Chiang Kai-shek, Adenauer, and Franco, who have signed, become left-wing forces of peace? So that is how matters stand! That is indeed a great discovery of the Soviet leaders!

Finding themselves unable to put up any defense for the tripartite treaty, the Soviet leaders resort to slandering China. One of the slanders is that China is opposed to the tripartite treaty because the Soviet Union has denied it the atom bomb. This is a deliberate distortion of China's position.

In our last statement we explained in detail how, as far back as 1959, the Soviet leaders made a gift to the United States of their refusal to provide China with the technical data required for the manufacture of nuclear weapons, but, for the sake of larger interests, we never mentioned this before, not even between fraternal parties. If it were not because the Soviet leaders have colluded with the U.S. imperialists in an effort to force China to undertake not to manufacture nuclear weapons, we would not have wanted to talk about this.

Our exposure has enraged the Soviet leaders, who declare that it amounts to divulgence of confidential documents and information relating to the defenses of the countries in the socialist camp, and that they will draw their own conclusions. Please do not pretend innocence. You know very well that long before we published our last statement you told the Americans the secrets between China and the Soviet Union concerning nuclear weapons.

As for drawing conclusions, have you not already done that long ago? Not only have you perfidiously and unilaterally scrapped the agreement on providing China with nuclear technical data, but you have blatantly given more and more military aid to the Indian reactionaries, who are hostile to China and have made incessant armed provocations against it. What is this if not your "own conclusions"?

The real point is that the Soviet leaders hold that China should not, and must not, manufacture nuclear weapons, and that only the few nuclear powers, and particularly U.S. imperialism, the enemy of the people of the whole world, are entitled to the continued production of nuclear weapons.

The Soviet statement asserts that China can rely on the nuclear weapons of the Soviet Union and need not manufacture them itself; that if it tries to manufacture them it will result in a great strain on China's economy.

Should or should not China itself master the means of resisting U.S. nuclear blackmail? True, if the Soviet leaders really practiced proletarian internationalism, it might not be necessary for China to manufacture its own nuclear weapons. But it is equally true that if the Soviet leaders really practiced proletarian internationalism, they would have no reason whatever for obstructing China from manufacturing nuclear weapons.

Is not China very poor and backward? Yes, it is. The Soviet leaders say, how can the Chinese be qualified to manufacture nuclear weapons when they eat watery soup out of a common bowl and do not even have trousers to wear? The Soviet leaders are perhaps too hasty in deriding China for its backwardness. They may or may not have judged right. But in any case, and even if we Chinese people are unable to produce an atom bomb for a hundred years, we will neither crawl to the baton of the Soviet leaders nor kneel before the nuclear blackmail of the U.S. imperialists.

The Soviet statement says that if China were to produce two or three atom bombs, the imperialists would target many more atom bombs on China. This is in effect instigating the imperialists to threaten China with atom bombs. Of course the fact that the U.S. imperialists may wish to aim more atom and hydrogen bombs at China merits attention and vigilance. But there is nothing terrifying about it. At this very moment the United States has many such bombs already poised against China. It will not make much difference if the United States listens to the Soviet leaders and adds a few more. The Chinese people will not tremble before U.S. nuclear threats. But one must ask: Where do the Soviet leaders place themselves in making such instigation?

In the eyes of the Soviet leaders, the whole world and the destiny of all mankind revolve around nuclear weapons. Therefore, they hold on tightly to their nuclear weapons, afraid that someone might take them away or come to possess them and so to break up their monopoly. They are very nervous. They attribute China's principled criticism of the tripartite treaty to its failure to obtain the atom bombs it desires.

We feel that this attitude of the Soviet leaders is ludicrous. It calls to mind the following ancient Chinese fable: Hui Tzu was prime minister of the state of Liang. Chuang Tzu was on his way to call on him. Somebody said to Hui Tzu, "Chuang Tzu is coming with the intention of taking over your place as prime minister." Hui Tzu became afraid and hunted for Chuang Tzu high and low for three days and three nights. Chuang Tzu appeared before Hui Tzu and said, "Have you heard about the southern bird, the phoenix? It set out from the South Sea to fly to the North Sea. It would not alight except on the wutung tree. It would eat nothing except the fruit of the bamboo. It would drink nothing except the purest spring water. An owl, which had gotten hold of a dead rat, looked up as the phoenix flew over and screeched to warn it off. Are you, too, not screeching at men, over your kingdom of Liang?"

The moral of this fable is that different people have different aspirations, and it is improper to measure the stature of great men by the yardstick of small men.

The main feature of the Soviet government's latest statement is its slander that we want socialism to win by means of thermonuclear war and that we would sacrifice 300 million Chinese and half of mankind in order to create a greater civilization on the corpses and the ruins. Railing at China, the Soviet statement asserts that China is carrying out "an inhuman policy" and following a "bestial conception."

This is really hair-raising stuff. How shocking! The Chinese Communists are nothing but a bunch of bloodthirsty monsters, worse than Hitler, worse than any tyrants past or present, and, needless to say, hundreds of times worse than the U.S. imperialists.

But how is this possible? What do the Soviet leaders base themselves on in making such fantastic charges against China? Their charges, however varied, boil down to two counts: First, that some responsible Chinese leaders have talked about the possibility that in a war people may die by hundreds of millions; second, that the Chinese journal *Red Flag* has made the assertion that the victorious people would create a beautiful future for themselves on the ruins of imperialism.

The references are to certain remarks made by Comrade Mao Tse-tung in his speech at the Moscow meeting of the Communist and Workers' Parties on November 18, 1957, and to a passage in the article "Long Live Leninism!" written by the editorial department of *Red Flag* [*Hung Ch'i,* April 22, 1960].

Let us now see what the Chinese Communist Party actually said. Comrade Mao Tse-tung said:

> It is my opinion that the international situation has now reached a new turning point. There are two winds in the world today, the east wind and the west wind. There is a Chinese saying, "either the east wind prevails over the west wind or the west wind prevails over the east wind." It is characteristic of the situation today, I believe, that the east wind is prevailing over the west wind. That is to say, the forces of socialism are overwhelmingly superior to the forces of imperialism.

Proceeding from that estimate, Comrade Mao Tse-tung pointed to the steadily growing possibility of preventing imperialism from launching a new world war. Comrade Mao Tse-tung then added:

> At present another situation has to be taken into account, namely, that the war-maniacs may drop atomic and hydrogen bombs everywhere. They drop them and we act after their fashion; thus there will be chaos and people will be lost. The question has to be considered for the worst. The political bureau of our party has held several sessions to discuss this question. If fighting breaks out now, China has got only hand grenades and not atomic bombs—which the Soviet Union has, though. Let us imagine, how many people will die if war should break out? Out of the world's population of 2,700,000, one-third—or, if more, half—may be lost. It is they and not we who want to fight; when a fight starts, atomic and hydrogen bombs may be dropped. I debated this question with a foreign statesman [Nehru]. He believed that if an atomic war was fought, the whole of mankind would be annihilated. I said that if the worst came to the worst and half of mankind died, the other half would remain while imperialism would be razed to the ground and the whole world would become socialist; in a number of years there would be again 2,700,000 people and definitely more. We Chinese have not yet completed our construction and we desire peace. However, if imperialism insists on fighting a war, we will have no alternative but to make up our minds and fight to the finish before going ahead with our construction. If every day you are afraid of war and war eventually comes, what will you do then? First, I have said that the east wind prevails over the west wind and that war will not break out, and now I have added these explanations about the situation in case war should break out. In this way, both possibilities have been taken into account.

The passage in "Long Live Leninism!" reads:

> We consistently oppose the launching of criminal war by imperialism, because imperialist wars would impose enormous sacrifices upon the peoples of various countries (including the peoples of the United States and other imperialist countries). But should the imperialists impose such sacrifices on them, we believe that, just as the experience of the Russian Revolution and the Chinese Revolution shows, those sacrifices would be rewarded. The victorious peoples would very swiftly create on the ruins of imperialism a civilization thousands of times higher than the capitalist system and a truly beautiful future for themselves.

The meaning of these words is very clear:

(1) China wants peace, and not war;

(2) It is the imperialists, and not we, who want to fight a war;

(3) A world war can be prevented;

(4) Even in the eventuality that imperialism should impose a war on the peoples of the world and inflict tragic losses on them, it is the imperialist system, and not mankind, that would perish, and the future of mankind would still be bright.

In effect, we make the point in these four sentences. These four sentences are interrelated. But the Soviet leaders have seized hold of half the sentence in which we mention the possibility that the peoples of the world might suffer tragic sacrifice, quoted it out of context, and turned the other three and a half sentences inside out. Hence the conclusion: China wants war, not peace; China, and not world imperialism, wants to fight a world war; a world war is inevitable; and China wants to launch a nuclear world war and bring about the death of half of mankind so as to attain a bright future for mankind. It is indeed pitiful that the leaders of a great power, and a great socialist power at that, should resort to such low fabrication.

But the lies told by the Soviet leaders are really too gross and fantastic. Anyone who uses his brains will ask, how can China launch a nuclear war if it does not have a single atom bomb? All revolutionaries throughout the world know that imperialism is the source of war. How can anyone imagine that socialist China will launch a world war? It is inconceivable.

The quoted remarks of Comrade Mao Tse-tung in 1957 were a reply to some people's view that mankind would be annihilated if imperialism unleashed a nuclear war. The Soviet leaders have spread this view over a number of years and are still spreading it. They say that if imperialism unleashes a nuclear war it will not only scorch but will burn everything to ashes, i.e., the 3 billion people of the world will all die. We do not agree with this pessimistic and despairing view of theirs. We say that if imperialism should unleash a nuclear war and the worst came to the worst, half of the world's population would be killed. We are optimistic about the future of mankind.

They say, our extreme supposition that half the world's population might die is a bestial conception. Does that not make their oft-repeated view, that all the 3 billion people of the world would die, doubly bestial?

While propagating the theory of the annihilation of mankind, they say that the people of the world will bury imperialism if imperialism forces a nuclear war on them. For instance, the open letter of the Central Committee of the CPSU of July 14 declared, "It stands to reason, of course, that if the imperialist madmen unleash a war, the peoples will sweep away capitalism and bury it." But people are bound to ask, if according to your theory all the 3 billion people in the world will die if imperialism unleashes a nuclear war, then who will remain to bury imperialism?

As a matter of fact, this lie of the Soviet leaders is not a new one, nor can they claim authorship. On October 1, and then on October 8, 1960, [James J.] Wadsworth, the U.S. delegate to the U.N. General Assembly, quoted out of context the sentences in "Long Live Leninism!" concerning the ruins of imperialism. He slanderously asserted that China "welcomes an atomic war," and wants a world war fought with hydrogen bombs," "if only that war promises the conquest of the world by communism." In his book "Socialism and War" published in 1960, Kardelj of the renegade Tito clique also slandered China as wanting to unleash a world war to promote world revolution. On September 2, 1960, the Soviet paper *Pravda* said in criticizing this book that Kardelj was helping the U.S. imperialist big guns and that "in substance, he repeats the slanders spread by the U.S. imperialists about the aggressiveness of People's China." Now the Soviet leaders have simply collected the spittle of the imperialists and the renegades. The U.S. imperialists had a try at this slander but then dropped it when they saw that no one paid it any attention. But the Soviet leaders are endlessly hammering away at the same lie, toning it up with color and life, and insisting on making people believe it.

Why do the Soviet leaders continuously repeat this big lie? Do they really believe that the imperialists would not launch another world war? Do they really believe that China wants to launch a world war? Clearly, this is not the crux of the matter. The crucial point is, what should be the policy in face of the U.S. imperialist nuclear blackmail and threats—resistance or capitulation? We stand for resistance, and so they say we want to launch a war and bring about the death of half of mankind. They even believe that whoever dares to presume that imperialism may launch a war wants to launch a war himself. Of course, the only way is capitulation and to capitulate before the imperialists act. In the final analysis, they are racking their brains and telling all these lies for the purpose of covering up their disreputable capitulationist stand.

The Soviet statement declares that "the appeals of the CPR leaders smack strongly of demagogy and adventurism," and that "to link the fate of the national liberation movement with an aggravation of international tension, with urging humanity to a world thermonuclear war, as the CPR leaders are doing, is like promising the peoples freedom after death." What the Soviet leaders mean is clear. Imperialism in possession of nuclear weapons must not be resisted. Should the oppressed peoples and nations resist and should the socialist countries support the resistance, that would be pushing mankind into a world thermonuclear war.

The Soviet leaders hold that "no problem of the revolutionary movement of the working class or the national liberation movement can now be considered in isolation from the struggle to preserve peace and avert a world thermonuclear war." The Soviet leaders hold that "local wars in our time are very dangerous, for any small local war might spark off the conflagration of a world war." The Soviet leaders hold that if the people of any country dare to wage a revolutionary war against imperialism, they are doing nothing but hankering after "dying beautifully" and engaging in a "movement for piling up corpses." The Soviet leaders hold that if a nuclear war should break out "in the case of many peoples the question of socialism would be eliminated altogether because they would have disappeared bodily from our planet." The Soviet leaders even hold that under the threat of a nuclear war Kennedy, the chieftain of U.S. imperialism, and people like him have "shown concern for the preservation of peace" and "try on their part to avert a war."

In short, in the opinion of the Soviet leaders, the emergence of nuclear weapons has changed everything; it has changed both the nature of imperialism and the nature of our epoch. Our epoch is no longer one of revolution as defined in the [1960] Moscow statement, but a nuclear epoch, a nuclear century.

In the July 14 [1963] Open Letter of the Central Committee of the CPSU, the Soviet leaders said, "The nuclear rocket weapons that were created in the middle of our century have changed old conceptions about wars." In reality, this means that, after the emergence of nuclear weapons, war is no longer the continuation of politics, there is no longer any difference between unjust and just wars, imperialism is no longer the source of war, and the peoples of various countries should no longer wage just wars against imperialist armed aggression and armed suppression by the reactionary regime for such just wars cannot possibly be won but will only bring about the annihilation of mankind. In the opinion of the Soviet leaders, in this nuclear century to remain alive is everything, and there is no aim in life. This is the philosophy of willing slaves which demands of the peoples of the world that they should submit to the tender mercies of imperialism. It is a reactionary theory in the service of imperialism. It is a truly bestial conception.

The views of the Soviet leaders referred to above are a total betrayal of Marxism-Leninism and are completely contradicted by the facts of history since the end of World War II. Except to the blind, it is clear that since the emergence of nuclear weapons, the imperialists have continued to resort to nuclear weapons, the imperialists have continued to resort to counter-revolutionary wars as a way to carry out their policies of opressing and enslaving the peoples of various countries, and that the countries and peoples suffering from aggression and oppression have continued to regard revolutionary wars as the way to oppose imperialism, aggression, and oppression and to win their independence and liberation. The history of the last 18 years is replete with wars of aggression and wars against aggression, with unjust and just wars. War is still the continuation of politics.

At the end of World War II, after it had dropped two atomic bombs on Hiroshima and Nagasaki in Japan, U.S. imperialism assumed that armed with this "ultimate weapon" it could ride roughshod over the world and do whatever it pleased. At the time there was a kind of fear-mentality among the Chinese people as well as among the peoples of other countries. U.S. imperialism, possessed of atomic weapons, appeared to them so powerful that they thought it could put down peoples' revolutions at will.

Precisely at that crucial moment, Comrade Mao Tse-tung said in his talk with the American correspondent Anna Louise Strong in 1946:

> The atom bomb is a paper tiger which the U.S. reactionaries use to scare people. It looks terrible, but in fact it isn't. Of course, the atom bomb is a weapon of mass slaughter, but the outcome of a war is decided by the people, not by one or two new types of weapon.
> All reactionaries are paper tigers. In appearance, the reactionaries are terrifying, but in reality they are not so powerful. From a long-term point of view, it is not the reactionaries but the people who are really powerful.

This Marxist-Leninist thesis of Comrade Mao Tse-tung's was a timely exposure of the U.S. imperialists' plot of atomic blackmail and armed the Chinese people and the revolutionary peoples of all countries against it. The victory after victory which the peoples of many countries have won in their revolutionary wars against the aggression and enslavement by the imperialists and their lackeys in the past seventeen years have repeatedly proved the correctness of this thesis.

While the U.S. imperialists still had a monopoly of nuclear weapons the Chinese people achieved the great victory of their revolution in defiance of U.S. imperialist blackmail and intimidation. While the U.S. imperialists still retained their nuclear superiority, they were not able to prevent the defeat of their war of aggression in Korea. In November, 1950, after the U.S. imperialists had met with serious reverses on the Korean battlefield, Truman, then president of the United States, cried for the use of atomic bombs and this immediately aroused indignant protests from the people of the whole world and also general panic and opposition from the allies of the United States. Furthermore, U.S. military personnel did not believe that the use of atomic weapons on the Korean battlefield would actually be effective. As a result, throughout the Korean war the U.S. imperialists never dared to use atomic weapons.

Following the armistice in Korea, the people of Viet-Nam were victorious in their revolutionary war against French imperialism. Even though it had atomic weapons, U.S. imperialism was unable to realize its plan of increasing its intervention in the war in Viet-Nam.

The people of Algeria, after more than seven years of hard and bitter struggle, were victorious in their war for national independence.

The people of Cuba, at the very gate of U.S. imperialism, won victory in their revolution through armed struggle. U.S. imperialism has never dared to declare that it would use nuclear weapons against the Cuban people.

The people's armed forces in Southern Viet-Nam are now carrying on a victorious struggle against the U.S. imperialists and their lackey, the Ngo Dinh Diem clique. Although the U.S. imperialists have employed a great variety of new weapons, they have not dared to use nuclear weapons. U.S. imperialism cannot stop the people's revolutionary struggles of various countries by means of nuclear weapons. The reason is that politically, recourse to this kind of weapons would place U.S. imperialism in a position of extreme isolation and militarily, the massive destructiveness of nuclear weapons limits their use, for in civil wars and wars of national independence, where the lines zigzag and the fighting is at close range, the use of nuclear weapons of mass destruction would inflict damage on both belligerents. In his speech delivered on December 16, 1959, Kennedy admitted that U.S. nuclear strength "cannot be used in so-called brushfire peripheral wars. It was not used in Korea, Indochina, Hungary, Suez, Lebanon, Quemoy, Tibet, or Laos. In short, it cannot prevent the communists from gradually nibbling away at the fringe of the free world's territory and strength, until our security is being steadily eroded in piecemeal fashion . . ." [ellipsis in original].

It is therefore evident that, provided the revolutionary people are not afraid of the imperialists' nuclear blackmail and persevere in their just struggles, they can gain victories in their revolutions. And such struggles and victories have not led to world war but have constantly weakened and effectively restrained imperialism, and thus have reduced the danger of the imperialists launching a world war and safeguarded world peace.

The interests of the people's revolutions and the interests of world peace are identical. It is a manifestation of the proletarian internationalism of the Chinese Communist Party when it gives full support to the daily growing national liberation movements in Asia, Africa, and Latin America. The Soviet leaders slander this stand of the Chinese Communist Party as being racist and accuse us of undermining the unity of the national liberation movement with the international proletariat. As a matter of fact, since you smear the national liberation movement as a "movement for piling up corpses" and as "promising the peoples freedom after death," what is the need of your talking about this unity? Is there any meaning in uniting with a pile of corpses? Your contempt for the colored peoples and the oppressed nations is a downright racist and reactionary nationalist viewpoint.

Imperialism, whose doom is sealed, cannot save itself by relying on nuclear weapons, nor can the socialist countries win victory in their struggle against imperialism by relying solely on nuclear weapons. We have always fully appreciated the important role played by the Soviet Union's possession of nuclear weapons in the struggle of the people of the world against the imperialist policies of aggression and war and for world peace.

But there is a limit to everything, and once the limit is exceeded, the thing is reduced to absurdity. It is a pity that in their attitude toward the Soviet Union's possession of nuclear weapons the Soviet leaders have exceeded the limit. The Soviet leaders insist on exaggerating the role of nuclear weapons and trust blindly in them, despise the masses, and have forgotten that the masses are the makers of history, and so they have degenerated into worshippers of nuclear weapons.

In June, 1960, during the meeting in Bucharest, the Soviet leader, Khrushchev, remarked that in the past they too had once organized a militia but that now, when they had modern weapons, these men were not troops but just human flesh. It is crystal clear that in the eyes of the Soviet leaders the 3 billion people of the world are nothing but rubbish, while the nuclear arms of the Soviet Union and the U.S. imperialists are infinitely powerful magic weapons. That is why they boast so much about what they call the decisive role of the Soviet nuclear weapons in the defense of world peace and completely deny the great significance of the people's anti-imperialist struggles throughout the world. On July 10, 1962, the Soviet leader said at the world conference for general disarmament and peace in Moscow that "the rocket-nuclear might of the Soviet Union serves as a decisive means of defending peace, and has already more than once saved mankind from a world war which the Western imperialist cliques attempted to unleash."

The latest statement of the Soviet Government is even more blatant in asserting that Soviet nuclear weapons played the decisive role in defeating the Anglo-French war of aggression against Egypt in 1956 and frustrating the plot of the U.S. armed threat against Syria in 1957 and the U.S.–British plot to send troops for intervention in Iraq in 1958. All these defeats suffered by the imperialists resulted primarily from the struggles of the Egyptian, Syrian, and Iraqi peoples. The firm support to these peoples by the people of the world, including the Soviet people, also played an important part. How then can all this be credited solely to Soviet nuclear weapons?

It is especially ridiculous that the Soviet statement also gives all the credit to Soviet nuclear weapons for the Chinese people's victory in smashing the armed provocations of U.S. imperialism in the Taiwan [Formosa] Strait in 1958. The Soviet paper *Red Star* [*Krasnaya zvezda*] even said on August 25, 1963, "The nuclear might of the Soviet Union, the very country which has now been abused by the slanderers of Peking, had saved millions of Chinese from nuclear death and defended the sovereignty, security and independence of their country."

What are the facts? In August and September of 1958, the situation in the Taiwan [Formosa] Strait was indeed very tense as a result of the aggression and provocations by the U.S. imperialists. The Soviet leaders expressed their support for China on September 7 and 19 respectively. Although at that time the situation in the Taiwan [Formosa] Strait was tense, there was no possibility that a nuclear war would break out and no need for the Soviet Union to support China with its nuclear weapons. It was only when it was clear that this was the situation that the Soviet leaders expressed their support for China.

We have not forgotten and will not forget the support which the Soviet people have given to China on the question of Taiwan over a long period. Likewise, however, we have not forgotten and will not forget what the Soviet leader Khrushchev said about the question of Taiwan after his visit to the United States in October, 1959. He said that the question of Taiwan was an incendiary factor in the international situation and that because the United States supported Chiang Kai-shek and the Soviet Union supported China, there resulted the atmosphere of an imminent great war. But what the Soviet Union stood for was the creation of all conditions to ease international tension and eliminate war. He further said that there was more than one way to solve every complicated question, depending on what basis you took. For example, after the October revolution, there was established in the Soviet far east the Far Eastern Republic, and Lenin recognized it at the time; this was a temporary concession and sacrifice, but later on it was united with Russia.

The meaning of this statement by the Soviet leader was quite clear. To put it bluntly, this was to ask China to agree to the U.S. scheme of creating "two Chinas."

This absurd view was of course rebutted and rejected by China, whereupon the Soviet leader made a series of speeches hinting that China was "craving for war like a cock for a fight," and, like Trotsky, wanted "neither peace nor war," etc.

In accordance with the procedure mutually agreed upon by the Soviet

Union and the United States, the Chiang Kai-shek clique has now signed the tripartite treaty and is swaggering as if it were a sovereign state. Not only has the Soviet leader asked the Chinese government to sign the same tripartite treaty with the Chiang Kai-shek clique spurned by the Chinese people, and thus to create a situation of two Chinas, he has also threatened that, if the Chinese government opposed this treaty and refused to be bound by it, the United States would help the Chiang Kai-shek clique to manufacture nuclear weapons. It turns out that in order to "save millions of Chinese from nuclear death," one China has to become two Chinas! It is evident that the Soviet leaders will stop at nothing in order to curry favor with the U.S. imperialists. The international position of the German Democratic Republic is beneath their notice and China's sovereignty and territorial integrity are also beneath their notice. Although the truth has been exposed so fully, they still assert that the nuclear strength of the Soviet Union guarantees China's independence and sovereignty. What effrontery!

Nuclear weapons in the hands of socialist countries should always be defensive weapons against the nuclear threats of the imperialists. In contrast to the imperialists, socialist countries have no need to, and must not, use nuclear weapons for blackmail or gambling. The question of using nuclear weapons is one that concerns the interests of millions upon millions of people; and the socialist countries must be extremely prudent on this question and never act recklessly. In this connection, both adventurism and capitulationism are extremely dangerous.

During the Caribbean crisis, the Soviet leaders committed both the error of adventurism and the error of capitulationism. Instead of criticizing themselves, they have prided themselves on the slap in their face, boasted of their "genuine proletarian internationalism" and proclaimed what they have called a "major victory of the policy of reason, of the forces of peace and socialism." They have wantonly attacked the Chinese Communist Party for the righteous position it took on this issue, alleging that China hoped for a head-on clash between the United States and the Soviet Union and tried to provoke a nuclear war. This is utterly loathesome.

The Soviet leaders never weary of asserting that there was a thermonuclear war crisis in the Caribbean Sea which was averted only because the Soviet leaders firmly pursued the policy of peaceful coexistence.

But the facts are there for everyone to see. Although the tension in the Caribbean Sea stemmed from the U.S. imperialist policy of aggression against Cuba and although there has been a continuing danger of an invasion of Cuba by the U.S. imperialists, nevertheless, before the Soviet leaders sent rockets into Cuba, there did not exist a crisis of the United States using nuclear weapons in the Caribbean Sea and of a nuclear war breaking out. If it should be said that such a crisis did arise, it was a result of the rash action of the Soviet leaders.

The Soviet leaders slanderously accuse China of hoping for a head-on clash between the United States and the Soviet Union. The question is, did we ask you to transport rockets to Cuba? The label of adventurism cannot be pinned on us. If the Marxist-Leninist line, which we always follow, had been acted on, there would never have been a question of shipping rockets to Cuba and the so-called nuclear war crisis would never have existed. Then, how could the question of adventurism have arisen?

We should like to ask the Soviet leaders, since the transport of rockets to Cuba was a matter of such great importance, did you ever consult about it with the Soviet people, or with the other socialist countries, or with the working class in capitalist countries? Without consulting anybody, you willfully embarked on a reckless course and irresponsibly played with the lives of millions upon millions of people. The errors were of your own making, so what ground is there for you to blame others?

There is no need whatsoever to transport rockets to Cuba in order to support the Cuban revolution. That was what the Soviet leaders said in the past, and it is also what they are saying now, and in very beautiful language. For instance, the Open Letter of July 14 of the Central Committee of the CPSU said that "in case of aggression by American imperialists we shall come to the assistance of the Cuban people from Soviet territory, just as we would have helped them from Cuban territory. True, in this case the rockets would take slightly longer in the flight, but their accuracy would not be impaired by this." That being so, why did you have to ship rockets to Cuba? Was your purpose really to defend the Cuban Revolution? Would it not be more correct to say that what you did in the name of defending the Cuban Revolution was in reality political gambling?

Anyone with common sense will ask: since the rockets were introduced, why did they have to be withdrawn afterward? And inasmuch as the rockets were afterward withdrawn, why did they have to be earlier introduced? According to you, there was a great deal of finesse in first putting them in, and then taking them out. The withdrawal of the Soviet rockets is said to have gained in exchange a guarantee from the United States that it would refrain from invading Cuba. The Americans have said there was no such guarantee. You have said there was. But where is the guarantee? Do you really believe that the United States will not invade Cuba again? Unfortunately, you do not seem to have much confidence in that.

The Soviet leaders have said that China was opposed to the withdrawal of the rockets from Cuba and to the efforts of the Soviet Union to avert a nuclear war. This is a completely groundless statement. We were totally opposed to your sending the rockets in, then why should we oppose their withdrawal?

It is understandable that you should have tried to extricate yourselves from the difficulties of your own creation, but we were resolutely opposed to your acceptance of the completely unjustifiable and humiliating terms which the U.S. imperialists advanced.

The Soviet leaders blame China for not having supported them as an ally should. You had better look up the documents. Was there anything you did right during the Caribbean crisis on which we did not support you? You are dissatisfied, but exactly what did you want us to support? Did you want us to support you in your decision to accept the inspection of Soviet ships on the high seas by the U.S. pirates? That would not do! If we had given you support on that we would have done a disservice to the great Soviet people. Did you want us to support you in your acceptance of the U.S. imperialists' demand for the "international inspection" of Cuba? That would not do! If we had given you support on that, we would have done a disservice to the great Cuban people.

In recklessly introducing the rockets into Cuba and then humiliatingly withdrawing them, the Soviet leaders moved from adventurism to capitulationism and brought disgrace to the Soviet people, the Cuban people, the people of the countries in the socialist camp, and the people of the whole world. They have inflicted unprecedented shame and humiliation on the international proletariat. All this has been unalterably written into history. No matter how the Soviet leaders lie or what sleight of hand they perform, they can never wash away their shame.

The capitulation of the Soviet leaders has inflated the aggressiveness and arrogance of the imperialists. After the Caribbean crisis, when the U.S. imperialists saw that their policy of nuclear blackmail had succeeded, they concluded that Moscow was more afraid of atomic war than Washington. Just like any fortune hunter who gets a windfall, the U.S. imperialists become overweeningly arrogant. Now that they fully understand the weaknesses of the Soviet leaders, they are using both tough and soft tactics to force them into further capitulation. The signing of the tripartite treaty is a hallmark of such further capitulation to U.S. imperialism on the part of the Soviet leaders.

The position and line of the Chinese Communist Party and the Chinese Government on the question of war and peace have always been clear and cannot be distorted.

We resolutely oppose world war and we resolutely defend world peace. Not long after World War II, Comrade Mao Tse-tung stated definitely that a third world war can be prevented. For over a decade, the Chinese people have been firmly persisting in the struggle to oppose the imperialist policies of aggression and war, to prevent a new world war, and to preserve world peace. We have consistently held that provided the peoples of the whole world become united, follow a correct line, and persevere in struggle, a new world war can be prevented, a nuclear war can be prevented, and world peace can be preserved.

It is our view that imperialism is the source of modern wars and that U.S. imperialism is the main force of aggression and war. Unless a resolute struggle is waged against the U.S. imperialist policies of aggression and war, defense of world peace is completely out of the question. If one prettifies U.S. imperialism and obscures from the peoples of the world the targets of this struggle, this will only endanger world peace.

It is our view that in order to strive for world peace, it is necessary to unite in joint efforts all the peace-loving forces of the world, namely, the socialist camp, the national liberation movement, the revolutionary movement of the peoples of all countries, and all the peace-loving countries and peoples. If one despises the force of the masses of the people and blindly trusts nuclear weapons as omnipotent, this will only endanger world peace.

It is our view that in order to strive for world peace, it is necessary to strengthen the unity of the socialist camp and enhance the strength of the national defenses of all the countries in the socialist camp. If one splits the socialist camp and weakens its defense forces, it will only endanger world peace.

It is our view that in order to strive for world peace, it is necessary to give full support to the national liberation movement and the revolutionary struggles of the peoples of all countries. The more these struggles develop, the more the imperialist forces will be weakened and the more possible it will be to prevent the imperialists from launching world war. If one refuses to support, and even sabotages, the national liberation movement and the revolutionary struggle of the peoples of all countries, this will only endanger world peace.

We consistently maintain that countries with different social systems should coexist peacefully. It was China which initiated the five principles of peaceful coexistence. It has made unremitting efforts for peaceful coexistence with countries having different social systems on the basis of the five principles. For the socialist countries, peaceful coexistence must in all circumstances be based on principles and must not depart from them. Negotiation is one form of struggle against imperialism. Necessary compromises can be made in negotiations so long as the principle of upholding the fundamental interests of the people is observed.

But if one regards negotiations as the main means, or even the sole means, of striving for peaceful coexistence and does not scruple to sell out the fundamental interests of the people in order to seek compromises with imperialism, that is not peaceful coexistence but capitulationist coexistence, and it will only result in endangering world peace.

We are in favor of general disarmament and hold that the imperialists can be forced to accept certain agreements on disarmament through the unremitting struggle of the peoples of all countries. We are of the opinion that the complete and thorough prohibition of nuclear weapons can be achieved while imperialism still exists, just as poison gas was prohibited. This is because the use of such a weapon of mass destruction is completely contrary to the will of the peoples and, moreover, would subject the users to destruction. However, general and complete disarmament can be realized only after imperialism, capitalism and all systems of exploitation have been eliminated. To make propaganda about the possibility of realizing "a world without weapons, without armed forces and without wars" through general and complete disarmament while imperialism still exists, is to deceive the peoples of the world and is detrimental to the struggle for world peace.

We hold that while affirming the growing possibility that imperialism can be prevented from launching a new world war, one should also recognize that the danger of a new world war still exists. Necessary preparations must be made against this danger. The better we are prepared, the less is the possibility that the imperialists will dare to launch such a war. If anyone stresses only one possibility—the possibility that imperialism will not launch such a war—tries to make the people of the world believe that no other possibility exists, and does not even dare think of the other possibility, that will only lull the vigilance of the world people, provide opportunities for imperialism to exploit, and increase the danger of world war.

In fighting imperialism we are of the opinion that, strategically and with regard to the whole, one must despise the enemy, dare to struggle against him, and dare to seize victory; at the same time, tactically and with regard to each specific struggle, one must take the enemy seriously and be prudent. If one does not take full account of the enemy tactically and is heedless and reckless, while strategically one dares not despise the enemy, it is inevitable that one will commit the error of adventurism in tactics and the error of capitulationism in strategy.

The position and line of the Chinese Communist Party and the Chinese Government on the question of war and peace are in full conformity with the revolutionary principles of the 1957 declaration and the 1960 statement. Theirs is a Marxist-Leninist line. Adherence to this line will lead both to victory for the people's revolutions and to victory for world peace. We maintain that the line pursued by the Soviet leaders is an anti-Marxist-Leninist line, one that runs counter to the revolutionary principles of the declaration and the statement. Adherence to this line will harm the fundamental interests of the people of all countries, and it will endanger world peace.

Our line on the question of war and peace is indeed the diametrical opposite of that of the Soviet leaders. The Soviet leaders are of course entitled to defend their own line; however, abuse is not debate and misrepresentation is not argument. Communists should always have respect for the facts and talk reason. It is for the Chinese people, the Soviet people, and the people of the whole world to judge which line is correct, ours or yours, and which line is wrong.

We note that the Soviet papers have published our statement of August 15. We hope you will continue this good practice and also publish our present statement.

Appendix D

The following is the full text (in the editor's translation) of an article by I. I. Yermashev, which appeared in the restricted-circulation Soviet General Staff journal *Voennaya mysl'* (*Military Thought*), No. 10, October, 1963, pp. 12–22.

The Peking Version of "Total Strategy"

The anti-Soviet campaign, conducted in China with extreme frenzy, has assumed unprecedented scale. There is no slanderous, lying fabrication that is not permitted in Chinese propaganda. The Chinese leaders evidently have been put in a fury by the circumstance that the Communist Party of the Soviet Union and the overwhelming majority of Marxist-Leninist parties of other countries have rejected the pretensions of the Chinese "wise men" to the role of unquestioned authorities on everything concerning Marxist-Leninist theory, the strategy and tactics of the international Communist movement. True, there is no basis for recognizing such pretensions on their part. It is not without value to analyze in this connection the essence of some of the "theoretical" views that Chinese propaganda attempts to thrust upon the Marxist-Leninist parties, in particular on the questions of military theory and military policy.

I

The Chinese leaders have their "views" on virtually all problems of contemporary theory and policy. They also have their views on the questions of military theory and military policy.

Military science, like all science, is extremely important. But there is bourgeois military science, and proletarian Marxist-Leninist military science. This situation does not require proof, because there is no dispute over the fact that military science is one of the social sciences, one of the most important branches. What can one say about the "military science" circulating in China? One cannot consider it proletarian-Marxist. In actual fact, that which in China is called "Marxist" military science is the product of an eclectic mixture. It borrows from Marxism recognition of the role of the masses, but only as a factor of *numbers*,* denying at the same time the decisive signifi-

* All italics in this translation appear as they are in the original Russian—R.L.G.

239

cance of the economic-material factor; it borrows voluntarism from petty-bourgeois thinkers, which in its crudest form is incarnated in subjective idealism. It is not difficult also to detect in Chinese "military science" components that are typically Chinese, preserved still from feudal times. Characteristically, it *faces the past, the Chinese past,* not recognizing any experience except the experience of China, despite the fact that this experience has only historical value, but is completely unsuitable in contemporary conditions; it is simply obsolete. And it became obsolete not merely by itself but as a consequence of radical changes in many objective conditions, including *the material bases of war* and especially of armaments. In this connection, the basic derivative factors have undergone changes: the military art, the organization of the armed forces, and others.

Chinese "military science" flatly contradicts all that. For it, there exist factors given once and for all, which is understandable if one holds to a metaphysical manner of thinking. We read, in an article concerning questions of strategy and tactics published in *Jen-min Jih-pao* [*People's Daily*] (Kao K'o, "Path of Victory in National Liberation War"), July 31 [1963], the following "discoveries": "Victory or defeat in wars are not decided by the factor of relative strengths and weaknesses, but by a comparison of the general sum total of the fundamental factors inherent in the combatant sides; are not determined by the relative military and economic potential at a given time, but by the character of the war for each side and the comparison of manpower and morale factors which stem therefrom."

"Strength" and "weakness" in war must be understood as material, and not spiritual, factors. Other conditions equal, victory will go to the stronger side and the weaker will suffer defeat. There can be no argument on this score. The fuzzy reference to a mysterious "general sum total of fundamental factors" does not save the author. If there is any thought at all in those words, it is to be found in the last clause of the excerpt cited. There it is said frankly that victory or defeat is decided by the character of the war for both sides, and manpower and morale factors, and not in the confrontation of military and economic potentials.

As we see, in the very definition of the requirements for victory, morale and political conditions are mainly emphasized (the character of the war, the morale factor), and the relationship of real material strengths and resources is downgraded. No one, of course, must be led astray by the author's remark "at any given time." In actuality, what is the meaning of his words: "victory or defeat are not determined by a comparison of the military and economic potential at a given time"? The strengths of the sides will always, at any given time (even if the process of conflict goes through numerous "given times"), be perceived only by means of comparison, and such comparisons are made for each side. The author's thought comes down to the fact that, to the extent that the relation of forces changes in the course of struggle, it is necessary to go to war even in case "at a given time," that is, speaking frankly, at the present time, the enemy is stronger, because in the course of struggle the relation of forces may change to the advantage of the weaker.

How has that miracle come to pass? Under what circumstances? The author's answer is very simple: under conditions of protracted war. He thus writes: "In everything it is necessary to base oneself on the factor of protractedness, and base oneself mainly on one's own strengths. Although that is an extremely difficult and tortuous path, demanding a certain cost and sacrifice, it is nonetheless the only reliable path able to lead to victory . . . It is a long and difficult process in the course of which *the weak wins over the strong*" (my italics—I. Ye.).

It is absurd to suppose that a war of attrition will, as it were, favor the weak and harm the strong. In such a war, the weak will be exhausted before the strong. All that is evident, if one stands on a scientific, materialist point of view. But the author of the article has no such understanding. He supposes that in the struggle of the weak against the strong what counts are not objective conditions, not the material factor, but subjective conditions—will, stamina, capability to go "the extremely difficult path," readiness for sacrifices. Doubtless these conditions are extremely important for victory. But do they operate, as Lenin emphasized, in the final analysis? He always put in the first place the material factors, weapons. The Peking author puts the factor of time in first place. There is no question but that time is a very important factor in war. But just the same, time is only a form of movement of matter, and it cannot replace any material factors. An example advanced in the article cited, the victory of China in a long protracted war with Japan, is not convincing. If Japan had not been tied down on many fronts in the Pacific Ocean, if the antifascist coalition had not taken the war to the territory of Japan, if the Soviet Army had not dealt complete defeat to the Japanese Army in Northeastern and Northern China, the might of Japanese imperialism would not have been broken, and the outcome of the war might have been different. China alone did not have the capabilities necessary to gain victory and throw the foe out of its homeland, despite the fact that the Chinese people conducted a heroic struggle against the Japanese aggressors and their exploits will go down in the history of mankind.

One cannot deny the important role of stamina and will in a war. But it is necessary not to involve oneself light-mindedly in a serious battle, counting on the idea that the enemy will grow weaker in the course of it, and the weak, developing willpower and stamina, will vanquish the strong. It is stupid to count in a happy-go-lucky fashion on chance. After all, in order for the weak to defeat the strong, he must in the course of the struggle become strong, and the strong must become weak. And that depends not at all on subjective factors—will and stamina—, but above all on objective—material, economic —factors.

In essence, the Chinese "theoreticians" separate war—a form of extreme violence—from its material base, and convert it into exclusively *an act of will*. It is therefore necessary to recall what F. Engels wrote on that subject in his polemic against Dühring. Engels' main theses, which have entered the treasure-trove of Marxist-Leninist science on war and the military art, come down to the fact that "violence is not a simple act of will, but demands very real prerequisites for its accomplishment, especially certain well-known tools, of which the more advanced hold an advantage over the less advanced, and further that these tools must be produced, and that already as a consequence of that fact the producer of more advanced tools of violence, *vulgo* ('speaking plainly'—[Russian] Editor) weapons, will be victorious over the producer of less advanced weapons; in a word, victory by violence is based in the production of armaments, and the production of armaments in turn is based on production in general, consequently . . . on 'economic strength,' on 'the economic situation,' on *material* resources, at the disposal of violence."

It would almost appear that Engels foresaw the possibility of the emergence from the ill-starred Dühring of the imitators in Peking! Engels' argumentation hits also the contemporary followers of the Berlin professor-metaphysician, attempting to make a "revolution in science" and suffering a complete failure.

Further, Engels wrote: "Nothing depends on economic conditions as much as the army and navy. Armaments, personnel, organization, tactics and strategy depend above all on the stage of production, and the means of communication, achieved at a given time. No 'free creation of the mind' of genius strategists has operated here in a revolutionizing manner, but invention of the best weapons and changes in soldiery." (K. Marx and F. Engels, *Collected Works* [Russian edition], Vol. 20, pp. 170 and 171.)

What is there in common between the Peking wise men and the great thoughts of Engels? Nothing! Ignoring the material, economic factors in war, the Peking home-grown "Marxists" inevitably slide into extreme idealism on such a cardinal question as the conduct of the war "of the weak against the strong." Standing on the ground of "Chinese Marxism," the Peking "theoretician" had to decide metaphysically the question of the role of such a factor of strength as size of population of combatant sides. As we have seen, he treats population size ("manpower resources") as a decisive factor, along with political-morale factors, determining victory or defeat. Moreover, manpower is the only material factor to which he gives attention, obviously since without people one cannot fight at all.

The size of the population, without doubt, is an important element in determining the strengths of sides. We stress, it is important; but not decisive. History bears witness to the fact that vast countries, with populations of hundreds of millions of people, have been enslaved by countries having incomparably smaller territory and population. The enslavement of India by England can serve as an example, English violence in China, and the defeat which little Japan also dealt to China in 1894–95. And how about the seizure and enslavement of the countries of Africa and South America by the imperialist powers of Europe?

What was responsible for the weakness of those countries, which found themselves under the heel of the imperialists? *Economic backwardness* gave birth also to military weakness. Recall the words of Lenin: ". . . the whole

East, with its hundreds of millions of toiling, exploited population, driven to the ultimate degree of human deprivation, placed in conditions where its physical and material strengths cannot compare decisively with the physical, material, and military strengths of any of the much smaller Western European states." (*Collected Works* [Russian edition], Vol. 33, p. 457.)

This is the Leninist evaluation of the real significance of *numbers* alone in determining the role of population in the struggle between enslaved peoples and the powers that enslave them. *Lenin considered as the decisive prerequisite for victory in this struggle the militant collaboration of the toilers of the countries of the East and of the countries of the West, especially the militant collaboration of the East with the Soviet land.* Lenin was not in any case an advocate of the slogan "reliance on one's own strengths," for that slogan leads to the disassociation of the struggling peoples, to their isolation from one another, to a weakening of the anti-imperialist front. On the contrary, Lenin told the peoples of the East, and all oppressed peoples, to unite their forces, to give assistance to one another, to hold strongly the principle of mutual aid in order jointly to carry on the struggle against imperialism. Addressing the peoples of the East, he wrote: "Only when the Indian, Chinese, Korean, Japanese, Persian, and Turkish workers and peasants hold out their hands to one another and proceed together in their common cause of liberation, only then will a decisive victory over the exploiters be achieved." (*Collected Works,* Vol. 31, p, 116.)

The slogan "reliance on one's own strengths" is an anti-Leninist, anti-Marxist, nationalist slogan, dictated by the same idealist [i.e., non-materialist —R.L.G.] views of the Chinese leaders. It is advanced with the definite political and tactical aim of separating the peoples of the oppressed countries from the camp of socialism [i.e., the Moscow-led bloc—R.L.G.], sowing among them the seeds of nationalism and chauvinism, in order to make political capital. Such slogans of the Chinese splitters [of the Communist movement—R.L.G.] are advantageous only to imperialism.

That which is propagated under the guise of "Marxist-Leninist military science" in the pages of the Chinese press, and especially in the newspaper of the Central Committee of the CCP [Communist Party of China] *Jen-min Jih-pao* [*People's Daily*] and the theoretical organ *Hung Ch'i* [*Red Flag*] in the name of the leadership of the CCP, is the purest adventurism on the questions of conducting armed conflict in our age.

II

On the main question—on the relationship of objective and subjective factors in the complex and multi-faceted process of conducting war—the Chinese leaders have slipped into reactionary positions of idealism, placing in preeminence the subjective over the objective, the ideal (will) over the material (economics), absolutizing the role of *numbers* and downgrading the role of material power, economics, and technology.

It is only logical that such idealistic, metaphysical views are affirmed among other things in the evaluation of the character and peculiarities of contemporary wars. In that connection, no one should be misled by the fact that in their anti-Soviet propaganda, in their slander against the Marxist-Leninist parties, the Peking leaders for reasons of demagogy and camouflage adopt Marxist terminology. In actual fact, cut off from Marxism, the Peking leaders deliberately cry out loudly of their "fidelity" to Marxism and the study of the class struggle relating to war.

Listen to the Chinese military "theoreticians." In *Hung Ch'i,* No. 16, August [1963], was published an article by Lu Chih-ch'ao, under the much-promising title "Examination of the Question of War Must Not Run Counter to the Marxist-Leninist Viewpoint on the Class Struggle." This article is a model of the metaphysical approach to the complex problems born of the contemporary stage of development of military affairs and the unprecedented growth of the killing and destructive power of modern weapons.

The scribblings of this Chinese author bear no relation whatsoever to the Marxist-Leninist view on the class struggle as the criterion for the correct evaluation of the character of a given war. His aim is quite different: to prompt the reader to the conclusion that those fighting imperialism must, as it were, always and everywhere prefer war as a means of policy.

In order to establish the character of a given war, as Lenin wrote, it is necessary to determine "what the war is being fought for, by *what* classes, for *what* political aim." (*Collected Works,* Vol. 23, p. 21.) Marxist-Leninists have considered and now consider as just only those wars that are conducted by the oppressed against the oppressor: the working class in alliance with the peasantry against the capitalists and landowners, oppressed peoples against colonizers. Such wars—civil wars, liberation wars—have their specific features: "as a rule, it is a war within one country. In connection with it the question of the use of the nuclear weapon does not arise. This weapon has so far never been used in such wars. And that is understandable, since there is often not even a defined front line dividing opponents. It was thus in Viet-Nam, in Cuba, in Algeria, and in other countries." (Statement of the Soviet Government, *Pravda,* September 22, 1963.)

The war of the states of the antifascist coalition against the bloc of fascist aggressors headed by Hitlerite Germany was just. Obviously, a war of the Soviet Union and the whole socialist commonwealth, if it had to defend itself against an attack by imperialism, would be a just war. In such a war capitalism would be destroyed. War between the states of the system of socialism and the bloc of imperialist aggressors would be a world war, and in it nuclear weapons would inevitably be widely used. That is its most important feature.

And how does the Chinese metaphysician-demagogue judge that indisputable proposition? He affirms: better than to wait, it is necessary to act "boldly," not hesitating before the costs no matter how great they should be. This position was unambiguously set forth by none other than Mao Tse-tung himself, at the meeting of the representatives of the Communist and Workers' parties in Moscow as early as 1957. All the subsequent development of this "idea" bears witness to the fact that it was no chance remark, but a considered conception.

Mao Tse-tung blandly declared that, in case of world nuclear war, in his opinion half the population of our planet, or perhaps more than half, would perish. What does that mean, half? That is one and a third to one and a half billion people! And what conclusion did the leader of the CCP draw from his calculations? Did he express alarm over the fact that the imperialists are preparing for mankind a bloody war of unprecedented scale? No! On the contrary, he distinctly left one to understand that he considered such a "development" completely acceptable for socialism. He set forth his point of view with an equanimity to the fate of *over a billion people,* mainly workers, impermissible for a Communist, and still more for a leader of the party. In his speech he said: ". . . If half of mankind is destroyed, then half will remain, while imperialism will be completely destroyed and there will be only socialism in the whole world, and in half a century or a century the population will again grow even more than that half."

Mao Tse-tung in essence called for a world nuclear war, presuming that it would have its "favorable" side: the hydrogen bomb in "one blow" would decide the main contradiction of our epoch—the contradition between the world system of socialism and the system of capitalism. And that thought is in fact propagated by the Chinese leaders and the Chinese press today too, advancing it at the same time in crying contradiction with their own evaluation, since despite elementary logic they contend that the might of nuclear weapons is, as it were, exaggerated. Thus, on the one hand the thermonuclear weapon would cause at least half the population of the world to perish, while on the other hand it is a "paper tiger"! It's not worth searching for logic in the Chinese "theoreticians"; they just haven't got it.

There's more than enough demagogy. The same Chinese author in *Hung Ch'i* declares: "Opportunists have recourse to propaganda of fear of war, of destructive war, of the devastation and horrors of war." What a brave man that author is! To him and his ilk nothing matters. . . .*

We see that discussions of the "class approach" are necessary to them only in order to drag in surreptitiously their propagation of war—of world war with the use of nuclear weapons.

The pretensions of the Peking dogmatists to the role of zealots of the class approach to problems of war are ridiculous. The problem of class relationship in respect to world war in our time of course remains. Of what does it consist? In pushing into such a war, provoking it, bringing it nearer in the name as it were of "speeding up" the fall of imperialism? Not in the slightest. Imperialism is doomed to perish, socialism will triumph in the whole world —that is an objective inevitability. The most powerful thing in speeding the fall of imperialism, in undermining its whole basis, is the growth of the economic power of the world socialist system, the development of the revolutionary and national-liberation movements. A Marxist understands that the faster and more inspiring is the tempo of growth of the socialist system, then

* Ellipses appear as in the original article—R.L.G.

the closer will come the hour of the final fall of imperialism. Precisely the path of economic competition, and not the path of war, will decide the main contradiction of the contemporary epoch—the contradiction between socialism and imperialism.

That is the correct class approach at the present time. It is necessary to unleash the highest tempo of Communist construction. But for that a stable peace is required.

For successful construction, a well-organized smooth rhythm of work has decisive significance. War, and all the more nuclear war, would create extraordinary difficulties, it would seriously impede the construction of communism in the U.S.S.R. and socialism in the other fraternal countries. That is why the theses advanced in the Statement of the Soviet Government published on September 22 [1963] have such exceptional importance: "Peace is the very first condition for the strengthening and spread of the positions of socialism in the world arena . . . Peace is the true ally of socialism, of the international workers movement, of the peoples struggling for national liberation. . . ." * Peace, and not atomic and hydrogen bombs!

Obviously, the interests of socialism are not dear to the Chinese leaders; the losses and devastation, the human sacrifices, which would be dealt to the socialist countries too in a world nuclear war do not alarm them.

Such a war would be a genuine catastrophe for peoples. It would not advance mankind, but on the contrary would throw mankind back. "In policy," the Statement of the Soviet Government declares, "it is necessary to proceed not from utopia, but from the fact that thermonuclear war will have catastrophic consequences for all peoples, for the whole world. All countries, even those that survive the war, would be thrown back in their development by decades, if not centuries. In a world that has suffered thermonuclear war, the question of the birth-rate also would not be like the Chinese leaders wish to imagine it. . . ."

Marxist-Leninists understand what the true class approach to the question of a new world war consists of in the contemporary situation: it consists in not permitting the unleashing of such a war. In contradistinction to the Chinese psuedo-Marxist fatalists, considering war as inevitable, Marxist-Leninists stand on the viewpoint that in our epoch there is no fatal inevitability of war, and they see their task to be defending the general peace and the future of all mankind by all measures, mobilizing the masses for the struggle against the criminal designs of the warmongers. Communists are the most determined opponents of world war, and in general opponents of wars between states. This is the basic distinction of the CPSU [Communist Party of the Soviet Union] and other Communist and Workers parties holding a genuine class position, from the adventurism of the Peking top leaders, covered over by empty phrases. It is, after all, clear that if imperialism unleashes a thermonuclear war it will have to be waged against all mankind, that, in the flames of nuclear explosions, tens, hundreds of millions of

* All ellipses appear as in the original article—R.L.G.

workers, our brothers, would perish, and not just capitalists, of whom there are not so many.

"Chinese Marxism" places its stakes not on the multifaceted development of the workers' class struggle adapted to the concrete conditions of place and time, not on the organization of the toiling masses, not on the winning over of the majority of the people to the side of the great cause of the revolutionary transformation of society, but on war, on thermonuclear world war. And no matter how much the Peking leaders disavow this fact, it is incontrovertible and remains to their indelible shame. He who, in our time, in fact trumpets thermonuclear war, conceding to it the "shortest path" to the victory of socialism, becomes the bearer of the infamous doctrine of genocide—the destruction of people. And no loud phrases about "class-ness" can conceal that fact.

III

The Chinese leaders, with the aim of camouflage, defend the point of view that, as it were, the only form of proletarian revolution has been and will remain revolutionary war, uprisings. A rejection of uprisings, they contend, is equivalent to rejecting revolution.

In the letter of the Central Committee of the CCP of June 14 [1963], in which the true views of the Chinese leaders are masked by a heavy smoke-screen of "revolutionary" phrases, we read: "Some say that revolution is entirely possible without wars too. Of what kind of wars are they speaking? Of national liberation and civil revolutionary wars, or of world wars? If they mean national liberation and civil revolutionary wars, then such assertions are in actual fact directed against revolutionary wars, that is, against revolution."

Here it is written, black on white, that without revolutionary wars, without armed uprisings, proletarian revolution is impossible. But Marxist-Leninists have always held that the proletarian revolution as a social revolution, as a concept, is broader than revolutionary war. Revolutionary war is a means, a form of achieving the proletarian revolution, and moreover not the only means or the only form.

The proletarian revolution includes: the revolutionary overthrow, the overthrow of the rule of capital; the suppression of resistance by the overthrown exploiters; the revolutionary transformation of society—the construction of socialism.

"Marxism," Lenin teaches us, "is distinguished from all primitive forms of socialism by the fact that it does not bind the movement to any single particular form of struggle." (*Collected Works*, Vol. 11, p. 186.)

The sorry Chinese Marxists cite Lenin and quote his words on the fact that the peaceful development of revolution is rarely found in history. Yes, Lenin wrote about that on the eve of October—in September, 1917. Here is his well-know thesis: "Any kind of peaceful development of revolution in general is an extremely rare thing." Lenin proceeded on the basis of the then available experience. And moreover he also spoke in the pre-October period for a peaceful transition of power to the Soviets, which "would make civil war in Russia impossible." (*Collected Works*, Vol. 26, pp. 18 and 17.) If one hews to the "views" of the Peking strategists of the "revolutionary" phrase, Lenin should be indicted for speaking out against revolution!

In order to present more clearly the anti-Marxist theories circulating in Peking, we shall note one more important example from the history of the proletarian movement. Well-known is the reference by Engels to the fact that the experience of revolutions of the nineteenth century confirmed that "real victory of an uprising over troops in street battle, that is a victory as between two armies in the field, is an extreme rarity." (K. Marx and F. Engels, *Collected Works*, Vol. 22, p. 540.) Was Engels right, or is it necessary according to the Peking instructions to expel him from Marxism for "revisionism"? Of course, Engels was right. *The experience of revolutions of the nineteenth century indicated that conclusion; nonetheless he advised the workers in no case to reject their right to revolution. (Ibid.*, p. 545.) And, as is well known, under other conditions the workers and their allies have in many countries exercised that right fully to the end.

That which was a rare occurrence in a past epoch has become, under changed concrete circumstances—in particular in the epoch of transition from capitalism to socialism—the rule, the norm. The transition of power to the working class and the overthrow of capitalism by peaceful means has occurred in many countries belonging to the camp of socialism, and was completed *without civil war,* despite what the Chinese leaders say. In other countries the victory of the working class in alliance with the peasantry has required a long armed conflict. Consequently, it would be absurd to stand on the proposition that there exists only one path to the victory of the proletariat, to the proletarian revolution—civil war.

The leaders of the CCP have abdicated from the instruction of Lenin: "Marxism must not in any circumstance be limited to the forms of struggle possible and extant at any given moment, recognizing the *inevitability* of new forms of struggle, unknown to people of that given period, with changes in the given social situation." (*Collected Works*, Vol. 11, p. 186.) They pretend too not to know another extremely important thesis of Lenin's on the fact that rejection of uprisings under particular concrete circumstances is not at all equivalent to rejecting revolution. Here is that thesis of Lenin's: ". . . history has shown that oppression cannot always be answered by uprising; but rejection of an uprising does not signify rejection of revolution." (*Collected Works*, Vol. 27, p. 27.) These clear words of Lenin, full of deep meaning, dispose on the spot of all "arguments" of the proponents who identify one form of struggle, an uprising, with the proletarian revolution.

The Central Committee of our party was entirely correct in showing the Chinese leaders that world revolution today proceeds through many paths, "which must not be counterposed to one another, but united, directed toward one aim—the overthrow of the rule of imperialism." (*Open Letter of the CC of the CPSU to Party Organizations, to All Communists of the Soviet Union,* State Political Publishing House, 1963, p. 44.)

The Chinese leaders, as we have already seen, stubbornly stand on their depraved point of view that one path exists for all countries and conditions: war, no matter even if it takes the lives of millions, tens, and hundreds of millions. Revolution, they consider, can be made any time—all one needs is to want to organize an uprising!

It would be erroneous to see in all that something specifically Chinese, national; it is not hard to detect in it characteristics of the ideology of *petty-bourgeois revolutionism* which, as Lenin taught us Communists, "resembles anarchism or borrows something from it, which whatever it is lacks something essential from the conditions and requirements of seasoned proletarian class struggle." (*Collected Works,* Vol. 31, p. 15.)

Precisely that "petty-bourgeois revolutionism," which recognizes no flexibility, no compromises in the course of the great battle of the working class against world imperialism, and which recognizes (in words, above all!) only "direct action" or, to use the term now in vogue in China, "no quarter given."

One must not forget that contemporary China is still just an enormous peasant country with a relatively small proportion of proletarian elements, with a young and not yet tempered working class, actually originating only in the last quarter century; a country in which there are still strong and living remnants, not completely eliminated, of the old ideology of small and very small property owners of the recent past and even elements of feudal ideology in customs, the family, and interpersonal relations. One cannot completely exclude the influence of all these petty-bourgeois social strata on the leaders, especially if these very leaders themselves also suffer from strokes of "extreme revolutionariness," especially in time of internal difficulties as a result of the adventurist course of the "speed up" [great leap forward] to socialism by crude administrative measures—all this is well known.

The disdainful attitude of the Peking "supermen" to those millions—tens and hundreds of millions—of human sacrifices, which they are prepared to sacrifice on the altar of their adventuristic, one may say "total strategy," is typical. This also shows their tie to the anarchists. "What are sacrifices to us. . . ," exclaimed Laurent Tailhade, one of the anarchist troubadors. "What does the destruction of indeterminate masses mean. . . ," he continued. Adducing these words of Tailhade, G. V. Plekhanov * noted: "Here is the real morality of the anarchists, the morality of the Caesars: 'sic volo, sic jubeo!' (As I wish, so do I command!)" (G. V. Plekhanov, *Collected Works,* Vol. IV, 1923, p. 244.)

There is, of course, a substantial quantitative difference, one may say, between anarchists such as those Plekhanov scorned and the anarchistically inclined Peking advocates of "direct action." The former could, at most, toss a pot full of explosive into a group of people gathered in some restaurant or theater. Their contemporary fellows, having incomparably greater resources and potentialities, propose to act not with a homemade explosive bomb, but with nuclear weapons, which they will build "relying on their own

---

* One of the founders of the Marxist movement in Russia in the latter part of the nineteenth century—R.L.G.

strength." And with the assistance of this weapon they intend to "shove" the tempo of historical development so as to "heap benefits" on mankind. These followers of anarchist doctrines should recall a comment of Engels: ". . . the victorious proletariat cannot force any happiness on any other nation, not supported by its own victory." (K. Marx, F. Engels, V. I. Lenin, *On Proletarian Internationalism* [Russian], State Political Publishing House, Moscow, 1957, p. 174.)

The essential condition for victory over world imperialism consists not in provoking nuclear war, but in the maximum consolidation and development of the world system of socialism, the further rise of its might, which will have revolutionizing influence on the wide masses of workers of the whole world and help them in the struggle against imperialism; in the preservation of the high combat readiness of the armed forces of the socialist states so as to repulse at any moment even the smallest attempt at an attack by world reaction.

A genuine revolutionary strategy has a good aim—saving mankind. An adventurist "strategy," a "total strategy" of the Peking style is pregnant with indescribable calamities for all peoples, including the Chinese people.

The propaganda war conducted with unheard-of licentiousness in China against the Soviet Union, the CPSU, and other Marxist-Leninist parties is an integral part of this "strategy." By their hostile tone, malicious impertinence, and dirty insinuations, articles in the Chinese press could "grace" any anti-Soviet, superreactionary, even fascist press paid from the secret coffers of the world black hundreds [ultra reactionaries in Czarist Russia—R.L.G.]. And all this is not the result of polemical venting, but, on the contrary, a cold-blooded realization of the definite plan of the leaders of the CCP [Chinese Communist Party], descending the path of extreme chauvinism of a racist ilk. A task has been set for their propaganda—to sow panic among the people, and to incite them to take on their shoulders a new burden, the burden of a nuclear arms race, into which the leaders of the CCP consider it necessary to drag much-suffering China.

But why is the top leadership of the CCP so rabid to tear off after the nuclear weapon? After all, not a single socialist state except China considers it necessary to have its "own" nuclear weapons, considering entirely correctly that the power of the Soviet nuclear forces reliably protects the entire socialist camp from attack. The leaders of the CCP do not believe in fraternal friendship with the other socialist countries and do not value this friendship, orienting themselves only on "their own strength." They consider that world thermonuclear war is inevitable and, attempting to hurry it along, they evidently suppose that the Chinese people will have the best chance since they are the most populous people on the earth. In case of the destruction of the majority of the peoples of the world [sic] and their states, their culture (and this, in the language of the Peking political hysterics, is called "the fall of imperialism") there would remain, in their opinion, the epoch of world domination by people of the yellow race. The Peking leaders have already come to terms with the idea of dividing people by race, by the color of their skin, rather than by class, social characteristics. Thus they have entered the path leading into the swamp of racism, with all of the consequences that flow from that. The Peking version of "total strategy" is the fruit of the reactionary utopia of the leaders of the CCP, who have broken with Marxism-Leninism.

When one acquaints himself closely with the theories of the Peking leaders and their practical activity in the international arena, it becomes clear that they put in first place not the interests of the peoples struggling for peace, socialism, and national liberation, but their own great power aims. When they call on the peoples not to consider the concrete situation, not to consider the potentiality and consequences of thermonuclear war, the true aims of the Chinese leaders stand all the further away from the interests of the struggle for the development of the international Communist movement, for the victory of socialism in all countries of the globe.

Notes

2. Armed Conflict in the Chinese
Borderlands, 1917–50

1. James William Morley, *The Japanese Thrust Into Siberia, 1918* (New York, 1954), Appendix N, p. 363.
2. Robert A. Rupen, *Mongols of the Twentieth Century* (Indiana University Publications Ural and Altaic Series, Vol. 37, Part I) (The Hague, 1964), pp. 135–36.
3. Rupen, *op. cit.*, p. 141. Ye. M. Zhukov (editor in chief), *Mezhdunarodnye otnosheniya na dal'nem vostoke (1840–1949)* (*International Relations in the Far East, 1840–1949*) (2d ed.; Moscow, 1956), p. 325, gives the date as February 4, 1921.
4. V. Dushen'kin, *Ot soldata do marshala, zhizn' i boevoi put' Marshala Sovetskogo Soyuzu V. K. Blyukhera* (*From Private to Marshal; The Life and Combat Career of Marshal of the Soviet Union V. K. Blücher*) (Moscow, 1960), p. 76.
5. Rupen, *op. cit.*, p. 144.
6. *Ibid.*
7. *Ibid.* Cf. Gerard M. Friters, *Outer Mongolia and Its International Position* (London, 1951), p. 122, who dates this or a similar appeal as August.
8. In treating official Sinkiang reactions to current political problems, heavy reliance has been placed in this account on Yang Tseng-hsin's compendium, *Pu-kuo-chai Wen-tu* (*Pu-kuo Studio Documents*) (Peking, 1921).
9. Aitchen K. Wu, *China and the Soviet Union: A Study of Sino-Soviet Relations* (New York, 1950), pp. 200–1.
10. John Erickson, *The Soviet High Command: A Military-Political History 1918–1941* (London, 1962), p. 241.
11. Following Zhukov, *op. cit.*, p. 413, and Dushen'kin, *op. cit.*, p. 102. Elsewhere the date August 7 appears.
12. For this account, reliance in the main is upon the eyewitness report of a sea captain as given to a U.S. vice consul at Harbin; see Department of State, *U.S. Foreign Relations, 1929* (Washington, 1944), III, 337–38. But see also Dushen'kin, *op. cit.*, pp. 105–6.
13. Dushen'kin, *op. cit.*, p. 106. Erickson, *op. cit.*, p. 242, states that the 5th Amur and 4th Volochaevka Regiments were assigned to the 2d Division, and that the battle continued until November 3.
14. Dushen'kin, *op. cit.*, p. 111, gives the strength of the ODVA group as 7,632 men, who were opposed by 16,000 Chinese. The cavalry force appears to have been a Buryat Mongol unit, but may have been Outer Mongolian.

15. *Ibid.* See similar reports by Zhukov, *op. cit.*, p. 413, and Erickson, *op. cit.*, p. 244.

16. Reports of November 24 and November 27 from the U.S. Consul at Harbin, *U.S. Foreign Relations, 1929*, III, 350, 357–58.

17. *U.S. Foreign Relations, 1929*, III, 345.

18. *U.S. Foreign Relations, 1929*, III, 380.

19. Erickson, *op. cit.*, p. 245.

20. Alexander Barmine, *One Who Survived* (New York, 1945), pp. 231–32.

21. Allen S. Whiting and General Sheng Shih-ts'ai, *Sinkiang: Pawn or Pivot?* (East Lansing, Mich., 1958), pp. 23, 160, and 193.

22. Zhukov, *op. cit.*, p. 467.

23. Erickson, *op. cit.*, pp. 449–51. For the 1936 disposition of forces, see J. M. Mackintosh in B. H. Liddell Hart (ed.), *The Red Army* (New York, 1956), p. 62.

24. *Ibid.*, p. 468.

25. Clark W. Tinch, "Quasi-War Between Japan and the U.S.S.R., 1937–1939," *World Politics*, January, 1951, p. 178.

26. *U.S. Foreign Relations, 1938* (Washington, 1954), III, 443.

27. See Dushen'kin, *op. cit.*, p. 126, for further description of the terrain.

28. *U.S. Foreign Relations, 1938*, III, 455.

29. Zhukov, *op. cit.*, p. 495; and see Martin Blumenson, "The Soviet Power Play at Changkufeng," *World Politics*, January, 1960, pp. 249 ff. Blumenson's work makes extensive use of U.S. Department of the Army, Office of Military History, USAFFE and U.S. 8th Army Historical Sections, series *Japanese Studies on Manchuria*, dealing with the Changkufeng affair. (Zhukov gives the date July 20, 1938.)

30. *U.S. Foreign Relations, 1938*, III, 457.

31. Blumenson, *op. cit.*, p. 256.

32. *Ibid.*, p. 257.

33. Dushen'kin, *op. cit.*, p. 127.

34. Zhukov, *op. cit.*, p. 495. See also U.S. Chargé at Moscow, *U.S. Foreign Relations, 1938*, III, 460–61. Zhukov identifies the attacking force as two infantry regiments of the 19th Division.

35. U.S. Chargé at Moscow, August 5, *U.S. Foreign Relations, 1938*, III, 468–69.

36. Dushen'kin, *op. cit.*, p. 131, is however fairly clear in his suggestion that Blücher remained in charge on the Far Eastern Front until the end of the Changkufeng affair.

37. *U.S. Foreign Relations, 1938*, III, 476–77.

38. U.S. Embassy Moscow's Despatch of September 15, cited in *ibid.*, pp. 484–85.

39. Max Beloff, *Foreign Policy of Soviet Russia, 1929–1941* (London, 1949), II (1936–41), 193, note 3.

40. Zhukov, *op. cit.*, p. 496, says that this offensive succeeded on August 7 in ejecting the Japanese from Changkufeng and throwing them outside the Soviet frontiers. Dushen'kin, *op. cit.*, p. 130, holds that Changkufeng was taken at 22:30 hours on August 6, 1938.

41. *U.S. Foreign Relations, 1938*, III, 477–78.

42. Erickson, *op. cit.*, 498–99; also Blumenson, *op. cit.*

43. Quoted by Blumenson, *op. cit.*, p. 259.

44. *Ibid.,* quoting the USAFFE and U.S. 8th Army studies.

45. *U.S. Foreign Relations, 1938,* III, 478.

46. For information permitting this deduction, see report by the U.S. Chargé at Moscow, August 15, of TASS communiqué regarding the military situation, *ibid.,* pp. 481–82; and report of First Secretary of the American Embassy at Peiping (Peking) August 17, transmitting information received from an AP correspondent just returned from the battle zone, *ibid.,* pp. 482–83.

47. Blumenson, *op. cit.,* p. 262.

48. *Ibid.*

49. Tinch, *op. cit.,* p. 181.

50. *U.S. Foreign Relations, 1938,* III, 479–81. See also, Tinch, *op. cit.*

51. F. C. Jones, *Japan's New Order in East Asia, Its Rise and Fall, 1937–1945* (London, 1954), p. 181.

52. Erickson, *op. cit.,* note, p. 517.

53. Accepting the date given in Dushen'kin, *op. cit.,* p. 131.

54. Zhukov, *op. cit.,* p. 507.

55. U.S. Embassy Moscow, *U.S. Foreign Relations, 1939,* III, 17.

56. *Ibid.,* pp. 46–47.

57. Tinch, *op cit.,* p. 185.

58. Zhukov, *op. cit.,* p. 507.

59. *Ibid.,* p. 508.

60. Erickson, *op. cit.,* p. 518. He has a detailed account of the battle of Nomonhan, with a map of the battle on p. 535.

61. Zhukov, *op. cit.,* p. 508.

62. *U.S. Foreign Relations, 1939,* III, 50.

63. *Ibid.,* p. 53.

64. *Ibid.,* pp. 70–71.

65. Tinch, *op. cit.,* p. 185.

66. Rupen, *op. cit.,* p. 259; see also Whiting and Sheng Shih-ts'ai, *op. cit.,* p. 115.

67. Chang Ta-chün, *Hsin-chiang Nei-mu (The Inside Story of Sinkiang)* (Hong Kong, 1956), pp. 138–39. See Owen Lattimore, *Pivot of Asia: Sinkiang and the Inner Asian Frontiers of China and Russia* (Boston, 1950), p. 81, for another version of Sheng's final démarche to Moscow.

68. Whiting and Sheng Shih-ts'ai, *op. cit.,* pp. 117–18.

3. Soviet Military Aid to Nationalist China, 1923–41

1. S. Tikhvinsky, in *Voenno-istoricheskii zhurnal (The Military Historical Journal),* No. 8, August, 1964, p. 107.

2. B. N. Ponomarev (ed.), *Politicheskii slovar' (The Political Dictionary)* (Moscow, 1958), p. 562.

3. Vladimir V. Yurzanov, *Stalnye soldaty: ocherki o voinakh narodno-osvoboditel'noi armii Kitaya (Steel Soldiers: Essays on the Warriors of the People's Liberation Army of China)* (Moscow, 1959), p. 9.

4. Franz L. Moedelhammer, *Moscow's Hand in the Far East* (Tokyo, 1938), p. 162.

5. F. F. Liu, *A Military History of Modern China, 1924–1949* (Princeton, N.J., 1956), p. 5.

6. V. Dushen'kin, *Ot soldata do marshala* (*From Private to Marshal*) (Moscow, 1960), p. 91; and Pyn Min, *Istoriya Kitaisko-Sovetskoi druzhby* (*History of Chinese-Soviet Friendship*) (Moscow, 1959), p. 197. The forward to the latter work identifies Pyn Min as a "Chinese historian," but the tenor of the book closely follows the Soviet line.

7. Cheng Tien-fong, *A History of Sino-Russian Relations* (Washington, D.C., 1957), p. 130.

8. Pyn Min, *op. cit.*, p. 118.

9. Liu, *op. cit.*, pp. 14 and 15. Chiang Kai-shek himself has said that 3,000 tons of Soviet military equipment were received in 1924 from the Russians. Chiang Kai-shek, *Soviet Russia in China* (New York, 1958), p. 272.

10. Louis Fischer, *The Soviets in World Affairs* (New York, 1960), p. 467.

11. A. I. Cherepanov, *Zapiski voennogo sovetnika v Kitae* (*Memoirs of a Soviet Military Advisor in China*) (Moscow, 1964), pp. 93, 95, and 96.

12. *Ibid.*, p. 32.

13. Dushen'kin, *op. cit.*, pp. 91–92.

14. Cheng Tien-fong, *op. cit.*, p. 130.

15. Cherepanov, *op. cit.*, p. 32.

16. Dushen'kin, *op. cit.*, p. 91.

17. Liu, *op. cit.*, p. 18.

18. Cheng Tien-fong, *op. cit.*

19. Cherepanov, *op. cit.*, p. 172.

20. Fischer, *op. cit.*, p. 485.

21. Cherepanov, *op. cit.*, p. 149.

22. *Ibid.*, p. 154.

23. *Ibid.*, p. 155.

24. *Ibid.*, pp. 224–25.

25. Clarence Martin Wilbur and Julie Lien-ying How, *Documents on Communism, Nationalism and Soviet Advisors in China, 1918–1927* (Papers seized in 1927 Peking Raid) (New York, 1956), pp. 212–13.

26. *Ibid.*, p. 21.

27. *Ibid.*, p. 215.

28. *Ibid.*, p. 216.

29. Pyn Min, *op. cit.*, p. 165.

30. Wilbur and How, *op. cit.*, p. 219.

31. Liu, *op. cit.*, pp. 26–27.

32. *Ibid.*

33. *Ibid.*, pp. 33–35.

34. Cherepanov, *op. cit.*, p. 283, and Dushen'kin, *op. cit.*, pp. 94–100. (The quotation is from p. 96.)

35. Harley F. MacNair, *China in Revolution* (Chicago, 1931), p. 108.

36. Cherepanov, *op. cit.*, p. 283.

37. Moedelhammer, *op. cit.*, p. 162.

38. Cherepanov, *op. cit.*, p. 273.

39. Moedelhammer, *op. cit.*, p. 167.

40. Pyn Min, *op. cit.*, p. 166.

41. George F. Kennan, *Russia and the West* (New York, 1962), p. 261.

42. Mikhail F. Yur'ev, *Krasnaya armiya Kitaya* (*The Red Army of China*) (Moscow, 1958), p. 3.

43. Liu, *op. cit.*, pp. 61, 62, and 67. For a description of German influence during this period, see Liu's Chapter 7.

44. Cherepanov, *op. cit.*, pp. 230, 274, and 275.

45. Chiang Kai-shek, *op. cit.*, p. 241.

46. A. A. Martynov, *Slavnaya narodno-osvoboditalnaya armiya Kitaya* (*The Glorious National Liberation Army of China*) (Moscow, 1957), pp. 6–7.

47. Arthur Young, *China and the Helping Hand, 1937–45* (Cambridge, 1964), p. 207. Chiang Kai-shek himself states (*op. cit.*, p. 272) that, from 1937 to 1941, China received 849 aircraft and considerable artillery. Cheng (*op. cit.*, p. 213) states that, by January, 1938, 300 million rubles worth of aircraft, tanks, and artillery had been sent to China by the U.S.S.R.

48. Edgar Snow, *The Battle for Asia* (New York, 1941), p. 181.

49. *Ibid.*, p. 182.

50. O. Edmund Clubb, *20th Century China* (New York, 1964), pp. 219–20.

51. Edgar O'Ballance, *The Red Army of China* (New York, 1962), p. 124.

4. The Soviet Intervention in Manchuria, 1945–46

1. See Saburo Hayashi in collaboration with Alvin Coox, *Kogun: The Japanese Army in the Pacific War*, translated from the Japanese (Quantico, Va., 1959), pp. 19–20.

2. *Istoriya velikoi otechestvennoi voiny Sovetskogo Soyuza, 1941–1945* (*History of the Great Fatherland War of the Soviet Union, 1941–1945*) (Moscow, 1963), V, 524–25. (Hereafter cited as *IVOVSS.*)

3. Marshal R. Malinovsky, *Krasnaya zvezda* (*Red Star*), September 2, 1965.

4. *Ibid.* This and other Soviet accounts give the Japanese increase in August, 1941, as 300,000 to 600,000; Colonel Hayashi, who was in a position to know, gives the figures 400,000 to 700,000 (*op. cit.*, p. 20). In all other respects, there is agreement in the Russian and Japanese accounts.

5. *Study of the Strategical and Tactical Peculiarities of Far Eastern Russia and Soviet Far East Forces* (Japanese Special Studies on Manchuria, Vol. XIII, Military History Section, Headquarters [U.S.] Army Forces Far East) (Tokyo, 1955), p. 43; and *Japanese Preparations for Operations in Manchuria, January 1943–August 1945* (Japanese Monograph No. 138, Military History Section, Headquarters [U.S.] Army Forces Far East) (Tokyo, 1953), pp. 82–89.

6. The most convenient authoritative summary source for these American-Soviet exchanges is in U.S. Department of Defense, *The Entry of the Soviet Union Into the War Against Japan: Military Plans, 1941–1945* (Washington, D.C., 1955). On the Moscow and Tehran conferences, as reported above, see this source, pp. 22–27, and see *Foreign Relations of the United States, 1943* (Washington, D.C., 1963), I, 513–781 for the Moscow Conference, and *Foreign Relations of the United States, The Conferences at Cairo and Tehran* (Washington, D.C., 1961), *passim.*

7. *Ibid.*, pp. 28–38. See also *Foreign Relations of the United States, The*

Conferences at Malta and Yalta, 1945 (Washington, D.C., 1955), pp. 361–83.

8. *Ibid.*, pp. 46–49.

9. *Ibid.*, pp. 38–45; the quotation cited is on p. 43. For the relevant background and discussions at Yalta, including the text of this JCS study, see *The Conferences at Malta and Yalta, 1945*, pp. 385–400 and 549–965 (the JCS paper is given in full on pp. 388–93).

10. Data from a reliable Japanese source.

11. *IVOVSS*, pp. 537–38.

12. *The Entry of the Soviet Union Into the War Against Japan*, pp. 60–61 and 72–74.

13. *Ibid.*, pp. 68–71.

14. *Ibid.*, pp. 76–89; the quotation cited is on p. 79.

15. *Ibid.*, p. 92.

16. *Ibid.*, p. 105. See also, for the revealing texts of the telegrams between Tokyo and the Japanese Ambassador in Moscow, *Foreign Relations of the United States, The Conference of Berlin (The Potsdam Conference), 1945* (Washington, D.C., 1960), II, 1248–55 and 1291–98.

17. See *Record of Operations Against Soviet Russia, Eastern Front (August, 1945)* (Japanese Monograph No. 154, Military History Section, Headquarters [U.S.] Army Forces Far East) (Tokyo, 1954), pp. 1–2.

18. *Ibid.*, pp. 2–3.

19. These data are taken from *Japanese Preparations for Operations in Manchuria (Prior to 1943)* (Japanese Monograph No. 77, Military History Section, Headquarters [U.S.] Army Forces Far East) (Tokyo, 1954), pp. 16–17 and 35–36, and the earlier cited *Study of Strategical and Tactical Peculiarities*, pp. 64–65.

20. See Marshal M. Zakharov, in *Voenno-istoricheskii zhurnal (The Military Historical Journal)*, Moscow, No. 9, September, 1960, pp. 15–16.

21. These data are taken from the official Soviet archives, as given in a detailed breakdown in "Campaign of the Soviet Armed Forces in the Far East in 1945," *Voenno-istoricheskii zhurnal*, No. 8, August, 1965, pp. 67–70; see also *IVOVSS*, p. 551. (Contemporary Japanese estimates, which were close on men and major matériel but far off on units, are given in *Study of Strategical and Tactical Peculiarities*, p. 112.)

22. *Japanese Preparations for Operations in Manchuria, January, 1943–August, 1945*, pp. 127 and 141–62; Hayashi, *Kogun*, pp. 173–74; and *Voenno-istoricheskii zhurnal*, No. 8, August, 1965, p. 69.

23. Various sources; see esp. *IVOVSS*, p. 548; Hayashi, *Kogun*, pp. 173–74; *Voenno-istoricheskii zhurnal*, No. 8, August, 1965, p. 69; and B. G. Sapozhnikov and V. B. Vorontsov, "The Liberation Mission of the U.S.S.R. in the Far East in the Years of the Second World War," *Istoriya SSSR (History of the U.S.S.R.)*, Moscow, No. 4, July–August, 1965, p. 35.

24. The best source for this evaluation, and source for most of the data cited above, is *Japanese Preparations for Operations in Manchuria, January, 1943–August, 1945*, esp. pp. 141–62. For a surprisingly frank Soviet admission of the shortcomings of the Kwantung Army, see *IVOVSS*, p. 549.

25. See, for example, *Study of Strategical and Tactical Peculiarities*, p. 117; and *Japanese Preparations for Operations in Manchuria, January, 1943–August, 1945*, p. 139.

26. *IVOVSS*, p. 552.

27. *Ibid.*, pp. 552 ff.; and see Marshal M. Zakharov, "The Campaign of the Soviet Armed Forces in the Far East (August–September, 1945)," *Voenno-istoricheskii zhurnal*, No. 9, September, 1960, pp. 11–12. Except as otherwise noted, the following summary of the military campaign generally draws from various published Soviet military works, including the *IVOVSS*.

28. For a more detailed account of the operations of the Trans-Baikal Front, see this author's "Marshal Malinovsky's Manchurian Campaign, August, 1945," in *Military Review*, October, 1966.

29. *Record of Operations Against Soviet Russia, Eastern Front*, pp. 70–71. See also the memoirs of Marshal K. A. Meretskov, "Combat Paths: 3—The Far Eastern . . . ," *Voprosy istorii* (*Problems of History*), Moscow, No. 2, February, 1966, pp. 101–9.

30. For a more detailed account of the Soviet landing operations in northern Korea, southern Sakhalin, and the Kuril Islands, see this author's article "Soviet Operations in the War with Japan (August, 1945)," in *United States Naval Institute Proceedings*, May, 1966. See also Captain First Rank G. Gelfond, *Sovetskii flot v voine s Yaponiei* (*The Soviet Navy in the War with Japan*) (Moscow, 1958), pp. 65–79; and A. Mitin, *Tikhookeanskii flot v velikoi otechestvennoi voine* (*The Pacific Fleet in the Great Fatherland War*) (Moscow, 1948), pp. 11–14. No good Japanese accounts of these landing operations are available.

31. *IVOVSS*, pp. 551–52, 562–69, and 575–78; *Record of Operations Against Soviet Russia—On Northern and Western Fronts of Manchuria, and in Northern Korea (August, 1945)* (Japanese Monograph No. 155) (Tokyo, 1954), pp. 172–84, and 205–16; Gelfond, *op. cit.*, pp. 138–70; and Captains First Rank N. V'yunenko and R. Mordvinov, *Voennye flotilli v velikoi otechestvennoi voine* (*The Naval Flotillas in the Great Fatherland War*) (Moscow, 1957), pp. 233–45.

32. For the Sakhalin and Kuril operations, see the author's above-cited article in *U.S. Naval Institute Proceedings*, May, 1966.

33. "The Campaign of the Soviet Armed Forces in the Far East in 1945," *Voenno-istoricheskii zhurnal*, No. 8, August, 1965, p. 68.

34. *Air Operations Record Against Soviet Russia* (Japanese Monograph No. 151, Military Historical Section, Headquarters [U.S.] Army Forces Far East) (Tokyo, 1952), pp. 25 and 33; *Record of Operations Against Soviet Russia, Eastern Front*, p. 99; and *IVOVSS*, pp. 548 and 549.

35. *Ibid.*, pp. 36–44.

36. *Ibid.*, pp. 36 and 42–46.

37. *IVOVSS*, pp. 552–53.

38. *Ibid.*, p. 551; *Voenno-istoricheskii zhurnal*, No. 8, August, 1965, p. 69; and see Admiral I. S. Yumashev, *Morskoi sbornik* (*Naval Journal*), No. 8, August, 1965, p. 16. For the Japanese forces, see *Naval Operations Against Soviet Russia* (Japanese Monograph No. 106, Military Historical Section, Headquarters, [U.S.] Army Forces Far East) (Tokyo, 1952), p. 10. (Note: This monograph is not accurate in its accounts of operations in the Kurils and Sakhalin.)

39. *IVOVSS*, pp. 578–81; and *Record of Operations Against Soviet Russia, Eastern Front*, pp. 18–25.

40. For the transfers, see *IVOVSS,* p. 560; for the ammunition expended, by fronts and totals, see *Voenno-istoricheskii zhurnal,* No. 8, August, 1965, p. 68.

41. Sovinformburo communiqué, *Pravda,* September 12, 1945; and *IVOSS,* p. 581.

42. Max Beloff, *Soviet Policy in the Far East, 1944–1951* (London, 1953), p. 143.

43. *IVOVSS,* p. 581.

44. See Appendix A for the texts of the Treaty and associated protocols of August 14, 1945.

45. For reviews of the Sino-Soviet treaty negotiations, see Tang Tsou, *America's Failure in China, 1941–50* (Chicago, 1963), pp. 270–87; and Herbert Feis, *The China Tangle* (Princeton, N.J., 1953), pp. 333–51.

46. See O. Edmund Clubb, "Manchuria in the Balance, 1945–1946," *Pacific Historical Review,* November, 1957, p. 379; and Feis, *op. cit.,* p. 383.

47. *Ibid.,* pp. 379–80.

48. See A. M. Dubinsky, "The Liberation Mission of the Soviet Union in the Far East (1945)," *Voprosy istorii (Problems of History),* August, 1965, p. 60; and see O. Edmund Clubb, *Twentieth Century China* (New York, 1964), pp. 260–62; Tang Tsou, *op. cit.,* pp. 331–32; and David Dallin, *Soviet Russia and the Far East* (London, 1949), pp. 249, 251, and 332.

49. See Tang Tsou, *op. cit.,* pp. 328–30; Dallin, *op. cit.,* p. 252; Feis, *op. cit.,* pp. 384–86; and Charles B. McLane, *Soviet Policy and the Chinese Communists, 1931–1946* (New York, 1958), pp. 210–11.

50. Feis, *op. cit.,* pp. 377–78.

51. *Krasnyi flot (Red Fleet),* Moscow, September 6, 1945; cited by Feis, *op. cit.,* p. 381, from a contemporary U.S. Embassy Moscow dispatch.

52. A. M. Dubinsky, *Voprosy istorii,* August, 1965, p. 59.

53. Tang Tsou, *op. cit.,* p. 330 and 332; and Feis, *op. cit.,* p. 387.

54. Tang Tsou, *op. cit.,* p. 332; Clubb, *op. cit.,* p. 263.

55. Feis, *op. cit.,* pp. 397 and 399.

56. Tang Tsou, *op. cit.,* pp. 333–34.

57. See Tang Tsou, *op. cit.,* pp. 335–37; Dallin, op. cit., pp. 244–46 and 318–20; and Max Beloff, *Soviet Policy in the Far East, 1944–1951,* pp. 38–41. For the U.S. notes and findings of the Pauley Commission, see *United States Relations with China,* pp. 596–604.

58. Quoted by Dallin, *op. cit.,* p. 245.

59. B. G. Sapozhnikov and V. B. Vorontsov, "The Liberation Mission of the U.S.S.R. in the Far East During the Years of the Second World War," *Istoriya SSS (History of the U.S.S.R.),* No. 4, July-August, 1965, p. 46.

60. Tang Tsou, *op. cit.,* pp. 334–35; and Beloff, *op. cit.,* pp. 41–47.

61. Clubb, *op. cit.,* p. 267; Tang Tsou, *op. cit.,* p. 334; and *United States Relations With China,* pp. 137 and 147.

62. *United States Relations With China,* p. 149; McLane, *op. cit.,* p. 228; Clubb, *op. cit.,* p. 268; Major Robert Rigg, "Campaign for the Northeast China Railway System (1946–1947)," *Military Review,* December, 1947, p. 29; and Tang Tsou, *op. cit.,* p. 338. The relative strength estimates of Rigg, who was in Changchun at the time, are used.

63. *United States Relations With China,* p. 151; McLane, *op. cit.,* p. 245; and Tang Tsou, *op. cit.,* p. 419.

64. Clubb, *op. cit.,* p. 279.

65. Rigg, *Military Review,* December, 1947, pp. 29–31; Clubb, *op. cit.,* pp. 268–71; and Liu Yun-an, *Demokraticheskoe i sotsialisticheskoe stroitel'stvo v severo-vostochnym Kitae* (*Democratic and Socialist Construction in Northeastern China*) (Moscow, 1957), p. 38.

66. For accounts of General Marshall's mediation efforts, see Tang Tsou, *op. cit.,* pp. 349–440; *United States Relations With China,* pp. 127–229; and Clubb, *op. cit.,* pp. 264–73.

67. Liu Yun-an, *op. cit.,* pp. 39–42.

68. Dallin, *op. cit.,* p. 326; Clubb, *op. cit.,* p. 278; and Rigg, *op. cit.,* pp. 31–32.

69. Clubb, *op. cit.,* pp. 279–280; Rigg, *op. cit.,* pp. 33–34; and *United States Relations With China,* p. 315.

70. Clubb, *op. cit.,* pp. 280–86; Liu Yun-an, *op. cit.,* pp. 44–45; *United States Relations With China,* pp. 315–18; and V. P. Ilyushechkin, "The Third Revolutionary Civil War in China, 1945–49," *Uchënye zapiski instituta vostokovedeniya* (Tom XI: *Kitaiskii sbornik*) (*Learned Journal of the Institute of Oriental Studies* [Vol. XI, *China Issue*]) (Moscow, 1955), pp. 117–41.

71. *United States Relations With China,* pp. 320–30.

72. *Ibid.,* p. 260; and Tang Tsou, *op. cit.,* pp. 454–62.

73. *Ibid.,* p. 266.

74. Liu Yun-an, *op. cit.,* pp. 45–47; Ilyushechkin, *Uchënye zapiski,* XI (1955), 144–45; V. I. Glunin, *Tret'ya grazhdanskaya revolyutsionnaya voina v Kitae (1946–1949)* (*The Third Revolutionary Civil War in China, 1946–1949*) (Moscow, 1958), pp. 138–40; and Clubb, *op. cit.,* pp. 289–90.

75. Glunin, *op. cit.,* pp. 138–40; and Ilyushechkin, *Uchënye zapiski,* XI (1955), 145.

76. For the texts of the 1950 Treaty and other related agreements of 1950, 1952, and 1954, see Appendix B.

77. Marshal R. Malinovsky, Order of the Day, *Radio Moscow,* September 2, 1965.

78. "A Victory for Our Politics, A Victory for Mao Tse-tung's Thinking," editorial from *Liberation Army Daily,* on *Radio Peking,* September 1, 1965; *Hsinhua,* August 15, 1965; Mao Tse-tung, "The Situation and Our Policy After the Victory in the War of Resistance Against Japan [August, 1945]," *Selected Works of Mao Tse-tung* (Peking, n.d.), IV, 11.

5. *Sino-Soviet Military Relations, 1945–66*

1. For example, Stalin informed Yugoslav Party leaders that he had advised the Chinese Communists to enter a coalition government. See Vladimir Dedijer, *Tito* (New York, 1953), p. 322.

2. These data are taken largely from Lieutenant Colonel Robert Rigg, *Red China's Fighting Hordes* (Harrisburg, Pa., 1952), pp. 100, 248, 251, 277, and 297. See also Max Beloff, *Soviet Policy in the Far East, 1944–1951* (New York, 1953), pp. 20–64; F. F. Liu, *A Military History of Modern China, 1924–1949* (Princeton, N.J., 1956), pp. 227–29; and General L. M.

Chassin, *La Conquète de la Chine par Mao Tse-tung* (Paris, 1952), *passim.*

3. Rigg, *op. cit.,* p. 255.

4. *Ibid.,* p. 276.

5. See Harold C. Hinton, "Communist China's Military Posture," *Current History,* September, 1962, pp. 150–51.

6. The full texts of the treaty and associated agreements are given in Appendix B.

7. This estimated figure is given by Rigg, *op. cit.,* p. 302.

8. Rigg (*op. cit.,* p. 321) notes that the Russians unofficially provided training to some Chinese Communist airmen in the U.S.S.R. in 1947–49. If true, this is the one exception to nonassistance from 1946 to 1950.

9. Allen S. Whiting, *China Crosses the Yalu* (New York, 1960), pp. iv–v *et passim.*

10. *Ibid.,* p. 135.

11. Rigg, *op. cit.,* pp. 323–24.

12. The piston light bombers were used in combat but once; a flight of ten sent down the North Korean coast was intercepted by U.S. jet fighters, and nine were destroyed.

13. Rigg, "Red Army in Retreat," *Current History,* January, 1957, p. 3.

14. Allen S. Whiting, " 'Contradictions' in the Moscow-Peking Axis," *Journal of Politics,* February, 1958, pp. 127–61.

15. Rigg, *Current History,* January, 1957, p. 3.

16. *Hsinhua,* June 18, 1957. See Greg MacGregor, "Peiping General Criticizes Soviet on Seized Plants," *The New York Times,* June 24, 1957.

17. See the text in Appendix B.

18. George A. Modelski, *Atomic Energy in the Communist Bloc* (Melbourne, 1959), pp. 181–95.

19. Rigg, *Current History,* January, 1957, p. 5.

20. *Ibid.,* p. 3.

21. See Edward Crankshaw, "Sino-Soviet Rift Held Very Deep," *Washington Post,* February 12, 1961.

22. Marshal Yeh Chien-ying, *NCNA* (New China News Agency release), Peking, July 27, 1955.

23. See the detailed account of the 1954–57 debate in Alice L. Hsieh, *Communist China's Strategy in the Nuclear Era* (New York, 1962), pp. 15–75.

24. *Ibid.,* pp. 72–75.

25. See *Hsinhua,* August 15, 1963, and September 1, 1963, and *Hung Ch'i* (*Red Flag*) and *Jen-min Jih-pao* (*People's Daily*), September 6, 1963.

26. See Hsieh, *Communist China's Strategy,* pp. 76–109; and Hsieh, "China, Russia and the Bomb," *The New Leader,* October 17, 1960.

27. *Ibid.* See also Donald S. Zagoria, *The Sino-Soviet Conflict, 1956–1961* (Princeton, N.J., 1962), pp. 169–71.

28. *Hung Ch'i* and *Jen-min Jih-pao,* September 6, 1965.

29. BBC monitoring, cited in *China Quartely,* April-June, 1964, p. 238.

30. *Radio Moscow,* July 10, 1964.

31. Hsieh, *Communist China's Strategy in the Nuclear Era,* pp. 109–10.

32. *Ibid.,* pp. 106–8.

33. *Ibid.,* p. 112. See also Zagoria, *op. cit.,* p. 192.

34. Hsieh, *op. cit.,* pp. 114 and 116. For discussion of the conference, see also Zagoria, *op. cit.,* pp. 189–94.

35. Hsieh, *op. cit.*, p. 116.

36. Zagoria, *op. cit.*, p. 193.

37. Yu Chao-li, in *Hung Ch'i*, August 16, 1958. See also *Liberation Army Daily*, October 24, 1958, and *Jen-min Jih-pao*, November 12, 1958.

38. *Hung Ch'i*, October 16, 1958.

39. See A. Kashin, "Chinese Military Doctrine," *Bulletin of the Institute for the Study of the USSR*, Munich, November, 1960, pp. 39–44.

40. See discussion in Chapter 7; and see Hsieh, *Communist China's Strategy*, pp. 119–36.

41. A. M. Rosenthal, "Warsaw Reports Soviet-China Pact," *The New York Times*, August 7, 1958, and "Soviet Atom Arms To Go To Peiping, Warsaw Learns," *The New York Times*, August 18, 1958.

42. See Hsieh, *Communist China's Strategy*, pp. 103–9 and 155–61.

43. Editorial, *Jen-min Jih-pao*, February 4, 1959.

44. Hsieh, *Communist China's Strategy*, p. 164.

45. David A. Charles, "The Dismissal of Marshal P'eng Teh-huai," *The China Quarterly*, October-December, 1961, pp. 63 ff.

46. *Ibid.*, pp. 64–65 and 74–75.

47. See Ronald Farquhar, "China Posts Go to 18 Rightists," *Washington Post*, April 18, 1959.

48. See the Institute for Strategic Studies, *The Military Balance, 1965–66* (London, 1965), pp. 9–10; *The Military Balance, 1964–65* (London, 1964), pp. 8–10; and *The Communist Bloc and the Western Alliances: The Military Balance, 1962–1963* (London, 1962), p. 8, and the same serial for 1963–64 (1963), pp. 9–10.

49. See Clare Hollingsworth, "China Soon to be Nuclear Power," *Manchester Guardian Weekly*, October 1, 1961; *China News* (Taiwan), July 10, 1962; Richard Frykland, "Chinese Reds Believed Building MiG Fighters," Washington *Evening Star*, December 31, 1964; Seymour Topping, "New Jet Fighters Detected in China," *The New York Times*, December 30, 1964; and Richard Frykland, "Joint Chiefs Minimize China's Military Power," Washington *Evening Star*, March 18, 1966. See also references cited in Note 48.

50. See references cited in Note 49; and see "Missile Submarine in Red China's Navy," *The New York Times*, November 14, 1965.

51. See Frykland, Washington *Evening Star*, March 18, 1966, citing Secretary of Defense Robert S. McNamara.

52. See Zagoria, *op. cit.*, pp. 335–36.

53. Marshal R. Malinovsky, *Tass*, January 24, 1962.

54. Editorial, *Pravda*, January 7, 1963.

55. *Pravda*, September 21 and 22, 1963.

56. Li Fu-Ch'un, *Hung Ch'i*, August 16, 1960.

57. Ch'en Yi, *NCNA*, January 5, 1962.

58. See *Kyodo*, Tokyo, October 28, 1963 (evening edition), and "Peking Foresees a Delay of Years on Atomic Bomb," *The New York Times*, October 29, 1963.

59. *Jen-min Jih-pao*, November 19, 1963.

60. "Internationalism is the Source of Victory in Revolutionary Struggle," editorial, *Pravda*, October 1, 1965.

61. *Kung Tso T'ung Hsün* (*Work Correspondence*), Peking, February 1, 1961.

62. CPPCC National Committee Message to the People's Council of the Sinkiang-Uighur Autonomous Region, *Radio Peking*, NCNA, September 29, 1965; and "Great Triumph for the Policy of National Solidarity of the Party," *Jen-min Jih-pao*, September 30, 1965.

63. Speech by Vice Premier Ho Lung in Urumchi, *Radio Peking*, September 30, 1965.

64. Victor Zorza, *The Guardian*, London, October 9, 1964.

65. Excerpts From a Secret CPSU Letter to All Party Organizations in the Soviet Union and to All Fraternal Communist Parties, in *Die Welt* (*The World*), Hamburg, March 21, 1966. The authenticity of the Letter as published in *Die Welt* has not been challenged.

66. Official English-language *Press Release* by the Chinese Communist Embassy in Stockholm of Ch'en Yi interview with the Danish News Agency, May 24, 1966.

67. In *Die Welt*, March 21, 1966.

68. *Ibid.*

69. *Ibid.*

6. The Eruption of Sino-Soviet
Politico-Military Problems, 1957–60

1. "The Soviet Army is the Example for the People's Armies of the World," New China News Agency (NCNA) release, *People's Daily, Survey of the China Mainland Press* (SCMP) (Hong Kong: U.S. Consulate General), No. 1647.

2. Broadcast speech, NCNA, *SCMP*, No. 1644.

3. NCNA, *SCMP*, No. 1649.

4. Speech at Soviet Embassy banquet, Peking, NCNA, November 7, 1957, *SCMP*, No. 1651.

5. Alice Langley Hsieh, *Communist China's Strategy in the Nuclear Era* (Englewood Cliffs, N.J., 1962), pp. 69–72.

6. *Chief-fang Chün Pao* (*Liberation Army Daily*), August 8, 1957, *SCMP*, No. 1692.

7. "New Training Program Promulgated by General Department of Supervision of Training," *Liberation Army Daily*, January 16, 1958. *SCMP*, No. 1786.

8. These statements appeared in mid-1958 in remarks by Marshal Chu Teh, Ch'en Yi, Ho Lung, and Nieh Jung-chen, and by the chief of the Air Force; and in various editorials in the *Liberation Army Daily* and in *Red Flag*.

9. Joint Publications Research Service (*JPRS*), Washington, D.C., translation study No. 1687–N, June 9, 1959.

10. *People's Daily, Current Background* (CB) (Hong Kong: U.S. Consulate General), No. 514. Ho was here listing what he held to have been one of the reasons for the failure of Chinese Communist military tactics in the Nanchang uprising of 1927. The other chief reason he listed was over-emphasis on weapons rather than on men. Ho went on to discuss Mao's struggles at that time (before his triumph over the Soviet-directed leadership of the Chinese Communist Party) against the "erroneous military line that existed at the time within the Party in the Red Army."

11. *People's Daily, SCMP*, No. 1831.

12. *JPRS*, No. 1357–N, March 16, 1959.

13. *JPRS*, No. 767–D, June 17, 1959.

14. *JPRS*, No. 1357–N, March 16, 1959.

15. *Pravda*, December 22, 1957.

16. Article by D. Shevlyagin, *Pravda*, January 7, 1958.

17. *Pravda*, April 6, 1958.

18. See, especially, "Everybody is a Soldier," *Red Flag*, October 16, 1958, *Extracts from Chinese Communist Magazines* (*ECCM*) (Hong Kong: U.S. Consulate General) No. 150.

19. See *People's Daily*, February 3, 1958, NCNA, *SCMP*, No. 1714; General Liu Ya-lou, May 23, 1958, *Liberation Army Daily*, *SCMP*, No. 1900; and Marshal Nieh Jung-chen, August 2, 1959, *People's Daily*, *SCMP* No. 1831.

20. *Kiangsu Ch'un-chung*, No. 5, October 1, 1958, *ECCM*, No. 150; *Liberation Army Daily*, July 1, August 1 and August 17, 1958, *SCMP*, No. 1881; and *JPRS*, No. 1357.

21. *Eighth Plenary Session of the Eighth Central Committee of the Communist Party of China* (Peking, 1949), p. 18.

22. *JPRS*, No. 2376, March 17, 1960, p. 6.

23. NCNA, May 27, 1958, *SCMP*, No. 1781.

24. See Russian arguments in *Pravda*, April 12, May 9, and June 4, 1958, and *Kommunist*, April, 1958: Chinese arguments in NCNA releases, in English, on May 5, 24, 27, and June 4, 1958, *SCMP*, Nos. 1767, 1781, and 1787, of May-June, 1958.

25. *Liberation Army Daily*, *SCMP*, No. 1900.

26. A judgment developed at some length by Hsieh, *op. cit.*

27. NCNA, *SCMP*, No. 1856.

28. *ECCM*, No. 150.

29. *SCMP*, No. 1907.

30. NCNA, *SCMP*, No. 1897.

31. *JPRS*, No. 779–D.

32. Statement to TASS questioner, *Pravda*, October 6, 1958.

33. On the occasion of a ceremony inaugurating China's first atomic reactor and cyclotron (built with Soviet assistance), NCNA, September 27, 1958, *SCMP*, No. 1865.

34. *Ibid.*, p. 37.

35. *Pravda*, November 15, 1958.

36. Yu Chao-li, "Peaceful Competition: An Inevitable Trend?" *Red Flag*, August 16, 1959, *ECCM*, No. 184, p. 5. The CCP Central Committee has made a practice of attaching this "author's" name [literally, "The Strength of Millions"] to especially important pronouncements in *Red Flag*.

37. September 30, 1959, *Pravda*, October 1, 1959.

38. *Pravda*, January 15, 1960.

7. The Limits of Alliance:
The Quemoy Crisis of 1958

1. J. Emmett Hughes, *America the Vincible* (Garden City, N.Y., 1959), p. 149.

2. See *Kommunist*, No. 13, September, 1960, p. 14.

3. For example, see *Sovetskii flot* (*Soviet Fleet*) and *Pravda*, August 27, 1958.

4. *Sovetskii flot*, August 28, 1958.

5. *Sovetskaya aviatsiya* (*Soviet Aviation*), August 28, 1958.
6. For example, *Pravda*, August 31, 1958.
7. *The New York Times*, September 5, 1958.
8. *Izvestiya*, September 9, 1958.
9. *The New York Times*, September 2, 1958.
10. *Radio Moscow*, September 9, 1958.
11. *Pravda*, September 13, 1958, and *Sovetskaya Rossiya* (*Soviet Russia*), September 16, 1958.
12. *Sovetskii flot*, August 28, 1958, and *Krasnaya zvezda* (*Red Star*), August 29, 1958.
13. *Izvestiya*, August 29, 1958.
14. *The New York Times*, August 29, 1958.
15. *Ibid.*
16. *Radio Tirana*, September 30, 1958.
17. As published in *Pravda*, September 9, 1958.
18. N. S. Khrushchev, in *Izvestiya*, September 12, 1958.
19. *Kommunist*, No. 12, August, 1958, p. 81.
20. *Sovetskaya aviatsiya*, September 6, 1958.
21. *Sovetskii flot*, September 16, 1958.
22. N. S. Khrushchev, *Pravda*, September 9, 1958.
23. N. S. Khrushchev, *Krasnaya zvezda*, September 21, 1958.
24. *Pravda*, September 28, 1958.
25. N. S. Khrushchev, *Pravda*, October 1, 1958.
26. *Sovetskii flot*, October 4, 1958.
27. *Radio Moscow*, October 1, 1958.
28. *Sovetskii flot*, October 4, 1958.
29. *Krasnaya zvezda*, September 21, 1958.
30. *Ibid.*, September 25, 1958.
31. Marshal of Tank Troops P. A. Rotmistrov, *Krasnaya zvezda*, September 14, 1958.
32. Marshal R. Ya. Malinovsky, *Krasnaya zvezda*, September 13, 1958.
33. *Ibid.*
34. Marshal I. S. Konev, *Radio Warsaw*, October 10, 1958.
35. *Sovetskii flot*, September 16, 1958.
36. A. I. Mikoyan, *Pravda*, November 7, 1958.
37. *Krasnaya zvezda*, February 15, 1959.
38. "Statement by the Spokesman of the Chinese Government," *Radio Peking*, September 1, 1963. The entire text is given in Appendix C.

8. The Sino-Soviet Nuclear Dialogue: 1963

1. "Open Letter from the Central Committee of the CPSU to Party Organizations, to All Communists of the Soviet Union," *Pravda*, July 14, 1963, in *Current Digest of the Soviet Press* (hereafter cited as *CDSP*), Vol. XV, No. 28, August 7, 1963.
2. "Two Different Lines on the Questions of War and Peace—Comment on the Open Letter of the Central Committee of the CPSU (V)," editorial in *Jen-min Jih-pao* (*People's Daily;* hereafter cited as *JMJP*) and *Hung Ch'i* (*Red Flag*), November 19, 1963.
3. "Statement by the Spokesman of the Chinese Government, September 1, 1963—A Comment on the Soviet Government's Statement of August 21,"

JMJP, September 1, 1963 (hereafter cited as "Chinese Government Statement of September 1, 1963"). The entire text is given in Appendix C.

4. N. Talensky, "On the Character of Modern Warfare," *International Affairs*, Moscow, October, 1960.

5. *Pravda*, June 6, 1962; January 17, 1963. In an article published in *Rabotnichesko delo (Worker's Affairs)*, Sofia, on October 10, 1963, Marshal A. I. Yeremenko stated: "According to the competent opinion of scientists, as a result of the first blow alone 700 to 800 million persons would be killed."

6. See, for example, Li Chih-min, "Resolute Struggles Must Be Carried Out Against U.S. Imperialism," *JMJP*, June 25, 1960.

7. Chinese Government Statement of September 1, 1963.

8. For a more detailed discussion of this material, see Alice Langley Hsieh, "China's Secret Military Papers: Military Doctrine and Strategy," *The China Quarterly*, April-June, 1964.

9. Marshal V. D. Sokolovsky, ed., *Soviet Military Strategy*, translated and annotated by H. S. Dinerstein, L. Goure, and T. W. Wolfe (Englewood Cliffs, N.J., 1963), p. 99

10. Lu Chih-ch'ao, "One Cannot Renounce the Marxist-Leninist Viewpoint of Class Struggle in Examining the Question of War," *Hung Ch'i*, August 15, 1963.

11. *The New York Times*, October 10, 1963.

12. Chinese Government Statement of September 1, 1963.

13. Leon Goure, *Soviet Limited War Doctrine*, The RAND Corporation, P–2744, May, 1963.

14. *Red Star*, November 2, 1963.

15. Yu Chao-li, "Imperialism Is the Source of War in Modern Times and the War for the People of All Countries to Struggle for Peace," *Hung Ch'i*, April 1, 1960.

16. "A Proposal Concerning the General Line of the International Communist Movement—June 14, 1963, Reply of the CC of the CCP to the March 30, 1963, Letter of the CC of the CPSU," *JMJP*, June 17, 1963.

17. Chinese Government Statement of September 1, 1963.

18. "Statement of the Soviet Government, August 21, 1963," *Pravda*, August 21, 1963, in *CDSP*, Vol. XV, No. 34, September 18, 1963 (hereafter cited as "Soviet Government Statement of August 21, 1963").

19. Chinese Government Statement of September 1, 1963.

20. "Statement by the Spokesman of the Chinese Government, August 15, 1963—A Comment on the Soviet Government's Statement of August 3, 1963," *JMJP*, August 15, 1963 (hereafter cited as "Chinese Government Statement of August 15, 1963").

21. "Statement of the Soviet Government, September 20, 1963," *Pravda*, September 21 and 22, 1963, in *CDSP*, Vol. XV, No. 38, October 16, 1963 (hereafter cited as "Soviet Government Statement of September 20, 1963").

22. "Statement of the Chinese Government, July 31, 1963," *JMJP*, July 31, 1963.

23. Chinese Government Statement of August 15, 1963.

24. Soviet Government Statement of August 21, 1963.

25. Soviet Government Statement of September 20, 1963.

26. Soviet Government Statement of August 21, 1963.

27. Soviet Government Statement of September 20, 1963.

28. Soviet Government Statement of August 21, 1963.

29. Chinese Government Statement of August 15, 1963.

30. Liao Cheng-chih, speech to rally in Peking on August 1, 1963, *Radio Peking,* Domestic Service, August 1, 1963.

31. Chinese Government Statement of September 1, 1963.

32. Chinese Government Statement of August 15, 1963.

33. Soviet Government Statement of August 21, 1963.

34. Chinese Government Statement of September 1, 1963.

35. Soviet Government Statement of August 21, 1963.

36. Chinese Government Statement of September 1, 1963.

37. Soviet Government Statement of August 21, 1963.

38. Colonel I. Sidel'nikov and Colonel V. Zmitrenko, *Krasnaya zvezda* (*Red Star*), September 19, 1963.

39. Soviet Government Statement of August 21, 1963.

40. Sidel'nikov and Zmitrenko, *Krasnaya zvezda,* September 19, 1963.

41. Soviet Government Statement of September 20, 1963.

42. *Ibid.*

43. "A Proposal Concerning the General Line of the International Communist Movement . . . ," *JMJP,* June 17, 1963; Chinese Government Statement of August 15, 1963.

44. *Washington Post,* December 8, 1963.

45. Chinese Government Statement of September 1, 1963.

46. Tokyo, KYODO, October 28, 1963.

47. For a more detailed consideration of possible Chinese uses of a nuclear capability, see Alice Langley Hsieh, *Communist China and Nuclear Force,* The RAND Corporation, P–2719–1, August, 1963.

48. Chinese Government Statement of August 15, 1963.

49. "The Origin and Development of the Differences between the Leadership of the CPSU and Ourselves—Comment on the Open Letter of the CC of the CPSU," editorial in *People's Daily* and *Red Flag,* September 6, 1963.

50. Available information does not permit the identification of the negotiators who may have signed the October 15, 1957, agreement. A delegation of the Supreme Soviet of the U.S.S.R., headed by A. B. Aristov, was in Peking at this time. (See *JMJP,* September 30, 1957.) A survey of the members of this delegation, however, hardly suggests that it would have had the authority to sign an agreement of this nature. That the negotiations may have been conducted over a period of time, and that their finalization coincided in some way with the visit to Moscow (October 18, 1957–January 19, 1958) of a Chinese scientific mission, headed by Kuo Mo-jo, President of the Chinese Academy of Sciences, is suggested in an interview Kuo gave to *New Times.* According to Kuo:

Last year our Party called on the people to launch a great campaign to master science. Six hundred scientists gathered in Peking and worked for six months drawing up a long-term program of scientific and technological progress. In this work we received much assistance from the Soviet Union, which sent a delegation under A. I. Mikhailov, director of the Information Institute of the U.S.S.R. Academy of Sciences, and the Soviet scientists and technicians in China at the time helped too. The outcome of these endeavors was our twelve-year program for the advancement of science. . . . Among the major tasks it maps out are the peaceful use of atomic energy, development of radio electronics and jet propulsion. . . . This May Premier Chou En-lai transmitted our twelve-year program to Premier Bulganin with the request that Soviet scientists should examine it. . . . The Soviet government at once responded to our request, setting up 26 consultation groups in which 640 Soviet scientists were active. They completed their work by October 20, and that was when our 120-man delegation came to Moscow.

(See *New Times*, Moscow, No. 50, December, 1957.)

51. *Life*, July 13, 1959, p. 36.

52. Allan Nanes, "The Armies of Red China," *Current History*, December, 1960, p. 342; Harold C. Hinton, "Communist China's Military Posture," *Current History*, September, 1962, p. 153.

53: See Chapter 5, above; and see Edward Crankshaw, *The Observer* (London), February 12–19, 1961.

54. David A. Charles, "The Dismissal of Marshal P'eng Teh-huai," *The China Quarterly*, No. 8, October-December, 1961, *passim*.

9. Politico-Military Issues in the Sino-Soviet Debate, 1963–65

1. I. Yermashev, "The Peking Version of 'Total Strategy,'" *Voennaya mysl'* (*Military Thought*), No. 10, October, 1963, p. 12.

2. *Ibid.*

3. See Marshal Vasily D. Sokolovsky *et al.* (eds.), *Voennaya strategiya* (Military Strategy) (Moscow, 1962), pp. 7–8; and the second edition (1963), p. 11, which not only deletes the fifth-century B.C. Chinese—previously described as "first" in this field—but states that there were (unidentified) initiators in this field "in the first to fourth centuries A.D."

4. Yermashev, *Voennaya mysl'*, No. 10, 1963, pp. 12–13.

5. *Ibid.*, p. 13.

6. *Ibid.*

7. *Ibid.*, pp. 13 and 14.

8. *Ibid.*, p. 15.

9. *Ibid.*

10. *Ibid.*, p. 14.

11. *Ibid.*, p. 15.

12. *Ibid.*

13. *Ibid.*, p. 22.

14. *Ibid.*, pp. 16–18.

15. *Ibid.*, p. 16.

16. *Ibid.*, p. 18.

17. *Ibid.*, p. 17.

18. *Ibid.*

19. *Ibid.*, pp. 16–17.

20. *Ibid.*, p. 20.

21. *Ibid.*, pp. 20–21.

22. *Ibid.*, p. 17.

23. *Ibid.*, p. 19.

24. *Ibid.*, p. 16.

25. *Ibid.*, p. 17.

26. *Ibid.*, p. 13.

27. *Ibid.*, p. 21.

28. *Ibid.*, p. 21.

29. *Ibid.*, p. 22.
30. *Ibid.*
31. *Ibid.*, p. 21.
32. See Raymond L. Garthoff, *Soviet Military Policy: A Historical Analysis* (New York, 1966), chapters 10, 11, and 12.
33. *Ibid.*, pp. 199–200.
34. Fan Hsiu-chu, "Struggle Between the Two Lines over the Question of Dealing with U.S. Imperialism," *Ta Kung Pao* (*The Impartial Daily*), Peking, July 26, 1965. See also "Refutation of the New Leaders of the CPSU on United Action," *Jen-min Jih-pao* (*People's Daily*) and *Hung Ch'i* (*Red Flag*), November 11, 1965.
35. Lin Piao, "Long Live the People's War," *Jen-min Jih-pao* and *Hung Ch'i*, September 3, 1965.
36. *Ibid.*

Bibliographical Note

The extensive footnote references to most of the chapters of this study provide a general guide to useful sources, as well as indicating the sources of particular information cited. This brief Note is intended to supplement them by highlighting some of the major studies in fields directly bearing on Sino-Soviet military relations.

CLUBB, O. EDMUND. *Twentieth Century China*. New York: Columbia University Press, 1964. 470 pp. The best general history of recent China, this volume provides the political context in which the Chinese have conducted politico-military relations with the Soviet Union.

GARTHOFF, RAYMOND L. *Soviet Strategy in the Nuclear Age*. Rev. ed. New York: Frederick A. Praeger, 1962. 301 pp. Analysis of developments in Soviet military strategy from 1953 through 1961.

GARTHOFF, RAYMOND L. *Soviet Military Policy: A Historical Analysis*. New York: Frederick A. Praeger, 1966. 276 pp. A comprehensive study of the role of military instruments and institutions in modern Russia, including particular attention to Soviet, Chinese, and other Communist views on the relation between war and revolution.

GRIFFITH, WILLIAM E. *The Sino-Soviet Rift*. Cambridge, Mass.: MIT Press, 1964. 508 pp. The development of the Sino-Soviet conflict from 1961 to 1964 is very well covered in this volume.

HALPERIN, MORTON H. *China and the Bomb*. New York: Frederick A. Praeger, 1965. 166 pp. The best single study of the role of the nascent Chinese nuclear weapons development program in Chinese foreign policy, including policy toward the Soviet Union.

HSIEH, ALICE LANGLEY. *Communist China's Strategy in the Nuclear Era*. Englewood Cliffs, N.J.: Prentice-Hall, 1962. 204 pp. The best account of Chinese Communist military strategy in the period from 1945 to 1960, this work is very useful background.

LIU, F. F. *A Military History of Modern China, 1924–1949*. Princeton, N.J.: Princeton University Press, 1956. 312 pp. The best general source for background on the military development of China, including relations with the Soviet Union, prior to the Communist victory on the mainland.

WOLFE, THOMAS W. *Soviet Strategy at the Crossroads*. Cambridge, Mass.: Harvard University Press, 1964. 362 pp. Analysis of developments in Soviet military strategy from 1962 through 1964.

ZAGORIA, DONALD S. *The Sino-Soviet Conflict, 1956–1961*. Princeton, N.J.: Princeton University Press, 1962. 484 pp. This is the most comprehensive account of the origins and emergence of the Sino-Soviet rift in the period from 1956 to 1961.

Index